STAGING RACE

STAGING RACE

Black Performers in
Turn of the Century America

KAREN SOTIROPOULOS

HARVARD UNIVERSITY PRESS
Cambridge, Massachusetts
London, England

First Harvard University Press paperback edition, 2008.

Library of Congress Cataloging-in-Publication Data

Sotiropoulos, Karen, 1963–
Staging race : black performers in turn of the century America /
Karen Sotiropoulos.
p. cm.
Includes bibliographical references and index.
ISBN 978-0-674-01940-9 (cloth : alk. paper)
ISBN 978-0-674-02760-2 (pbk.)
1. African Americans in the performing arts.
2. Performing arts—Political aspects—United States—19th century.
3. Performing arts—Political aspects—United States—20th century.
I. Title.

PN2270.A35S67   2006
791'.089'96073—dc22   2005050384

Designed by Gwen Nefsky Frankfeldt

To the memory of my yiayia and her sisters

Contents

Illustrations

Illustrations

Acknowledgments

I'VE DEDICATED this book to the memory of my grandmother and her sisters in part because learning their life stories—lives that spanned Greece and America—in no small way inspired my decision to become a historian. The dedication, however, extends to my entire family, who cheered me along this road, however rocky and unknown the path. I may not have found my way to this project had it not been for my father's love of jazz, and I cannot overstate how thankful I am to both him and my mother. My parents celebrated my accomplishments, eased my disappointments, and faithfully read every word of my book; I could not have completed this book without the constancy of their love and support.

At the CUNY Graduate Center, I was graced with a dissertation committee of distinguished scholars whose very different perspectives helped me to shape my project: James V. Hatch, Robin D. G. Kelley, David Nasaw, Colin Palmer, and Judith Stein. Special thanks go to David, who directed the dissertation and whose insight on conceptualization and attention to the detail of writing kept my book from being both smaller and duller. Heartfelt thanks to Robin, whose ability to help me envision where my argument was going always amazed me, and whose unflagging belief in me, enthusiasm for the study of daily life, and commitment to scholarship and struggle continue to inspire. Equally important were the friends and colleagues who sustained me emotionally, spiritually, politically, and intellectually during my years in graduate school. The insights and loving friendships of Dan Evans and Sarah Mercer Judson made graduate school bearable, and our conversations over the years have enriched my life and work more than they could possibly imagine. Special thanks go as well to Kevin Bourke, not only for his dry wit and many (many) years of friendship, but also for his expert editing of early drafts that saved me (and all subsequent readers) from innumerable grammatical and stylistic errors.

As much as *Staging Race* was made in New York, the book benefited immensely from my move to Cleveland. Cleveland State University supported me with the New Faculty Research Development and Established Full-Time Faculty Effort Development Awards. My Cleveland colleagues and students encouraged my work with their enthusiasm, whether shared in the classroom, at public lectures, or in comments on draft after draft. I am eternally grateful to Rhonda Y. Williams, whose careful reading and always right-on comments sharpened the manuscript in untold ways. Aided by a heavy dose of caffeine and chocolate, conversations with Rhonda made completing this book more joyful than I could have imagined and reaffirmed the relationship between love, struggle, and the production of knowledge. I am indebted to Gregory Conerly for his nuanced understanding of black popular culture, steadfast support, infectious laughter, and lively discussions that still shape my thinking. I am equally thankful to Mary Wren Bivins for her enthusiasm for my work, her boundless historical imagination, and for sending me packing—intellectually and physically—on my trip to Africa. Many thanks to Gillian Johns, who helped me see new layers of irony in the scripts I was sure I already knew inside and out. CSU graduate students Kim Carey, Jan Gornall, Angela Newman, and Dawn Wooten coaxed me along as they read portions or just listened to me as I tried out my ideas in class; CSU research assistants Susan Hall and Cindy Sprinzl helped proofread and fact-check in the final stages. Thanks to Abu Nasara, without whom I surely wouldn't have such a speedy computer to write on, and to Cindy Shairba, who went above and beyond the call of administrative duty in helping with various steps of the process, including facilitating grants, wrapping up the final package, celebrating its completion, and helping me stay calm through it all.

I am grateful to Susan Curtis and Shane White, both of whom carefully read the entire manuscript and provided detailed and insightful comments. The many other scholars who commented on portions of the manuscript and helped me along the way include Jim Borchert, Scot Brown, Lewis Erenberg, Mitch Kachun, Ellen Noonan, Debbie Pearl, Sylvain B.

Poosson, Sterling Stuckey, Sherrie Tucker, Bob Wheeler, and Deborah Gray White. I am thankful as well to Victor Yankah and his colleagues in the English Department at the University of Cape Coast, Ghana, who helped me better intuit the coming together of American dreams and African realities. At Harvard University Press, David Lobenstine started me off on this project with his own enthusiastic support and Joyce Seltzer saw it to completion with her expert guidance. Thanks as well to the staffs of the Schomburg Center for Research in Black Culture and the Billy Rose Theater Collection of the New York Public Library. Special thanks to Linden Anderson, Antony Toussaint, and Mary Yearwood of the Schomburg for their assistance in photo research and reproduction, to Lela Sewall-Williams at the Moorland-Spingarn Research Center at Howard University for her assistance with the Cook papers, and to the staff in Special Collections at the University of Iowa for assistance with the Keith-Albee Collection.

There is no way I can include everyone in the village it took to write this book, but there are a few more folks I want to mention. My comrades on the editorial collective of the *Radical History Review* remain a base of support and an unvarying reminder of the kind of scholar and teacher I strive to be. The E. P. Thompson Dissertation Fellowship in History helped immensely by enabling me to lighten my teaching load as a graduate student. No less important was the support of Myrna Chase (who served as chair of the department at Baruch College where I was adjuncting at the time); she always made sure scheduling allowed me to keep my scholarship a priority—a collegiality that was critical when funding was inadequate. Remembering Karen Deaver's support for me in the early years of graduate school still cheers me, and Barbara Shenton's love of tap has always reminded me of the resilience and reach of black dance. Ellen Wallenstein continues to bring to life with her own magnificent images the creative space where *Staging Race* was born. Dan Gunnells taught me more about the necessity of theorizing daily life than I cared to know, and I am grateful for that "beyond all ending." I cannot forget to give treats to Ginny and all our two-legged and four-legged friends at the Tompkins Square Park dog run, where chapters were edited, computer troubles mulled over, and daily life made. Lastly, gratitude and love to Lanell, who magically arrived as the book went to press to light up my world with his smiles.

Monster applause to all.

STAGING RACE

INTRODUCTION

Politics, Not Minstrelsy

THERE ARE two, now perhaps three, eras when black art has been understood as overtly political: the Harlem Renaissance of the 1920s, the Black Arts Movement of the 1960s and 1970s, and the rap and hip hop musical cultures of the 1980s and 1990s. Artists like Langston Hughes, Amiri Baraka, and Chuck D have become synonymous with their respective eras, and no one doubts that their artistic endeavors were inseparable from their political aspirations, or that their politics engaged a black agenda representing the voices of their generation. Black artists from other eras are more often described as precursors to one of these periods, as emblematic of an era's end, or as followers of the artists that came before them. Outside of these epochal moments, rarely are black artists—and the art that they made—described as constitutive of and emblematic of their own generation.

This book is about one such unrecognized cohort of artists, young men and women born in the years after the Civil War and coming of age with the rise of Jim Crow in the 1890s. They brought black music and dance to the popular stages and dance halls of America's burgeoning cities at the same time that intellectuals and activists like Ida B. Wells and W. E. B. Du Bois were developing new strategies in the struggle for the citizenship rights that Emancipation and Reconstruction had failed to bring. For black Americans, the 1890s ushered in a decade of shrinking possibilities, and artists and activists alike desperately sought any avenue for advancement. Artists found such a path on the popular stage—a forum made lucrative by the rise of commercial culture. Urban industrial America had brought about an unprecedented expansion of nightlife and offered entertainers numerous possibilities—possibilities that black artists were ready to exploit.[1]

This generation of black American artists struggled to make art, to make money, and to advance racial interests in the years between the World's Columbian Exposition of 1893 and the Great Migration of World War I. African Americans faced a formidable task as they confronted an era marked by increased racial violence, constitutionally upheld segregation laws, widespread disfranchisement, and a social Darwinism that hailed Anglo-Saxonism as the height of civilization and derided Africans as "primitive" and "savage." Participation in public life required the careful monitoring and appeasing of white audiences, and artists conformed to white expectation by using the conventions of the newly popular vaudeville stage—including blackface makeup—in their productions. While blacking up was arguably dangerous in its implications, the artists played to the white desire for racist stereotypes in order to participate in the theater. Always conscious that they were performing stage types, however, they manipulated the stage mask in innovative ways that helped them forge a space for dialogue with their black audiences—dialogue that included both assertions of black nationhood and critique of the racism that perpetuated stereotyped imagery.

Work on the popular stage made African American performers hyperconscious of the veil, of that "peculiar sensation" that Du Bois had described during the same years of "always looking at one's self through the eyes of others." By necessity, this generation of black artists grounded their work in this "double-consciousness." Du Bois did not have stage artists in mind when he so eloquently described black America's psyche in *Souls of Black Folk*. On the contrary, at the time, he adamantly denounced popular amusements as "unwholesome" and as a threat to racial progress. But the artists who made their way to the turn-of-the-century popular stage were not all that different from Du Bois; they were of the same generation, hailed from similar backgrounds, envisioned themselves as race leaders, and believed that appreciation for black creative expression was an integral part of racial advancement. Their most dramatic difference lay in their level of enthusiasm for America's budding urban leisure culture—a difference intimately connected to their lives as artists. To make their art public, the men and women of this generation had to grapple with and partly accept a nascent entertainment business mired in the racism of Jim Crow America.

Turn-of-the-century black performers migrated from the emerging cities of the South and West to New York City, the nation's theater capital. Unlike the vast majority of African Americans, they grew up in urban areas and came from relative privilege. Most of the leading performers' parents were comparatively well-off financially, and had expressed great hope that Emancipation would bring full citizenship rights. The young artists, however, encountered a federal government that turned its back on the rights of freedpeople, allowed rampant racist violence, upheld segregation laws as constitutional, and rendered the Fourteenth and Fifteenth Amendments meaningless. They came of age at a time when 90 percent of African Americans still resided in southern states, with more than 80 percent of those working in agriculture, largely as non-wage-earning sharecroppers. They witnessed the rise of ideologies of racial hierarchy and social Darwinism as well as an entertainment business that promulgated racist stereotypes.[2]

White men had blackened their faces in the 1830s, thereby beginning white America's love affair with blackface minstrelsy, but the widespread success of popular amusements at the turn of the twentieth century seared these images into the American psyche. With the introduction of mass production, stereotyped imagery appeared everywhere from song sheets to food labels, making the blackfaced minstrel a permanent part of the American landscape. Over the years, minstrel imagery has reflected and reinforced white supremacy and has caused black America immeasurable pain. Yet shortly after the Civil War, black performers capitalized on white America's desire for minstrel shows, marketing themselves as authentic "darkies" and Ethiopian delineators. Later, black vaudevillians, male and female, blacked up, while many others played "darky" roles without the use of makeup. Some minstrel troupes had set their shows outdoors in simulated plantations, entertaining whites with fictive scenes of the Old South. Although these "plantation shows" faded away, the prevalence and persistence of racist stereotypes continued to plague black artists. Still, the market for minstrel imagery offered them a way—although a very narrowly circumscribed way—to make money and art.[3]

Two leading comedians at the turn of the century, Bert Williams and Ernest Hogan, blacked up as well, but they did so on the newly popular vaudeville stage. Once described by his white colleague W. C. Fields as "the funniest man I ever saw, and the saddest man I ever knew," Williams too felt the constrictions of Jim Crow and the burden of stereotyped imagery. But along with his black colleagues, Williams strove to overcome the limits of the minstrel genre. Black vaudevillians pleased white theater managers and white audiences with their antics, but they were just as concerned with furthering race progress as they were with their own fame and fortune. Minstrelsy, said Williams, was "a thing of the past . . . to cork your face and talk politics is not minstrelsy."[4]

Fully engaged in contemporary issues, Williams and his colleagues brought a black political agenda to their stage productions, even though they worked in commercial theater. Most prominently, when the dominant culture understood Africa solely as the "dark" continent of "primitivism" and "savagery," the company led by Williams and his partner, George Walker, produced musical comedies addressing African Americans' interest in emigrating to Liberia and their pride in Ethiopia's independence during Europe's late-nineteenth-century scramble to colonize Africa. In other full-length shows, as well as individual sketches and songs, this generation of artists celebrated black communities, denounced Jim Crow, and critiqued black elite pretension—all behind the minstrel mask. Armed with their overt political content and inventive manipulation of stage types, these artists represented their offstage daily reality on vaudeville and musical comedy stages.

Black vaudevillians quickly became some of the most visible African Americans in the world, and thus, increasingly saw themselves as particularly well positioned to represent the race nationally and internationally. They countered their theatrical representation by making a clear distinction between their stage personas and their offstage role as respectable professionals. Throughout their careers, they hoped that white America would embrace them as professional actors playing stage types, and that such acceptance would lead to the inclusion of African Americans in the body politic.

In part, members of this generation could imagine such a possibility because they came of age just when the meanings of work and play were being radically transformed. Urban industrial society and the rise of commercialized leisure brought a new sphere of engagement for Americans, black and white, native and foreign-born. Electricity lighted theaters and city streets, as well as propelled streetcars and amusement rides. With increased leisure time and the wonders of technology, urban pioneers embraced a spirit of hopefulness at the dawn of the new century—a modern spirit epitomized by the brilliantly lit marquees that christened Broadway the Great White Way and the quarter of a million lights that turned night into day at Coney Island's Luna Park. Popular amusements like dance halls, amusement parks, and vaudeville theaters were becoming a part of daily life for most city dwellers, and these new amusements played a significant role in moving American culture from a nineteenth-century Victorian propriety to a twentieth-century embrace of novelty. This new sphere of engagement was unashamedly secular, encouraging the mingling of unmarried men and women, and thus it challenged nineteenth-century sexual mores. Activities considered vulgar and the sole province of the working classes became acceptable among America's middle classes by World War I. Indeed, participation in the new public culture became one of the most prominent markers of modernity (at least for white Americans), while the city became America's hope for its future—as yet unmapped, but promising the pursuit of progress, wealth, and previously unimaginable happiness.[5]

Cities had long played a prominent role in African American visions of freedom, and in the years following the Civil War, black Americans migrated when they could in search of the greater social openness of urban life. Although the major demographic shift known as the Great Migration that occurred during World War I was still years away, African Americans constituted roughly 2 percent of the population in cities like New York and Chicago at the turn of the century. Jim Crow lived in the North as well as the South, of course, and de facto segregation meant black and white Americans lived, for the most part, in separate neighborhoods. Popular theater too segregated African Americans as audience members, and brutally mocked them onstage. To earn bookings, black entertainers had to please white managers, who knew that white orchestra patrons longed to laugh at "darky" acts. During those same performances, black performers hoped to impress their black audiences watching from balcony seating, themselves yearning to celebrate the black performers on stage.

It is difficult to depict what actually went on inside a vaudeville theater a century ago. Snippets of reviews from the black and white press, sparse managers' reports, rare personal recollections, song sheets, and a few re-corded jokes are all that remain. In the case of full-length shows, there are scripts to draw on, but performers often departed from those scripts, im-provising as they interacted with different audiences. Only by drawing together all of these vestiges of the past does a picture emerge of a world rich with black applause as well as white. Theater critics often identified where, as well as when, laughter and applause erupted, and white critics were particularly attentive to moments when black audiences in the bal-cony laughed but whites remained silent. These moments made all too clear that black performers had told jokes that went literally and figura-tively over the heads of their white audiences.

Black audiences were well aware that the black performers they ap-plauded were acting, and were incorporating stereotype to negotiate within an extraordinarily tight cultural, social, and political space—a point most likely understood even by African Americans ambivalent about the artists' methods. A comedian's success intimately depended on a perceptible audi-ence response, and vaudeville encouraged communication between audi-ences and performers. When black performers played to black audiences—even though they were segregated—they hoped these audiences would re-spond to their performance less as a "darky" act, and more as commentary on their own lives in a racist society. Black patrons likely cheered the way that these comedians rose to fame; these artists used the segregated the-ater to divert white audiences with their stereotyped antics, enacting a sur-vival technique that many black Americans used daily—or at the very least, a technique that engaged their imaginations daily. Stereotyped imagery comes down to us as fixed through images seen on food labels, on song sheets, and in film, but in the hands of skilled black comedians at the turn of the century, it was something much more malleable. Watching together from the balcony, black audiences witnessed their own people reflect on and critique American life under Jim Crow, all the while achieving fame via a very modern and newly respectable profession.

Two black weeklies, the *Indianapolis Freeman* and the *New York Age,* pub-lished extensive theater reviews and stage commentary attesting to the breadth and strength of black audience support for black performers. Both newspapers commented on the national theatrical scene and had na-tional audiences, with *Freeman* editors proclaiming their paper "a national race paper" in 1893. Sprinkled through the papers were advertisements ex-plaining where the paper could be purchased whether in Norfolk, Pittsburgh, or Knoxville. *Freeman* owner and editor E. C. Knox had a particular interest in theatrical news, in part because he also owned a publishing company that marketed the sheet music of songs made popular on the show circuit.[6] His paper was the first black weekly to include extensive theatrical comment. The *New York Age* eventually caught up to the *Freeman*, and began including its own weekly theatrical page when Lester Walton joined its staff in 1908. Both papers served a purpose broader than simply critiquing the shows. Rather they reported extensively on the careers and offstage lives of performers, and fully participated in the project of establishing these entertainers as respectable professionals and race leaders. African American writers and editors transformed the pages of the black press into a central vehicle for building national political institutions, and the theatrical pages placed the performing world within this framework of race progress.

The world that black artists and theater critics made was interconnected with that of activists and intellectuals like Ida B. Wells and W. E. B. Du Bois. Wells, in particular, searched for a stage to make her views public, even traveling to England to awaken white America to the horrors of racist violence: the white press finally paid attention when she lectured abroad against lynching.[7] Together with Frederick Douglass, she managed to turn Chicago's World's Fair of 1893 into a hub of political organizing. Artists like Paul Laurence Dunbar and Will Marion Cook joined activists that summer and sought to use the slim space available at the fair to celebrate black cultural production. Artists and activists alike hoped that venues like the world's fair would help them attract and influence new audiences in rapidly urbanizing America. Performing artists hoped further that commercial theater would expand to offer them opportunities to perform. Just two years after the Chicago Fair, Booker T. Washington gained national attention with a speech in Atlanta and became America's most familiar black spokesperson, despite increasing criticism from Du Bois and Wells, among others. More powerful in print, Du Bois published *Souls of Black Folk* in 1903, making his criticism of Booker T. Washington's ideas public and declaring that the problem of the twentieth century would be the problem of the color line. That same year, vaudevillians Bert Williams and George Walker broke the color line on Broadway by heading the first black company to perform on the Great White Way with their full-length African-themed musical comedy, *In Dahomey*.

With the rise of Jim Crow, black artists and intellectuals sought to develop new ways to challenge modern white supremacy: both groups formalized their networks with a whole host of organizations, and made their ideas public through a myriad of publications and presentations. Du Bois imagined that a "talented tenth" of educated elite African Americans were best suited to lead the race, and black activists formed organizations like the National Association of Colored Women (1896), the Niagara Movement (1905), and the National Association for the Advancement of Colored People (1909). Black performing artists similarly envisioned their cultural production as instrumental to racial advancement, and they founded groups like the Frogs (1908), the Colored Vaudeville Benevolent Association (1909), and the Clef Club (1910). Yet although black popular artists might have pictured their project as partly political and themselves as possible race leaders, they were not necessarily accepted as such by most black professionals and activists. At least publicly, Du Bois and most of the prominent talented-tenth spokespeople initially condemned popular amusements—along with the modern city—as rife with possibilities for sin, degradation, illness, and the downfall of the race. But this new cohort of black professionals—the early twentieth-century black middle class—did not desire a return to the Victorian standards of the nineteenth century; rather, they sought to mediate the hazards of modern life through a politics of "uplift" and "respectability."[8] They paid careful attention to the influence of a growing leisure culture and weighed when and how to take part in such activities themselves without sacrificing their status or dignity.

Modern culture is often seen as a time when Americans threw off Victorian constraints and embraced a lifestyle that featured looser sexual norms and rampant commercialism.[9] As such, modern culture was inextricably entwined with race politics. The near-universal racial segregation of public space allowed whites to feel secure among their own while experiencing novel and sensual forms of entertainment. White husbands did not worry when their unescorted wives took in a vaudeville show between daily shopping errands because the theater was seen as a safe space. At night, white men and women alike could be assured that they would sit next to white patrons, whether native or foreign-born, no matter whom they applauded onstage. During the prewar dance craze, black all-male bands played off to the side, and modern whites unburdened themselves from the "requirements" of civilization by dancing to the rhythms of black music, secure that black Americans would not share the dance floor and endanger their sense of separateness. Mastering the steps of the so-named modern dances, white moderns would dance to black music as long as they could dance with other whites. Thus, black music had earned a central place among white moderns, giving them a sense of themselves as up-to-date, not only as intellectual and technological leaders, but as social progressives who discarded Victorian self-control for public exuberance and passion. But even as white Americans enjoyed dancing to black music, they shunted black musicians to the sidelines, more often categorizing them as folk artists—emotional, primitive, and the antithesis of modernity.

Like their white contemporaries, a new generation of African Americans shed nineteenth-century Victorian sensibilities and bristled at the conventions of their parents. As African Americans, however, they could not easily shake off social constraints and release themselves into music deemed primitive. Black artists had made black music and dance popular, and had made black culture a desirable, even respectable, consumer item before World War I, but in no small way, the social space in which to represent it was as segregated as physical space under Jim Crow. Pervasive racism left black performers with the problem of presenting a respectable and professional—and modern—black identity in a culture that saw everything black as laughable and primitive, and everything respectable, civilized, and modern as white.

African Americans were hyperconscious of how much their self-presentation on stage would be read through stereotype and how a modern sensibility required distancing oneself from pervasive black imagery. Black entertainers consciously used racist stereotypes in their performances in part to distance themselves from these images, since it was abundantly clear (at least to themselves and their black audiences) that they were *performing* these roles, not embracing them as representative behavior. They sought to show their audiences how much they were skilled actors—professionals—playing stereotypes in an effort to expose the fictions within the imagery. Indeed, through careful attention to public presentation both onstage and off, black entertainers not only won white audiences, but also raised the status of their performances to such a degree that their social and professional world became a central mediating institution for an emerging black middle class. Artists' stage success enabled them to purchase some of the first brownstones in Harlem available to African Americans, and their organizations' fundraising events, held uptown, became central to the social world of Harlem's new black professional class. In the years just prior to World War I, Du Bois still castigated vaudeville as an "unwholesome" activity and assessed leisure as "wholesome" only when it took place under the auspices of the church or YMCA, but even he had begun to participate in some urban amusements. In 1913, at the New York State Emancipation Celebration, he too danced the night away as he was honored as among the "One-Hundred Distinguished Freedmen" alongside blackface comedian Bert Williams.

Artists and activists alike had employed strategies that they hoped would not only achieve citizenship rights, but also gain them equal acceptance as twentieth-century professionals and intellectuals, as urban progressives, and as cosmopolitan city folk—in effect, as modern Americans. Although clearly different in the theories they espoused, and often at odds in how they pursued their goals, both entertainers and activists were similar in their attention to negotiating the racist landscape of modern mass culture. The ways that black stage performers drew attention to their offstage lives as respected actors actually resembled the larger "uplift" project of middle-class African Americans, who sought to present themselves as respectable and up-to-date in a dominant culture burdened by traditional racist stereotypes. Often proponents of racial uplift distanced themselves from public leisure activities deemed "too black," like ragtime music and dance, in an effort to present the race as respectable to white eyes. This distancing increased as members of the more established northern black middle class sought to distinguish themselves from ever greater numbers of black working-class migrants from the South. Whether performers (or promoters of racial uplift for that matter) actually furthered race progress or not, the strategies they employed to maintain dignity and self-respect reveal a distinctive approach to challenging American racism at the onset of Jim Crow.

Will Marion Cook's "Swing Along"—written for *In Dahomey*—perhaps best exemplifies the mindset of black artists. In this song, Cook used dialect speech to encourage his black audiences to "lif' a' yo' heads up high, Wif' pride an' gladness beamin' from yo' eye." He told them to "swing along" despite the pervasive white gaze; to "swing along" even though "white fo'ks jealous when you'se walkin' two by two"; to "swing along" despite the horrors and dehumanization of life under Jim Crow. Paul

Laurence Dunbar, James Weldon Johnson, and George Walker, along with the other artists of their generation, swung along toward Chicago and the world's fair in 1893 full of hope that their voices would be heard. From there, they transcended local vaudeville stages to bring their art to Broadway and beyond, gave birth to new musical styles as well as a public presence that would take the country by storm, and helped lead a black professional class into the twentieth century. Before the Great Migration of World War I, and hardly ignorant as to the realities of Jim Crow racism, they toured the country, selling their song and urging their people to be proud and make their own way in white America.

11111111

Minstrel Men and the World's Fair

I labor hard, and toil and sweat,
While others dream within the dell;
But even while my brow is wet,
I sing my song, and all is well.

PAUL LAURENCE DUNBAR,
"THE POET AND HIS SONG,"
1896

WITH ONLY twenty cents to his name and a quartet of singers that had "exactly nothing among them," W. C. Handy and his troupe left Alabama in 1892 with their "heads set on Chicago and the Columbian Exposition"—that is, determined to sing their way to the Chicago World's Fair. Handy, who later published the first blues song in 1912, asserted with all the exuberance of his nineteen years, "Money was no holdback when you could sing." Lacking money for train fare, the group hopped aboard a tank car at the local railroad yard for the first leg of the journey. Handy recalled that the brakeman tried to get rid of the stowaways by repeatedly throwing them off the train when it stopped, and by threatening to kick them off when the train was in motion. Once he dropped the young men off in a town known to be especially dangerous for blacks. Handy and his quartet, fearing for their lives, began to sing "When the Summer Breeze Was Blowing." Their delivery prompted the hostile brakeman to yell, "Why didn't you *say* you could sing?"—then he invited them back on board.[1]

The next morning, while relaxing in the shade during a breakfast stop in Decatur, Handy noticed "a group of white ladies walking down toward the levee of the Tennessee River with picnic baskets and colorful parasols" on their way to an excursion boat picnic. He approached one of the women with a business card he had prepared before leaving Birmingham, and she promptly hired his quartet to entertain her group for ten dollars. Through connections made on the excursion boat, Handy earned references that endeared the singers to railroad staff for the remainder of the trip. As he remembered, "Serenades and kindred entertainments, with the small fees,

W. C. Handy, Hampton Cornet Band Uniform, 1892.

(Photographs and Prints Division, Schomburg Center for Research in Black Culture, The New York Public Library, Astor, Lenox and Tilden Foundations.)

gifts and handouts that went with them, kept us rolling along on our way." But although they successfully sang their way north, they arrived in Chicago only to discover that the fair had been postponed until the following year.[2]

Handy was not alone in pinning his hopes on the Columbian Exposition. Actor George Walker, who would perform on Broadway in 1902, told of how he abandoned a stint traveling with medicine shows, hoping to launch his performing career in Chicago that year. "Lawrence, Kansas was where I got my start," he reported, "and the first money I ever made was doing a medicine turn. I had to get up on a wooden platform and sing songs to draw a crowd to boost Dr. Blank's Cure-'Em-While-You-Wait-Dandelion-Tonic. I got twenty-five cents in money and took the rest in tonic. As tonic was not substantial food I left Lawrence and drifted to Chicago. There I tried to convince managers that I could act, but as the meals didn't come regularly I quit the profession and got a job as bell boy at the Great Northern hotel where I remained during the World's Fair."[3]

Paul Laurence Dunbar and James Weldon Johnson, two black American writers who were to join Walker and Handy in transforming popular entertainment before World War I, also ventured to Chicago in 1893. Dunbar left a job running an elevator in Dayton, Ohio, with hopes of finding an audience for his poetry as well as better employment. His local newspaper had encouraged his travel by asking him to write a column on "Dayton at the Fair." Once in Chicago, Dunbar secured a series of menial jobs preparing the grounds for opening day before finding more desirable employment as a hotel waiter. Following a friend's advice that blacks were being hired as washroom caretakers, he left the hotel job for one on the fairgrounds. Johnson had fewer pretensions of working as an artist while in Chicago. He and his fellow students from Atlanta University ventured north to enjoy the spectacle and "to earn money for the coming school year." As university students, they obtained some of the better-paying jobs such as those in carpentry, and earned three to four dollars a day helping to prepare the grounds. Later, they worked alongside white college students as "chairboys," pushing sightseers in four-wheeled chairs to and from exhibits, earning a percentage of the seventy-five-cent-an-hour fee.[4]

These four black men, ranging in age from nineteen through twenty-two, shared similar experiences as they joined many other African Americans who too hoped that opportunities were to be had at the fair, however much its political culture—and, indeed, that of all of America—excluded them.[5] Chicago's extravaganza took place during the rise of Jim Crow—an era characterized by Constitutionally recognized racial segregation, widespread disfranchisement, and horrific racial violence; two or three African Americans were reported lynched every week. Thus, these black artists brimming with hope headed to the giant exposition during what has been called the nadir of American race relations.

Black Americans were as eager as white Americans to witness the much publicized exhibition, which promised to demonstrate four hundred years of progress since Columbus had first set foot in the New World. Erected seven miles south of the downtown loop, on the marshlands of Lake Michigan, the 633-acre Columbian Exhibition heralded the rise of the city and its accompanying industrialism as America's triumph. After the Civil War, the United States had aggressively begun its march on the path of industrial capitalism, and a quarter-century later was eager to display its glories. The war that ended slavery had been waged to protect the freedom of industrialists as much as, if not more than, to guarantee the rights of the newly freed, and it was the products of industrialism, rather than the triumph of emancipation, that the Columbian Exposition would honor.

African Americans, over 90 percent of whom still lived in the South, were far removed from America's industrial successes. The waning national commitment to Reconstruction had left four million freedpeople and their descendants toiling in agriculture without earning wages. Reconstruction's end marked the start of a new undeclared civil war—that between wage labor and industrial capitalism. Many of the federal troops that left the South in 1877, for example, were immediately redeployed to suppress the first national labor uprising: the great railroad strike. Waging such economic battles would consume national interests throughout the 1880s. With the country on the brink of financial panic and with fresh memories of local militias, federal troops, and private security guards suppressing strikers, government and industrial leaders eagerly united in 1893 to demonstrate the greatness of industrial progress and the promise of urban life despite these conflicts.

To sell their dream, they built the White City—a metropolitan utopia made up of two hundred buildings with a court of honor at its center. This central plaza was complete with a large reflecting pool, an elaborate fountain, a gilded statue, and a monumental archway. Over forty individual states and more than twenty foreign countries exhibited wares at their own buildings, but without a doubt, the main draw was the fourteen grand buildings that introduced the American public to beaux-arts architecture. These white neoclassical buildings paid homage to European design and origin, and as the exhibition board's first president, Lyman Gage, promised, visitors saw beautiful buildings with flashing sunlight bouncing off of gilded pinnacles and domes. Set against the expansive waters of Lake Michigan, Gage explained, the White City would "link the beautiful with the sublime, the present with the past, the finite with the infinite." James Weldon Johnson recorded the sight for his Atlanta University classmates. "No one who has not seen it, can form any idea of the immensity and grandeur of the exposition; nor can I give any adequate description of it . . . one standing under the Peristyle and looking down the Court of Honor, surrounded by magnificent buildings with their chaste white columns and gilded domes glittering in the sunlight . . . might easily imagine himself in a fairy city." Twenty-seven million fairgoers joined Johnson in visiting the "fairy city" between May and October of 1893; for the price of admission, they would see a vision of urban life that somehow erased the sounds and smells of nearby stockyards. The idealized city was free of labor battles, dirt, and poverty; it was truly America's first Disneyland.[6]

This fictive city was meant to evoke the promise of America, a theme echoed by other traditions the exhibition wrote into the national narrative. Although the fair was not scheduled to open until the following May, its dedication was set for October 12, 1892, and in its honor, President Harrison declared Columbus Day a national holiday. The fair brought America its Pledge of Allegiance, an oath written and promoted by editors of *The Youth's Companion,* one of the nation's largest circulating weeklies. At the October ceremony, a hundred thousand people witnessed the first recitation of the newly authored pledge while a parade of schoolgirls, dressed in red, white, and blue, marched in the formation of the flag. Millions of schoolchildren around the country joined in pledging allegiance to the flag that Columbus Day, making the grand event in Chicago reverberate across the nation.[7]

More than patriotism and utopian exhibitions drew audiences to Chicago that year, however. Rather, visitors excitedly ventured to the fair for adventure and recreation. For example, they eagerly anticipated visiting the Midway Plaisance—a one-mile long, six-hundred-foot wide strip of commercial amusements. This honky-tonk section of the fair not only offered fleeting pleasures for audiences, but also helped to firmly establish a national narrative linking culture, technology, progress, and consumption. On the midway, America's popular culture was for sale. The contrast with the White City was immediately apparent. No grand beaux-arts buildings appeared on the commercial strip. Rather, exhibitors built a variety of structures including sheds, stalls, and tents for their concessions; they used wood or canvas, overdecorating them in bright colors and plastering them with billboard and poster advertisements. The midway featured a confusing hodgepodge of exhibits, including rides, food stalls, haunted houses, and stage shows; fairgoers could see sports demonstrations, animal acts, and even Houdini escaping from a locked box. For a nickel, midway patrons could experience the latest amusement technology: they listened to Edison's Talking Machine and peered into the Anschutz Tachyscope to see projected moving images. In contrast to the planned serenity of light and water of the court of honor, midway barkers hawked their wares, adding a boisterous commercial soundtrack to the spectacle. The undisputed highlight was the grand two-hundred-foot wheel created by George Ferris; patrons paid fifty cents to ride twice around—or double what they had paid for admission.[8]

Aside from its fun and games, the midway also sponsored exhibits marketed as educational. On the midway, anthropology met commerce and gave birth to a series of "living exhibits" of peoples from around the world. Having been inspired by the "living villages" of Africans and Asians presented at the 1889 Paris Exposition's "colonial city," Harvard anthropologists and Smithsonian curators brought peoples from such places as Egypt, Dahomey, and Samoa to Chicago. They built simulated native villages where the foreigners would stay, and they presented these exhibits as educational displays of world history and culture. Visitors could enjoy a recreated Viennese street, Turkish bazaar, South Sea island hut, or Tunisian village; they could observe Egyptian swordsmen, Dahomean drummers, and Sudanese sheiks. North African dancers became well-known through a woman called "Little Egypt, the Darling of the Nile" who performed the "danse du ventre" on the "Streets of Cairo."[9] It must have been a particularly fascinating summer with such an international crowd encamped together in Chicago, but any convivial interactions among the foreigners, or with the Americans they met, were ultimately overshadowed by how they were displayed. As the *Youth's Companion* announced, "This illustration of primitive life will make more apparent the material progress made in America during the past four hundred years."[10]

The geography of exhibits tells part of the story of the fair's interpretation of American progress. Commercial ties to Japan—viewed by many as the "Yankees of the East"—earned them a choice exhibit space adjacent to a Parisian café and far removed from the midway. The nation invested over six hundred thousand dollars to pay Japanese workers and to cover construction costs. However, China, just a decade removed from the Exclusion Act, had a less enviable location. When it refused to send a commissioner, "patriotic and commercially interested" Chinese individuals in America leased exhibit space on the midway near the Captive Balloon concession and the Ice Railway. Set up between entertainment facilities, the Chinese exhibit joined the other "living villages" on the midway as a place of amusement rather than respect.[11] Moreover, the darker peoples of the globe were generally presented as antithetical to the civilized modernity celebrated at the Exhibition. A contemporary literary critic described the midway as a "sliding scale of humanity," suggesting that visitors view the exhibits so as "to behold them in the ascending scale, in the progressive movement; thus we can march forward with them starting with the lowest specimens of humanity, and reaching continually upward to the highest stage." One enamored white women reflected, "Viewing man in his primitive state, black, half-clad, it occurs to you why you are the only race not on display; the exhibit is for you, and you are the crowning glory of it all."[12]

While the actual fair in Chicago lasted only six months, its legacy stayed with America well into the twentieth century. Souvenir albums, popular novels, theatrical performances, along with the Pledge of Allegiance and Columbus Day, all helped to rewrite the American narrative; the White City encouraged a City Beautiful movement of neoclassical beaux-arts architecture, and the midway facilitated the spread of faith in progress and industrial might, which bolstered Jim Crow racism at home and American imperialist politics abroad. Chicago's midway was such a huge success that subsequent fairs, notably Atlanta (1895), Buffalo (1901), and St. Louis (1904), all included larger and more profitable midways. Fair midways eventually became staples of American summer vacations through their amusement park spin-offs, from Coney Island to Great Adventure. Their legacy too included the climate of racism pervading Chicago's fair. While ethnological exhibits did not appear regularly at amusement parks, games such as the "African Dodger" did, at least until World War I. To play this game, also called "Hit the Coon," patrons paid to throw a ball at a black worker for prizes.[13]

The significance of the Exposition was not lost on African Americans, and a vocal black leadership argued vociferously for black representation in Chicago as soon as fair organizers announced their plans for the extravaganza. Since the exposition was a paean to American progress and supported by congressional funds, black leaders declared they should be able to exhibit African American achievements since Emancipation. African Americans themselves had been celebrating their emancipation and advocating for freedom at public festivals as early as 1808, when the slave trade was abolished.[14] But despite black America's pleas, the National Board of Commissioners barred African Americans from planning committees and diverted their exhibit proposals to individual state boards. In practice that meant most African Americans had to appeal for representation to south-ern states, which were hardly willing to highlight black achievement. The Mississippi building at the fair actually sported drawings of plantation life with what one black Mississippian called "a typical 'Aunt Dinah' busily engaged in filling her basket" with cotton, and at the Louisiana build-ing, reenactors of the slave South sold miniature cotton balls as souvenirs. The black press dubbed the Columbian Exposition alternately the "great American white elephant" and "the white American's World's Fair," reflect-ing its clear exclusion of African Americans from contemporary American life.[15]

It would be two years later in Atlanta before a black man, Booker T. Washington, finally took to an exposition stage, but not to tout black achievement. Addressing a segregated audience at the Cotton States and International Exposition, Washington told blacks not to "underestimate the importance of cultivating friendly relations with the Southern white man" and urged his people to "cast their buckets down" where they were. The speech catapulted him into the national spotlight but earned him much criticism—especially from northern black leaders—for his accommo-dation to the white South. Washington's tone, however, reflected the tenor of American race relations. In Chicago, black Americans had earned only token (and ineffectual) representation on the planning board, as well as the right to hold a separate day of celebration called Colored American Day or Jubilee Day.

Despite almost wholesale exclusion from the fair's main events and at-tractions, one African American did work steadily at an exhibit demon-strating industrial progress at the Chicago exposition. She actually con-tributed to the making of another American myth, one that would plague American households throughout the twentieth century. Aunt Jemima—the loving, smiling, hardworking cook of southern lore—was born at the Columbian Exposition. She was the advertising card for the owners of the R. T. Davis Milling Company, who early on understood the power of com-pany logos in mass marketing consumer goods. If the boom in railroad building accelerated the development of a national market, the tremen-dous growth in print media circulated advertising images at an even faster speed. The Davis Company had earlier procured the trademark for the im-age of Aunt Jemima, but it was in Chicago that they turned their trade-mark into a real person. The flour millers hired Nancy Green, a fifty-nine-year-old domestic worker who had been born into slavery on a Kentucky plantation, to portray Aunt Jemima. She greeted guests and cooked pancakes at Davis's booth, an exhibit designed to look like a giant flour barrel. A souvenir button with her smiling face and the caption "I'se in town, honey" ensured that Aunt Jemima was as well-known as the Pledge of Allegiance by the fair's end.[16] Green portrayed an exaggeration of real black circumstance, even if not black contentment; she was a minstrel performer who reinforced the mammy stereotype and sold southern race relations, along with pancake mix, on a mass scale.

Of Midways and Minstrelsy

It was Chris Rutt who "discovered" Aunt Jemima in 1889. He had inherited a bankrupt flour mill, and was in search of a brand name for his pancake flour when he saw a white man in drag and blackface singing "Old Aunt Jemima, oh! Oh! OH!" during the cakewalk finale of a minstrel show. Rutt's company failed, but he registered the Aunt Jemima trademark and sold it to Davis, who made the image so successful that in 1903 he renamed his company Aunt Jemima Mills. The image's success rested on the widespread popularity of blackface minstrelsy, a form of theater that took off in the 1830s when some white men blacked up their faces to play African American characters on stage. The first professional white minstrel troupe, the Virginia Minstrels, performed in 1843, many others followed, and by the 1880s and the era of the Chicago World's Fair, minstrelsy was undeniably America's most popular form of entertainment. The minstrel stage ensured mass distribution of the mammy image along with the other standard images of racist stereotype; it gave America Jim Crow and Sambo (the "plantation darky") as well as Zip Coon ("the urban dandy").

According to legend, one of minstrelsy's originators, a white actor named Thomas Dartmouth "Daddy" Rice, developed the minstrel character known as Jim Crow in 1830 after he happened upon either a black stable hand or an elderly African American man suffering from rheumatism. Rice donned blackface makeup, copied the man's song and dance, and then mimicked the routine on stage singing, "Eb'ry time I weel about / And jump Jim Crow." In reality, Rice likely drew from a variety of performances by both black and white budding entertainers in the New York

City neighborhood where he lived, among whom crossing racial boundaries in performance was not uncommon. The character Jim Crow first appeared in black song and dance, often as a trickster figure, and Rice surely based his act on the mix of black cultural styles he witnessed rather than from a sole encounter.[17] The apocryphal foundation myth, however, encapsulates well minstrelsy's transformation into an overwhelmingly racist form of popular entertainment. In the decades before the Civil War, minstrelsy's popularity—and its mockery of African Americans—rose in response to abolitionist sentiment, a trend that continued with Emancipation and Reconstruction. The staged Jim Crow came to resemble Sambo, the "plantation darky" stereotype that helped reassure whites that blacks were content on the plantation. Jim Crow's popular counterpart on the minstrel stage was "Zip Coon"—an urban buffoon who derided free blacks and insinuated that African Americans were unfit for freedom and urban life.

Minstrel shows around the time of the Civil War typically opened with a "walk around," during which four or more blackfaced performers took turns singing before arranging themselves in a semicircle. An interlocutor sat in the center and bantered with the endmen (Tambo and Bones). The endmen played the roles of comedic buffoons and mocked the interlocutor's pomposity in speech laden with malapropisms; in turn, the interlocutor corrected the endmen's ignorance, thus allowing for multiple jokes to be made at the expense of African Americans. The second part of the minstrel show, or "olio," included a variety of skits, including song and dance numbers and acrobats, but its distinctive feature was a stump speech in which one character belittled issues like women's rights or emancipation in ways sure to elicit laughter from the audience, which was composed of predominantly white working-class males. The third act (where Rutt "met" Aunt Jemima) usually consisted of a one-act skit, almost invariably set on a southern plantation with the entire troupe dressed in "darky" costumes; after the war, this skit typically ended with a rendition of a cakewalk.[18]

When Rutt first encountered the character of Aunt Jemima, he saw a white man in blackface and drag, but it was Billy Kersands, a black minstrel performer, who wrote the song. Born enslaved in 1842 in Baton Rouge, Louisiana, Kersands made his way to New York City after Emancipation and went big on the minstrel stage singing "Old Aunt Jemima" with one of the first widely successful black troupes, Callender's Famous

Georgia Minstrels. After the Civil War, increasing numbers of black men sought to capitalize on America's racism by marketing themselves as "genuine," "real," or "bona-fide" "Negroes." To further distinguish themselves from white troupes, they did not, as a rule, blacken their faces, except for the two endmen who played buffoonish characters. Kersands, who did black up on stage, had performed "Old Aunt Jemima" over two thousand times by 1877, and he became exceedingly well-known. His colleague, black performer Tom Fletcher, once said, "A minstrel show without Billy Kersands was like a circus without elephants," and W. C. Handy remembered Kersands as a man who "could make a mule laugh."[19]

Kersands, like many black minstrel performers, was popular with black as well as white audiences, in part because songs such as "Old Aunt Jemima" held more than one meaning. In one verse of the song, the enslaved black woman sang about how her mistress promised to free her when she died; unfortunately, as the story went, her mistress lived so long she grew bald and "swore she would not die at all." Kersands drew this story directly from a slave song—lyrics that were probably familiar to most nineteenth-century African Americans. "My ole missus promise me / W'en she died, sh'd set me free / She lived so long dat 'er head got bal' / An' she give out'n de notion a-dyin at all."[20] The cakewalk had also evolved out of the experiences of Africans enslaved in America. It grew from the ring shout, a style of worship and dance that survived the Middle Passage. The dance developed when enslaved blacks were forced to perform for their owners, and in response, mocked their white audience by exaggerating European dance styles. Such black double-entendre underlay much of black expressive culture and played a central role in the lives and work of black minstrels.

Most whites only saw what Rutt saw—a mammy signaling southern warmth and hospitality. Capitalizing on this belief, black performers often named their troupes as if they had just walked off the plantation; the Georgia Slave Brothers and Georgia Slave Troupe Minstrels were two examples. These black minstrel performances—sometimes known as plantation shows—became immensely popular in the 1880s; they provided whites with a voyeuristic peek into plantation life in the Old South, and reached their height in 1895 with Nate Salisbury's *Black America*. This show was the brainchild of Billy McClain, a successful black performer who wanted to provide desperately needed summer work for actors since most theaters closed during the hottest months. Together, in one of the many uneasy partnerships that characterized black entertainment, a black actor and a white manager transformed a New York park into "the likeness of a southern plantation." As Tom Fletcher described, "Bales of cotton were brought in and a cotton gin in working order set up. Poultry and live stock were brought in and real cabins built, a large part of the company using these cabins as living quarters for the season." No script survives to explain what the cast of five hundred actually did in *Black America*, but numerous singers, dancers, and athletes, as well as the men from the U.S. Ninth Cavalry, were all employed for the show.[21]

Salisbury, the show's manager, however, billed *Black America* as "an ethnological exhibit of unique interest" whose cast was not made up of actors, but rather of "participants" from Virginia and the Carolinas. Reviewers reinforced this myth with one critic attesting, "One of the chief charms of the exhibition is its naturalness," another explaining that "all the features of Southern plantation life, cotton picking and pressing and the cabin life of negroes are faithfully and picturesquely re-produced," and yet another writing, "There are some 300 negro men and women in the organization and they were brought direct from the fields and plantations of the South and put before the Northern people, presenting animated scenes of rural simplicity in Dixie." In *Black America*, attested another, "the true Southern darkey is seen just as one might see him in a journey to the land of cotton through a car window."[22]

Fair midways offered ideal venues for plantation shows, and the same year that *Black America* toured, Atlanta exhibitors decided to include just such a show on their midway, with Buffalo (1901) and St. Louis (1904) following with even larger productions. Not unlike the living villages from overseas, these exhibits purported to be authentic. Actors were instructed to "act naturally," with Salisbury dictating, "Any one of the 400 participants attempting affectation will be instantly discharged." He told the press that "these people are no more difficult to manage than other people" and that "though free to go about they seem to have little love or curiosity about strange cities . . . as a rule, they don't go outside the colony, spending their time loafing about or sleeping, chatting or playing cards, really living a life which to their race must be ideal in its well fed freedom from responsibility, and its daily gratification of simple, honest vanity." Skip Dundy, who managed the show at Buffalo's fair, even sent his "participants" to a special "performance school in Charleston run by Fred McClellan, another blossoming showman" so that they could learn how to "act like darkies." And likewise, the R. T. Davis Milling Company marketed Nancy Green as if she really were Aunt Jemima, a fictional character. Like a minstrel showman, Davis circulated the myth that Green had been a loyal cook on a Louisiana plantation whose remarkable pancakes wooed Union troops, allowing her owners to escape. The myth of a real Aunt Jemima persisted well into the twentieth century, even surviving Nancy Green, who died in 1923.[23]

The living villages of foreign peoples were often as fictional as Aunt Jemima and the plantation shows. At San Francisco's Mid-Winter Fair of 1894, Bert Williams and George Walker—soon to become black vaudeville's leading comedy duo—worked at Dahomey's exhibit filling in for the West Africans whose ship had been delayed. On the "Streets of Cairo" it is unclear how many—if any—of the "hootchy kootchy" dancers were Egyptian. Even when native peoples populated the exhibits, fair managers determined presentation; "real African life in a real African village" was often fiction. For instance, Chicago's fair managers had hired a group of Samoans for their midway. To their dismay, the Samoans had given one another haircuts and had begun wearing some American clothing. Eager to show the "savage" and "childlike" past of nonwhite peoples, management required the Samoans to forgo their new haircuts and clothing if they wanted to keep their jobs on the exhibit. To the relief of one reporter, "the Samoans [were] making a heroic and laudable effort to resume their natural state of barbarism."[24]

Since many whites publicly linked the midway representations of Africans to African American life, these exhibits proved especially problematic for black Americans. One white critic wrote of the Dahomey exhibit in *Frank Leslie's Popular Monthly*, "Sixty-nine of them are here in all their barbaric ugliness, blacker than buried midnight and as degraded as the animals which prowl the jungles of their dark land . . . in these wild people we can easily detect many characteristics of the American negro." In a series of cartoons laden with stereotyped imagery, *Harper's Weekly* depicted an African American family, the Johnsons, visiting the fair and viewing the African exhibit. One drawing showed Mr. Johnson shaking hands with one of the African men in the Dahomey village, and included a caption of his wife's words: "Ezwell Johnson, stop shakin' Han's wid dat Heaten! You

Bert Williams and George Walker, ca. 1900.

(Photographs and Prints Division, Schomburg Center for Research in Black Culture,
The New York Public Library, Astor, Lenox and Tilden Foundations.)

want de hull Fair ter t'ink you's found a poo' relation?" Another cartoon in the series placed Mr. Johnson in the Kentucky exhibit rather than viewing it, as if to suggest that black Americans belonged on the plantation. Whether in Chicago, Atlanta, Buffalo, San Francisco, or St. Louis, black Americans confronted this sort of pervasive racist stereotype. After viewing the exhibits in St. Louis, Booker T. Washington's secretary, Emmett Scott, commented, "As at Chicago where the African Dahomey Village . . . was the sole representation of the Negro people, so at St. Louis . . . 'A Southern Plantation,' showing Negro life before the War of the Rebellion, is all there is to let the world know we are in existence."[25]

Despite having to confront exclusion and overwhelming stereotypes, African Americans could engage in their own ways with the international crowd. Little documentation of a black transnational dialogue exists, but with one hundred West Africans spending the summer in Chicago, black Americans had a unique opportunity to meet Africans face-to-face. Meeting Africans at the West Coast fair shaped the careers of Bert Williams and George Walker, the San Francisco "Dahomeans." "It was there, for the first time, that we were brought into close touch with native Africans," explained Walker, and "we were not long in deciding that if we ever reached the point of having a show of our own, we would delineate and feature native African characters as far as we could."[26]

The Black World and the White City

Despite the undeniably racist political culture of the fair, young artists like Paul Laurence Dunbar excitedly ventured to Chicago in 1893 knowing that even though exposition officials blocked official representation of black America, there was little the board could do to halt participation entirely. Dunbar, along with James Weldon Johnson and George Walker, may have been further motivated to travel to Chicago by the news that the grandfather of nineteenth-century black politics, Frederick Douglass, would be in Chicago all summer. Douglass had accepted a position as fair commissioner to represent Haiti, an office the nation bestowed on him in thanks for his service as U.S. consul to the country from 1889 through 1891. With Douglass at the helm, black Americans took advantage of the fair's international focus, in a sense entering through the doors the revolutionary black republic of Haiti had opened. African Americans had often looked abroad when stymied by American racism. Emigration to Africa, Haiti, or elsewhere in the Americas was one way they responded to the horrors of slavery, and later, Jim Crow. Black Americans thus could look to the larger black world for representation in Chicago.

Douglass was not known for advocating emigration, but rather for fighting racism at home. Still, his public service to the United States as an ambassador brought him more recognition from the Haitian government than from his own. Haiti's pavilion was one of the first completed, and Douglass gave an inaugural speech there on January 3, 1893, nearly four months before the fair officially opened. The building was a one-and-a-half-story wooden structure with a central dome and broad veranda located near the pavilions of Germany, Sweden, and Poland. Although the building was more modest than those of its neighbors, Douglass celebrated its location as "one of the finest" on the fairgrounds, in part because of its proximity to displays from "the greatest nations on earth," and most likely, for its distance from the midway. In addition to providing office space for Douglass and other Haitian officials, the pavilion displayed the black republic's agricultural products. In his dedication speech, Douglass hailed Haiti as the "only self-made Black Republic in the world" and declared that the "free and independent" nation would influence "the destiny of the African race" in the United States and elsewhere.[27]

After his inaugural speeches, Douglass went home to Washington, but he returned to Chicago in April to preside over the pavilion as well as to organize a protest against African American exclusion from the fair. In the fall of 1892, when it had become abundantly clear that the world's fair was to be an event for white Americans only, Douglass assisted antilynching advocate Ida B. Wells in her efforts to produce a pamphlet titled *The Reason Why the Colored American Is Not in the World's Columbian Exposition.* He also supported the planning of a day-long celebration of black achievement at the fair called alternately Colored American Day or Jubilee Day, which was scheduled for August 25 and intended to counter black exclusion from the exhibition. Throughout the spring and summer, debates were waged between Douglass and Wells and in the black press over the merits of the planned day of celebration. While Jubilee Day fit well within the fair culture (other nations, including Haiti, had their own special days scheduled), many black Americans who understood that fair officials had hoped to quell black protest by supporting the day adamantly opposed it as a capitulation to segregation. One group of black Chicagoans, for example, insisted that since "there is to be no 'white American citizen's day,' why should there be a 'colored' American citizen's day?" The *Indianapolis Freeman* more stridently declared, "No nigger day wanted."[28]

This publicity most likely further encouraged artists like Paul Laurence Dunbar to head for Chicago, and under Douglass's magnanimous leadership, black America lost little time in turning the Haitian pavilion into a place to gather, to organize politically, and, for some, to sell a song. Dunbar was one of many African Americans who met Douglass there, and their collaboration, however brief, forever changed his life. He had made his way to the Haitian pavilion after befriending Douglass's grandson, Joseph, shortly after arriving in Chicago. Joseph eagerly introduced the poet to his grandfather, and the elder Douglass was so impressed by Dunbar that he hired him on the spot as his assistant, paying him five dollars a day out of his own pocket and thus rescuing Dunbar from the series of menial jobs he had held since arriving in Chicago. It was also at the fair that Dunbar met Will Marion Cook, a twenty-four-year-old composer and violinist for whose music he would later write lyrics. Cook credited Douglass—"the greatest of our Supermen . . . the lover of all humanity, especially the greatly gifted"—for introducing him to the poet. The two would collaborate on two musical comedies together, *Clorindy* (1898) and *Jes Lak White Fo'ks* (1900), before joining with George Walker and Bert Williams (the San Francisco "Dahomeans") to write many of the songs for the Broadway-bound *In Dahomey* (1902). Not only did Dunbar meet Cook in Chicago, but also while there his first book of poems, *Oak and Ivy*, likely found its way into the hands of *Atlantic Monthly* editor William Dean Howells. Dunbar had not known of Howells's interest at the time, even telling Ida Wells at the end of the fair, "I guess there is nothing for me to do, Miss Wells, but to go back to Dayton and be an elevator boy again." But reviews by Howells would earn Dunbar recognition as a poet; as Wells wrote, Dunbar had "left his elevator cage never to return."[29]

Will Marion Cook had been partially responsible for conceptualizing Colored American Day, an event he imagined could highlight his musical composition along with that of other African American artists. Frederick Douglass had long been friends with Cook's Oberlin-educated parents, and he was well aware of Cook's musical talents: Cook had played in a

Paul Laurence Dunbar, n.d.

(Photographs and Prints Division, Schomburg Center for Research in Black Culture, The New York Public Library, Astor, Lenox and Tilden Foundations.)

Washington, D.C., orchestra, and Douglass had been so impressed with Cook's playing that he had helped send him abroad for a European musical education. Consequently, in February 1893, Douglass threw his support behind Colored American Day, and began to solicit funds to have Cook's opera based on *Uncle Tom's Cabin* produced for the event.[30]

Cook and Dunbar were just two of many young African Americans now daily engaged in Chicago with some of the most vocal black activists of the 1890s as they debated the feasibility of Colored American Day and Wells's pamphlet. The issues that divided African Americans over both projects reflected the dilemmas that black artists and intellectuals confronted daily as they sought to represent black identity in a deeply racist society. Wells had feared that visitors to the fair would read African American absence as incompetence and lack of distinction, and she sought funds to publish her pamphlet in several languages so that American and foreign visitors alike could read about the realities of black life in the context of American racism. Meanwhile, *Freeman* editors countered that while African Americans suffered from racial discrimination, they demeaned only themselves by publicly admitting it to foreign visitors at the fair. The *Methodist Union* agreed, saying that since no other group would print such a booklet, *The Reason Why* would "make negroes the butt of ridicule in the eyes . . . of the world." This line of reasoning echoed the fear felt by many black Americans that drawing any attention to black life and experience would be misinterpreted by whites, and would only serve to reinforce the common stereotype. This sentiment was clearly expressed by a *Denver Statesmen* reporter who cautioned that the "collection of nickels and dimes from washerwomen furnished ammunition to believers in the infantile mental and financial capacity of Negroes."[31] That poorly paid domestic workers donated funds in support of the pamphlet conveys their dedication to establishing a black presence at the fair. Pervasive racism, however, left black editors ambivalent about such acts, fearing how white interpretations would reflect on their own image.

Such criticisms made raising funds for the pamphlet far more difficult than expected; it would not be published until August 30, and then only in English with French and German translations of the preface. Still, Wells managed to distribute thousands of copies from her office at the Haitian pavilion before the end of the fair. Visitors who read just the preface learned that Wells and Douglass both described the fair as a "white sepulcher." Those reading further were introduced to Douglass's powerful words describing the realities of American racism: "We would like, for instance, to tell our visitors that the moral progress of the American people has kept even pace with their enterprise and their material civilization . . . that two hundred and sixty years of progress and enlightenment have banished barbarism and race hate from the United States . . . that the souls of Negroes are held to be as precious in the sight of God, as are the souls of white men," and "that here Negroes are not tortured, shot, hanged or burned to death, merely on suspicion of crime and without ever seeing a judge."[32] Such powerful language demonstrated that there was another voice at the fair—one initiated by African Americans, full of social protest, and specifically addressing a black agenda.

Still, Douglass and especially Wells must have been disappointed that the pamphlet was not ready for Colored American Day. Over the summer, Wells had joined the voices of opposition to the separate day of celebration, as she became increasingly concerned with how the image of African Americans enjoying themselves at the fair might reinforce the status quo under Jim Crow. She decried exposition officials "seeking to entice lower-class Negroes by providing two thousand watermelons." Wells feared that

Will Marion Cook,
ca. 1900.

(Photographs and Prints Division,
Schomburg Center for Research in
Black Culture, The New York Public
Library, Astor, Lenox and Tilden
Foundations.)

"the sight of the horde that would be attracted there by the dazzling pros-
pect of plenty of free watermelons to eat, will give our enemies all the illustration they wish as excuse for not treating the Afro-American with
the equality of other citizens." Her fears were realized when a cartoon in
World's Fair Puck announced "Darkies Day at the Fair" featuring drawings
of minstrel figures grasping for "ice cold water millions." Two years later,
just such an event would be enacted on stage; an entire cast of minstrel

performers "broke ranks and descended on the melons, 'uninhibitedly' breaking them open and gorging themselves on the sweet contents."[33]

Douglass continued to support Colored American Day throughout the summer, however, and argued that the day offered the opportunity to display "the real position" of African Americans. He explained, "All we have ever received has come to us in small concessions and it is not the part of wisdom to despise the day of small things." His disagreement with Wells reflected, in part, generational differences in understanding how the still nascent businesses in amusements worked. Wells, more attuned to the reach of mass markets, feared how events would be read by white audiences. Douglass, whose long career had earned him unprecedented success with white audiences, assumed that he could do the same with any public speaking engagement, and he feared that opting out of this day would reinforce claims of black incompetence. He continued to believe, along with other sponsors of the event, that African Americans attending the event would be able to show whites that they were "refined, dignified and cultured."[34]

It is no wonder that Douglass believed whites would be a respectful audience on Colored American Day, since his popularity among whites was unprecedented by late-nineteenth-century standards. White interest in meeting Douglass actually played a significant role in securing his space in the White City. "The peculiar thing," Wells later wrote, "was that nearly all day long (the Haiti building) was crowded with American white people who came to pay their respects to this black man whom his own country had refused to honor." He was, she explained, "literally swamped by white persons who wanted to shake his hand, tell of some former time when they heard him speak, or narrate some instance of the anti-slavery agitation in which they or their parents had taken part."[35] While Wells and Douglass disagreed over the best way to reach white audiences, they both saw that white enthusiasm for Douglass offered them rare access to public space in racially segregated America.

Despite widespread criticism in the black press, Colored American Day attracted many African Americans; some reports claim that over two-thirds of the 2,500 attendees that day were black. Further, the day was actually the last in a series of events specifically addressing the black world that summer. It was scheduled just a little over a week after Haiti's day of celebration, and only days after the end of a weeklong conference called the Congress on Africa. Thus for ten days in August there were events scheduled that specifically addressed the black world and that drew large African American audiences. Patrons were likely to attend all events, and at least one speaker, Bishop Henry McNeal Turner, presided at both the Congress on Africa and on Colored American Day. The August date fit well too with a longer history of Freedom Day Celebrations—since 1838, festivals had been held on August 1 honoring West Indian emancipation.[36] Considering the way the celebration reached out to the larger black world and the enthusiastic response of African Americans, it is easy to understand why Douglass and others supported Colored American Day.

The Congress on Africa was sponsored by white and black missionary efforts, including those of the controversial American Colonization Society (ACS)—an organization first set up by whites in 1816 in a misguided antislavery effort that sought to send free blacks back to Africa. While such paternalist and racist sponsorship determined the tenor of much of the conference, African Americans expected that some of the presentations would specifically address a black agenda on Africa, especially since emigrationist Turner was scheduled to speak. Turner worked with the ACS seeking funds for his own efforts to move African Americans to Liberia—a country founded by the organization. He had just returned from well-publicized travels in West Africa and saw the fair as an ideal venue to promote his plans for emigration. Despite the ambivalence and outright disgust of many northern blacks toward Turner's continued affiliation with the ACS, few could ignore the effects of his words. At one discussion about the "African in America," he announced that the first man, Adam, had been black. While this statement understandably pleased many blacks in the audience, it shocked whites and won him a prominent story in the *Chicago Tribune*. This story increased publicity for his emigration dreams, as well as earned him more support from black activists, even those like Douglass who were generally opposed to emigration.[37] That Turner was set to speak on Colored American Day must have encouraged more black participation.

When the day arrived, Joseph Douglass, Paul Laurence Dunbar, and vocalist Harry T. Burleigh were among the artists who joined Turner and Douglass on stage. (Cook's enthusiasm may have waned over the year, since there is no evidence that he attended the celebration or that any of his compositions were performed in August.) Dunbar read "Colored Americans," a poem he had prepared especially for the day. This poem, not unlike Wells's pamphlet, makes a claim to African American rights to citizenship:

> And their deeds shall find a record
> In the registry of Fame;
> For their blood has cleansed completely
> Every blot of Slavery's shame.
> So all honor and all glory
> To those noble sons of Ham
> The gallant colored soldiers
> Who fought for Uncle Sam!

Reportedly, when Dunbar finished reading, and it was announced that his verse was original, the applause from the predominantly black audience was deafening—a response that helped to fulfill Douglass's hopes for black participation at the fair.[38]

Still, Wells's fears were realized when Douglass rose to the platform to address "The Race Problem in America." When he spoke, some whites in the audience heckled him when it became clear this was not the minstrel show they had hoped to see. When the jeers and catcalls did not cease, Douglass pushed aside the speech and bellowed: "We fought for your country. We ask that we be treated as well as those who fought against your country. We love your country. We ask that you treat us as well as those who love but a part of it." Douglass addressed the reason why African Americans had no representation at the fair, and rebutted "with scorn and indignation the allegation . . . that our small participation in this World's Columbian exposition is due either to our ignorance or to our want of public spirit." African Americans were "outside of the World's Fair," explained Douglass, only because they were excluded from every respectable calling. Making reference to the Civil War, he asked whites in the audience, "Why in Heaven's name do you take to your breast the serpent that once stung, and crush down the race that grasped the saber and helped make the nation one and the exposition possible?"[39]

Douglass's words won Wells over, and she later conceded in her autobiography that Douglass was the wiser man to have participated in the event. She recalled that after having read the text of his speech, she "swelled with pride over his masterly presentation of our case" and "went straight out to the Fair and begged his pardon for presuming in my youth and inexperience to criticize him." Dunbar too was moved. When Douglass died just two years later, he remembered him in a poem: "He dared the lightning in the lightning's track / And answered thunder with his thunder back . . . He kept his counsel as he kept his path / 'T was for his race, not for himself, he spoke." Their views, however, were not necessarily widespread. Even though the black press published selections of Douglass's impromptu and powerful speech, many papers remained ambivalent about the entire event. The *Indianapolis Freeman* dismissed the day as a "dismal failure," although the paper commended the musical portion as a "glittering success." Disputes over attendance surfaced with the *Freeman* claiming that fewer than one thousand blacks attended, and the *Topeka Call* estimating that several thousand entered the grounds on Jubilee Day. The *Cleveland Gazette* reported that the day "was a farce. Hardly one of the prominent persons advertised to participate—to speak, sing and play—was present." This paper also reported that "even the promised watermelons were conspicuously absent."[40]

The debates that surrounded Colored American Day raise issues critical to African Americans—and even more crucial for African American artists—as they sought a voice in public culture. Douglass had won large white audiences over the course of the nineteenth century, and indisputably held court at the Haitian pavilion, but he was nearing the end of his life at the time of the fair. Wells, born in 1862, had launched her antislavery campaign in the early 1890s and was far more attuned to the political culture of Jim Crow. Even more attentive to the rapid changes of urban industrial society were many black artists. The most successful part of Colored American Day was the program of poetry and music, with Dunbar and Burleigh both garnering much applause. In 1893 selling a song proved easier than earning equal representation or demonstrating accomplishment in the professions, in part because musical ability itself fit with the white belief that blacks were emotional—and thus naturally musical—but not intellectual. In no small way, such a belief allowed artists a little more latitude as they searched for public venues where they could perform at the beginning of the twentieth century.

Hokum

As this generation of artists came of age, they confronted Jim Crow racism, but they also witnessed the rise of businesses in commercial amusement. With the new culture industries, audience demand often determined success more than did government edict. While the leaders of the Chicago Exposition had hoped to foster civic virtue and herald Western progress with the world's fair, the new amusement leaders sought above all to entertain as many Americans as possible. Midway entrepreneurs, theater impresarios, and other commercial promoters marketed their wares as educational and respectable, but they were most interested in box office receipts. The rise of commercial amusement meant that African American performing artists could sell their music and dance to fairgoers who ventured off the grounds and into local theaters and taverns. W. C. Handy expressed this new spirit well when he declared, "Money was no holdback when you could sing." Although perhaps an overstatement, Handy did achieve his goal of traveling from Alabama to Chicago by singing for white audiences. He had headed to the world's fair filled with hope, and the fair's midway—although plainly based on ideologies of racial hierarchy—fully inaugurated America's businesses in commercial culture. In doing so, the amusement business presented black artists with new ways to reach mass audiences. Entry to this entertainment world, however, demanded capitulation to the dominant language of racism and accommodation to the use of racist stereotype that had only become ever more pervasive in American society after the Civil War.

Even while they continued to use stage conventions reminiscent of minstrelsy, African American artists regarded the myriad of new cultural venues as opportunities to transform some of these nineteenth-century stereotypes. They managed to do this in one of the first shows that departed from the minstrel format—the white-managed, but black-acted, *Creole Show*. Manager Sam T. Jack had already earned recognition for this show, which had opened in Massachusetts in 1890 but made the big time during its run in Chicago during the world's fair. Advertised as "the Grandest Entertainment under the Canopy of Heaven, Silks, Satins, Glitter and Gold," the *Creole Show* differed from minstrelsy in several ways. Most important for African Americans, promoters marketed the show as entertainment rather than ethnology; Jack described it as a performance rather than as a depiction of authentic African American life. While it still roughly followed the format of early minstrel shows, the show favorably cast black characters as urban and included female performers. Jack's decision to represent urban black folk broke with postbellum minstrel traditions that had generally depicted African Americans as exhibiting the "peaceful" and "simple" lost rural world of the Old Plantation. His urban characters differed as well from that of the antebellum "Zip Coon," the minstrel invention meant to deride free blacks. Although blackface comedy was used throughout Jack's show, the new urban focus, together with the acknowledgment that the show was entertainment, allowed African American actors more room to manipulate characterizations. Virtually left out of the White City and lampooned on the midway, African Americans were included in the *Creole Show* as an integral part of urban life.

Moreover, black women in the show took the stage and partnered with men to perform the cakewalk finale, an act typically performed by men in drag on the minstrel stage. Later incarnations of the show included several song and dance teams as well as blackface comedians who would soon become celebrities on the increasingly popular vaudeville circuit.[41] With its foregrounding of female performers and decidedly urban setting, the *Creole Show* actually resembled a vaudeville extravaganza more than a minstrel performance. Vaudeville, from the French "voix de ville," was the "voice of the city."

Vaudeville was just getting off the ground in the 1880s when entertainment entrepreneurs began to see that American audiences hankered for affordable entertainment irrespective of educational value. It sought to attract the widest possible audiences by offering "something for everyone." Although comedy was its mainstay, vaudeville's success rested on both the mixing of a wide variety of acts together in one program and the running of continuous shows at low prices. Promoters had secured its success by attracting women as well as men to its audiences. Its short sketches avoided the bawdiness of burlesque, making it cheap and accessible "family" entertainment. For ten, twenty, or thirty cents, America's growing urban populations could see song and dance teams, animal acts, jugglers, sports demonstrations, operatic skits—and, of course, comic duos—all on vaudeville's stages.[42] The *Creole Show* was one of the first shows produced along these lines and featuring a black cast.

Over several years of touring, the *Creole Show* produced nearly forty actors who became stars. While no direct evidence exists that Paul Laurence Dunbar, Will Marion Cook, James Weldon Johnson, or George Walker saw the production, they would soon be combining their talents with several *Creole Show* artists, including Bob Cole, Irving Jones, and Jesse Shipp. Will Marion Cook first worked with actor and stage manager Bob Cole and his breakthrough all-black stock company at Worth's Museum in New York City (1897). Cole then teamed up with fellow *Creole Show* actor Billy Johnson to produce *A Trip to Coontown* (1898), considered the first full-length black-produced musical comedy, before he formed a song-writing and stage partnership with the brothers James Weldon and J. Rosamond Johnson. Irving Jones would star in Cook's and Dunbar's *Jes Lak White Fo'ks* (1900), and later, Jesse Shipp would join the two composers to write and star in *In Dahomey* (1902) by Williams and Walker. These artists felt hopeful, given the positive reception to Jack's show in Chicago, that they all would enjoy theatrical careers by the end of the century, and indeed they did.

While not a part of the official Columbian Exposition, the *Creole Show* garnered the attention of white and black fairgoers as well as promoters and artists. Urban audiences—the new consumers of culture—made the show a success. Audiences clamored so much for this type of popular music that managers had to change the official programs they had planned: earlier schedules highlighting work by European composers and limiting work by American composers were scrapped. Fair organizers, for example, had selected Theodore Thomas, the conductor of the Chicago Symphony Orchestra, to coordinate music, and under his leadership such groups as the Boston Symphony Orchestra and the St. Paul–Minneapolis Choral Association performed the music of Bach, Handel, Mendelssohn, Brahms, and Wagner. But attendance for these symphony concerts was "abysmal"; orchestras typically played "to only about 50 people" and vacant seats were "the rule." Fairgoers wanted to listen to the tunes they had heard at the various cafés along the midway or in the surrounding environs of Chicago. "Classic [*sic*] music is not popular in the west," reported one Missourian. Fairgoers, this critic reported, preferred "the gay colors, fascinating sights, and music of every description from the Dahomey tom-toms to the German garden bands." Thomas eventually resigned from his position, and the Chicago *Inter Ocean* enthused: "At last there is to be some popular music at the Fair and plenty of it."[43]

Music had, in part, become more "popular" because of innovations in

Bob Cole, James
Weldon Johnson, and
J. Rosamond Johnson,
ca. 1900.

(Photographs and Prints
Division, Schomburg Center
for Research in Black Culture,
The New York Public Library,
Astor, Lenox and Tilden
Foundations.)

production and marketing that made selling song sheets profitable business. By the time of the fair, a business in sheet music publishing had taken off, and Isidore Witmark, the publisher who two years later was to sign a contract for songs from Cook's and Dunbar's *Clorindy,* set up a branch office in Chicago specifically to take advantage of the business boom. Looking back, many critics believe that the new popular music that appeared that year constituted the early strains of what became known as ragtime. One critic announced in 1898, "Not until the 'midways' of our recent expositions stimulated general appreciation of Oriental rhythms did 'rag-time' find supporters throughout the country." Another reflected in 1913, "It has been said that 'rag-time' first appeared in our music-halls about the time of the Chicago World's Fair." Folklorist Henry Edward Krehbiel wrote in 1914, too, that he perceived "similarities between ragtime and the African music he had heard some years earlier at the 1893 Chicago World's Fair." While it is not known whether Scott Joplin attended the fair, he later wrote that 1893 was a significant year for white Americans' interest in ragtime.[44]

While white audiences were ready in 1893 to listen to tunes played by black musicians or to those emanating from the African villages at the fair, they were hardly ready to embrace black expressive culture as a whole. The music had yet to earn its name as ragtime, and it was only later that critics identified the fair as ragtime's generator. Cook and Dunbar's *Clorindy* would be one of many shows later caught up in debates over the naming of black music; the show's tunes would be named "rags" as often as they were called "coon songs." White audiences still viewed these tunes as primitive, as reflecting the musical style of a less-civilized people. Just as white fairgoers attending Colored American Day did not appreciate the event as a celebration of black culture or achievement, white audiences did not recognize the magnificence of black composers or the skill of black actors. Such biased reception left black Americans the narrowest of paths for self-presentation.

Black artists, in part because they specialized in performance, were able to both navigate this constricted path and open new avenues for advancement. African American musicians and performers combined their artistic skills with an inventive manipulation of the market, and made black expressive culture respectable entertainment before World War I. They took advantage of whites' desire for reassuring stereotypes and readily used the nascent culture industries to lure audiences. On the most basic level this strategy rested on reinforcing the stereotypes that had confined them. But, unlike Douglass on Colored American Day, these African American artists self-consciously played to white racist desires in order to gain a hearing. Among black performers such self-consciousness in method became a defining feature of their work. In a sense, they made their engagement with racist stereotypes itself part of the performance.

In his autobiography, W. C. Handy remembered that his aunt once responded to his complaint that bands made so many mistakes in playing his songs by saying: "Honey, white folks like to hear colored folks make mistakes." Handy quipped of this incident, "In this one remark can be hidden the source or secret of jazz." He explained how he incorporated such white expectation into his band's performances. Upon arrival in town, the band "would often pull the 'musicians' strike' out of our bag of tricks." Handy explained: "During this well-rehearsed feature each musician would, when his turn came, pretend to quarrel with someone else and quit the band in a huff, when, to the dismay of the innocent yokels, the band had dwindled to almost nothing, a policeman who had been 'fixed' and planted at a convenient spot would come up and ask questions. This would lead to a fight between some of the remaining musicians, and the officer would promptly arrest them." Handy and his musicians knew that a white audience would gather at the sight of this scuffle, and the troupe would "burst into song," winning over their audience. And "what singing it was," recalled Handy. "Our hokum hooked them."[45]

Handy took a different route than Cook, Dunbar, and the black vaude-villians who brought ragtime and black musical comedy to national atten-tion, but he shared with them similar methods of marketing black creative expression in commercial culture. This generation of black artists used a variety of tactics in different venues, but what underlay their endeavors was a hyperconsciousness of how they were seen by whites, and equally, of how much they would play to that gaze in order to win audiences. In 1936, the Harlem Renaissance writer Alain Locke reflected that black "musical comedy made its way by luring its audience with comedy farce and then ambushing and conquering them with music."[46]

Handy and this generation of young artists were not simply interested in selling their songs to survive, however. Rather they hoped to participate in America's new urban culture and in doing so, to facilitate race progress. As bohemian counterparts to Wells and her pamphlet, the young artists thought that by playing to the racist stereotypes, they would be able first to hook white audiences, then build their careers, and ultimately, educate America out of racism. In part, they succeeded. These artists made it to Broadway; they formed networks that launched a burgeoning stage profes-sion for African Americans; they became integral to the formation of mod-ern black urban communities; and they brought black expressive culture— the syncopated sounds of black music—to national and international au-diences. As Handy eloquently put it, "If morning stars sing together, who shall say that minstrel men may not lead parades through pearly gates and up streets of gold?"[47]

What the minstrel men could not control was how tightly the grip of Jim Crow would continue to strangle their efforts. While they could carefully manipulate stage images, they could not as easily monitor what whites thought of African Americans outside the theaters. Threatened by increased black populations in America's cities, most white Americans, na-tive and foreign-born alike, continued to demand that African Americans act subservient and behave as minstrels and buffoons wherever they en-countered them. As much as black artists hoped to show white audiences that their stage shows were indeed performances by gifted African Ameri-cans, most whites remained wedded to their belief that African Americans were "darkies" offstage as well as on.

2222222

Vaudeville Stages
and Black Bohemia

We want our folks, the Negroes, to like us. Over and above
the money and the prestige is a love for the race. We feel
that in a degree we represent the race and every hair's
breadth of achievement we make is to its credit.

GEORGE WALKER,
CHICAGO INTER OCEAN,
1909

O N THE night of August 15, 1900, in the middle of a New York City
heat wave, African American vaudevillian Ernest Hogan had just
completed an impromptu curbside performance of his song "All Coons
Look Alike to Me" when he encountered a mob of five hundred white New
Yorkers, armed with clubs and stones, crying alternately "get the niggers"
and "get Hogan and Williams and Walker and Cole and Johnson!" The
mob chased him down Broadway, from Forty-fourth Street, near the theater where he had performed, to Thirty-seventh Street where he escaped
into the open door of the Marlborough Hotel. That same night of racial
violence, another white mob sacked a nearby saloon owned by pugilist
"Barbados" Joe Walcott, beating its occupants, and "were heard to scream
for the heads of Williams and Walker," who frequented the place. In a related act of violence, a gang "of small boys armed with sticks and rocks"
emitted "wild cries and juvenile uproar" as they "savagely thumped and
whacked" a billboard announcing Bert Williams's show, "dragging the
board from its moorings." Clearly, the public visibility of black performers
made them targets of white New Yorkers' racial hostility as well as applause.[1]

In what was the worst episode of racial violence in the city since the
Draft Riots of 1863, members of the New York City Police Department
joined white street gangs in randomly attacking African Americans and
mobbing electric streetcars in search of victims. Mobs targeted the streets
where most black New Yorkers resided, a range of blocks that ran between

the West Thirties and West Fifties. At Thirty-fourth Street, they succeeded in pulling performer George Walker from a Sixth Avenue streetcar. Both he and Hogan sustained injuries from these attacks, with Walker narrowly escaping certain death by running into the hotel. Poet Paul Laurence Dunbar had also been in New York at the time, later reporting that he had been robbed during the fray.[2] Their experiences that night made it clear to these young artists that they may have hooked white audiences with hokum onstage, but on the street, they were just as vulnerable to white hostility as any other African American, perhaps even more so.

An interracial fight at a police funeral had sparked the violence that night, but the underlying cause of the riot was white fear of a black population that had grown more than 40 percent between 1890 and 1900.[3] After the Civil War, African Americans were on the move; an estimated 200,000 black southerners left for northern and midwestern cities between 1870 and 1910, and an even larger number moved from rural regions to southern cities. The black urban population of the South quadrupled between 1860 and 1910; the black populations of Atlanta and Nashville both grew by more than 25,000 between the war's end and 1890. White urban populations, both native and foreign-born, were also growing at a phenomenal rate, and the rapid migration and immigration resulted in racial conflicts over residential and community space, as well as over job availability and political power. Riots broke out in Wilmington in 1898, Atlanta in 1906, and Springfield, Illinois, in 1908. Later, with the increased employment opportunities of World War I, an estimated half million more blacks would head north before 1920; this demographic shift, known as the Great Migration, would give rise to another wave of urban riots, notably in St. Louis in 1917 and Chicago in 1919.

In New York City that August night, although whites indiscriminately attacked any blacks they encountered, they cried specifically for the heads of black performers—perhaps the few African Americans they knew by name. White mobs thus targeted the same black performers whom fellow white New Yorkers cheered nightly on vaudeville stages. As long as Ernest Hogan, Bert Williams, and George Walker remained on stage, objectified and confined by their role as entertainers, they found some amount of safety and even commercial success. Once these same performers stepped offstage, however, no "coon" act would protect them from white violence or exempt them from the manifestations of Jim Crow. Rather, on the street, their success was a sign of just how increasingly visible and power-ful the African American urban population was becoming.

It was during this era, known for increased racial violence and con-tests over public space, that performing artists saw the popular stage as presenting new possibilities for advancement. To a large extent, they were right. The *Creole Show*'s success in 1893 encouraged more white managers to hire black acts, and likewise, persuaded more black entertainers to pur-sue stage careers. Jack's show inspired John W. Isham's *Octoroons* (1895) and Sissieretta Jones's *Black Patti's Troubadours* (1896), musical revues that toured the country, acted and managed by African Americans. These shows generally included a mélange of operatic selections along with comedic skits and song-and-dance numbers. Isham's second show, *Oriental America* (1896), even enjoyed a brief run in a Broadway theater.[4] These black per-formers, many of them *Creole Show* veterans, had not been invited to the White City, but they now set their sights on Broadway—the "Great White Way." Black performers toured the vaudeville circuits and brought all-black musical comedy to the preeminent street of American theater in 1903 with Williams and Walker's *In Dahomey*, and became a significant presence in American popular theater for much of the decade. In doing so, they carved out new social, cultural, and political spaces for black urban communities in the hostile, and often violent, world of Jim Crow America.

On Stages and Streets

By the early twentieth century, vaudeville had replaced minstrelsy as Amer-ica's favorite form of popular theater. White acts far outnumbered black ones on vaudeville programs since management typically limited black performers to just one spot per show, but black acts were a staple of Amer-ican vaudeville nonetheless. Moreover, vaudeville had become big busi-ness. Vaudeville's early popularity encouraged theatrical management to form booking agencies, and in the 1890s, a number of such syndicates de-termined programming. Benjamin F. Keith and Edward F. Albee ran the largest and most well-known syndicate, one that originated with Keith's first vaudeville theater in Boston in the 1880s. By 1893, Keith and Albee had expanded their reach to Providence and New York City, and by 1902, they were booking acts in theaters across the country, including in Wash-ington, D.C., Cleveland, and Detroit.[5]

Keith and Albee regularly included a black act on each program, and since they were known for running one of the better-paid and more respectable circuits, black performers sometimes appeared at Keith houses even after they had already made a name for themselves on Broadway. Ernest Hogan appeared occasionally at Keith theaters, as would Bert Williams much later, after George Walker fell ill in 1909. When the Williams and Walker Company toured nationally and internationally with *In Dahomey* (1902–1903) and *Abyssinia* (1906), Dan Avery and Charles Hart, two former company members, played Keith houses as Williams and Walker imitators; similarly, Williams and Walker Glee Clubs of former cast members performed hit songs from the shows on the Keith circuit. Bob Cole and J. Rosamond Johnson too were Keith regulars, as was the *Creole Show* dance team Dora Dean and Charles Johnson. Other popular black Keith acts were the comedy duos of Cooper and Bailey, Murphy and Slater, Brown and Nevarro, and a group consisting of three women and two men who called themselves the Watermelon Trust.[6]

Vaudeville continued to reflect and reinforce the racism of the larger society, and to perform onstage black artists had to incorporate much racist imagery. Although African American performers had become a presence on the vaudeville stage by the first decade of the twentieth century, black stereotypes were still pervasive, having well outlived the minstrel stage and Midway Plaisance. Most leading performers billed themselves as "coon" entertainers at one time or another, and of the prominent comedians, Bert Williams and Ernest Hogan both wore blackface makeup to play buffoonish characters. Williams billed the 1896 act that made him and his partner, George Walker, famous in New York City the "Two Real Coons." That same year, Ernest Hogan's song "All Coons Look Alike to Me" took off with the vaudeville act that he toured. Bob Cole too played a "darky" role in *A Trip to Coontown* (1898), although he did so without the use of makeup. This necessary manipulation of stereotype was to constrain black public performance throughout these artists' lifetimes.

Although black stereotypes were by far the most heinous, African Americans were not the only group to be singled out. Vaudeville mirrored the heterogeneity of New York City, and comics regularly mocked people of Italian, Jewish, Irish, and Chinese descent. There was a significant difference, however, between the stereotyping of black Americans and the ridicule of European immigrants. White vaudevillians, whatever their nationality, could move indiscriminately among caricatures of any ethnic or racial group, while for the most part, African American comedians were confined to black characters. Only infrequently would black vaudevillians be called on to play Italian and Jewish characters, and with somewhat more regularity, Chinese characters. In a similar vein, the theater guaranteed whites a secure place. Because blacks were segregated in the balcony, whites could be assured that whomever they laughed at onstage, they would be laughing with someone white. Italian and Jewish immigrants seated together could mutually enjoy the foibles of a greenhorn whatever his nationality. Moreover, they could just as easily bond by contrasting themselves with the periodic images of blackness onstage, images they likely assumed were representative of the black patrons in the balcony.[7]

Bert Williams and George Walker were to dominate black vaudeville and then musical comedy during the first decade of the twentieth century with their skillful manipulation of stereotypes and formidable artistic talent. Williams and Walker's performances included an exchange of jokes and songs interspersed with stylized dance steps and pantomime. Walker played the straight man to Williams's funny man, and he became known for his dapper style, while Williams perfected the role of someone perpetually down on his luck. Williams staged dialect speech, buffoonery, and clumsiness to portray this "Jonah Man"—a character he once described as someone who would be stuck holding a fork if it were raining soup. Both men were admired for their dance steps; Walker for his fancy high-stepping, and Williams for a more eccentric dance—a step once described as a "sort of shuffle, combining rubberlegs with rotating hips." After a year as a duo, Williams and Walker introduced two women to their act: Stella Wiley, who would later perform with and wed Bob Cole, and Aida Reed Overton, who would later star with and wed George Walker. With Wiley and Overton, Williams and Walker could conclude their act with a cakewalk, and their rendition of the dance was so successful that critics hailed them as largely responsible for its popularization. Comedy was their stronghold, however, and they arranged their cakewalk competition so that the graceful Walker would outdo the clumsy Williams. Walker would walk offstage with both women, leaving Williams—forever the Jonah Man—alone.[8]

Williams and Walker were at the forefront of this generation of performers who sought to entertain, but who also saw the popular stage as an arena where they could push against stereotypes, something largely impossible—and fairly dangerous—to do on the street. By taking part in this new public culture of theater entertainment, they hoped to advance the race by representing black Americans as urban, skilled, and respectable—in stark contrast to nineteenth-century plantation imagery. They may have been playing to segregated audiences and relegated to vaudeville stages instead of serious drama, but they were able to blur the lines between "coon acts" and operetta, and between respectability and stereotype, when they transformed their "coon acts" into full-length musical comedy. Hogan starred on Broadway in *Clorindy* (1898), a musical mélange that Will Marion Cook had originally written for Williams and Walker (whose vaudeville performance schedules conflicted with the show's opening night). And Bob Cole's *A Trip to Coontown* took the stage that same year. Cole's show foretold the shift from vaudeville to musical comedy, much as the *Creole Show* had earlier marked the shift from minstrelsy to vaudeville. "Gone was the uff-dah of the minstrel," Cook declared in response to *Clorindy*'s success. "Negroes were at last on Broadway, and there to stay!"[9] Although Cook's exuberance may have been a bit overstated, the stage welcomed these black actors and encouraged them to manage their own troupes and produce their own shows.

In part, black performers saw opportunity on the vaudeville stage because the venue itself challenged traditional lines of respectability, offering newer, sanitized theatrical spaces suitable for middle-class as well as working-class audiences. Promoters explicitly marketed their shows as entertainment suitable for the entire family and distanced them from the burlesque skits associated with saloon culture. Since the content of shows on the Keith circuit became known as "clean," just appearing at a Keith house conferred some amount of respectability on an act. Like almost all white managers and critics, Keith managers regularly referred to black acts as "coon acts," and when praising black performers, they commended them for doing what came "naturally"—that is, playing the "darky." Yet they included black entertainers on their rosters because they were professionals who pleased audiences.

Despite adverse conditions, some performers managed to elicit real praise for their artistry from whites. One white critic distinguished Williams as an actor. "Whether serious, grotesque or just simply funny," he reported, "this dark-skinned man demonstrated again that he is one of the most finished *actors* on the American stage." Keith regulars Cole and Johnson received accolades from management as "unquestionably the best colored team of their kind in the business . . . big hit . . . so much so that it causes a big wait in the bill on account of so many curtain calls which they took." One Buffalo manager credited the team as "making the most refined of negro acts," and often managers wrote of their success with no reference to color at all. The Boston manager simply reported that Cole and Johnson were so well-known that "they got a big reception when they came on and were encored for every song."[10] Since the overwhelming number of white critics and management referred to African Americans as "coons" and their acts as "coon acts," the use of "negro" and "colored" here is significant. African Americans used both terms fairly regularly at the time, with the National Association for the Advancement of Colored People choosing its own name in 1909, whereas the general public more often used derogatory epithets.

Equally striking was the reception of the dance team of Charles Johnson and Dora Dean. At a time when any story of African American romance was treated as farce, managers almost always referred to this song-and-dance team as a "colored" rather than "coon" act. The pair had met while they both performed with the *Creole Show* in St. Louis, and they were credited as being the first black dance team to play Broadway as well as the first dance team, white or black, to wear evening clothes on stage. Dean's gowns cost more than a thousand dollars each at the peak of her success, and she and Johnson were often lauded as the "best dressed team in vaudeville." One New York manager reported booking in 1902 a "colored man and woman in one of the hardest places on the bill, where I felt pretty certain they were going to fall down, but they made practically the hit of the afternoon . . . as usual, the woman's dresses was one of the features of the act." Dressing well clearly had an effect, and acceptance and appreciation of their costume by the white audience indicated a new level of tolerance. George Walker became well-known for his extravagant wardrobe, and Cole and Johnson wore black tie, as did the all-male Williams and Walker Glee Club. Such dress dignified the performances and Keith management rarely referred to them as "coon acts." A particularly successful tour of the glee club prompted a Pittsburgh manager to describe the fifteen formally dressed members as "the most gentlemanly colored people we have ever played," and a New York manager to report that the choral group received "monster applause throughout the entire act."[11]

Bob Cole (standing) and J. Rosamond Johnson (at piano), ca. 1900.
(Billy Rose Theater Collection, The New York Public Library for the Performing Arts,
Astor, Lenox and Tilden Foundations.)

Despite this onstage success—and more likely because of it—these performing men and women came to represent an offstage presence that many whites perceived as threatening. In segregated theaters, whites could watch black performers but not have to sit next to black patrons. On the streets of cities around the country, however, blacks were becoming a more visible and permanent presence, and whites continued to resort to violence to maintain segregation and uphold white supremacy. While the riot of 1900 was the most brutal episode recorded in the North, several other incidents around the country indicate that the threat of violence was a fact of daily life for black performers, especially as they toured the South. Once, in Georgia, Williams and Walker's clothes were stolen and they had to leave town dressed in burlap sacks—an event they found so frightening and humiliating that they vowed not to tour the South again. Ernest Hogan once had to flee the Deep South after punching an angry white man who threatened him for mistakenly going to the white box office to collect the money owed him. And when the Black Patti Troubadours toured Georgia, local white Elks confronted cast members who were wearing their Elk pins. One of the Georgians said, "You niggers can't wear them pins in this town and you've got to take them off." The thug started to cut the pin off a cast member's coat when the actor complied and removed it himself.[12]

While performers certainly did not want to court violence, they sometimes attempted to use their fame and public visibility to enlighten whites. George Walker told one white interviewer about an incident that made it clear just how much whites saw him as spectacle whether on the street or the stage. Two men had encountered him on a streetcar, and proceeded to ask him why he wore such "flashy clothes and that large diamond ring." Walker understood that "it was not unusual for a white man to ask a darky what would seem to many as rather personal questions." He told the men, "In many cases white people would not believe that I was George Walker, if I did not wear them. The general public expects to see me as a flashy sort of a darky and I do not disappoint them as far as appearance goes." He made clear that he wore the clothes in part because he could afford them, but that they were also important as "a matter of business as well as personal pride or vanity, as you might call it. I admire nice clothes and like to take pride in the wearing of them, but I do hope I don't create a false or haughty impression on any one who sees me." When the streetcar stopped, the men invited Walker for a drink, and, at first, Walker accepted.

Publicity portrait of Dora Dean and Charles Johnson, Cakewalk Dance Team, 1901.
(Helen Armstead-Johnson Theater Photograph Collection, Photographs and Prints Division, Schomburg Center for Research in Black Culture, The New York Public Library, Astor, Lenox and Tilden Foundations.)

As they headed toward a nearby café, one of Walker's new hosts said that he had never drunk "with a nigger before, but would make this an exception." Walker quickly responded, "I thank you very much for the kind invitation, but I can only drink with you as a man and not an exception."[13]

Stories similar to Walker's encounter abounded as black troupes took to the road, playing venues as far west as Utah and Oregon. The stories show how much the street was often another stage for African Americans, one where whites expected them to perform "properly." Black theater critic Sylvester Russell noted that in many places across the nation, and even more so when shows traveled through Canada, white populations "only see one black person a year" and they then expect that person to do everything from dancing the cakewalk to singing a ditty. When Russell entered a hotel in Quebec province "dressed to kill," he was approached by a French-Canadian youth who requested, "You'll do the cakewalk before you go away, won't you?" Not wanting to play to the expectation that he would dance, Russell shot back, "No, I don't need any cake!"[14]

Incidents like these made artists aware of their representative roles as African Americans and convinced them that their work could help educate whites about black peoples' lives, culture, and aspirations. During an era of shrinking possibilities, this generation saw the stage, and the travel and notoriety associated with theatrical life, as a way to gain a presence in public culture. Although leading performers certainly pursued financial success and individual fame, they also came to see themselves as modern race leaders. "I venture to think and dare to state," announced Aida Overton Walker, "that our profession does more toward the alleviation of color prejudice than any other profession among colored people." She continued, "The fact of the matter is this, that we come in contact with more white people in a week than other professional colored people meet in a year and more than some meet in a whole decade."[15]

Black Bohemia

This generation of artists committed themselves to building a cultural and intellectual base that would nurture black talent and advance the race. Once Williams and Walker had attained some amount of success in New York with their 1896 vaudeville act, their "first move was to hire a flat in Fifty-third Street, furnish it, and throw our doors open to all colored men who possessed theatrical and musical ability and ambition." They wanted to provide a space where "all professional colored people could meet and exchange views and feel perfectly at home," and their own flat became "the headquarters of all artistic young men of our race who were stage struck."[16] Walker explained that "by having these men around" he and Williams "had an opportunity to study the musical and theatrical ability of the most talented members of our race."[17] By the time of their last show together, *Bandana Land* (1909), they had built a vibrant network of black artists.

Social and residential segregation had made it impossible for black performers to foster ties with white vaudevillians who resided in the buildings surrounding Union and Madison squares, then the center of New York's vaudeville scene. Not only could white performers network with each other, but by living near the Keith offices, they greatly increased their chances of earning bookings.[18] Though black entertainers fostered a vibrant performing community themselves, it was located in West Side African American neighborhoods far from vaudeville's business center, making it even more difficult for black actors to gain access to theatrical management. But the network of performers did involve and engage them in the larger, and growing, black community of New York. Fifty-third Street west of Eighth Avenue, known as the most "culturally stylish" black area of the city, became the center of the black theatrical world offstage and was later dubbed "Black Broadway" and "Black Bohemia."[19]

The rich artistic and social world that Williams and Walker had fostered in their own apartment spread to a nearby hotel run by Jimmie Marshall at 127–129 West Fifty-third Street. Commonly known as the Marshall, this was one of two popular "hotels" operated by African Americans on the street. The Maceo (named after the Afro-Cuban revolutionary Antonio Maceo) catered to the clergy and businessmen; and the popular Marshall quickly became the headquarters of actors and musicians. A converted four-story brownstone that had formerly been a private residence, the Marshall was more a rooming house and restaurant than a formal hotel. Several performers roomed there, but many others lived nearby and gathered in the dining room to eat, drink, talk, and try out their ideas. Seating for Sunday night dinners, which featured a four-piece orchestra, was booked days in advance, and the Marshall "gradually became New York's center for Negro artists." Impressed by the social world they discovered there in 1899, the Johnson brothers, James Weldon and J. Rosamond, immediately secured a room. James Weldon reveled in the unprecedented sight of "crowds of well-dressed colored men and women lounging and chatting in the parlors, loitering over their coffee and cigarettes while they talked or listened to the music." Johnson declared that before the Marshall opened, "there was scarcely a decent restaurant in New York in which Negroes could eat" and that "these hotels brought about a sudden social change" by introducing "a fashionable sort of life that hitherto had not existed."[20]

Running the Marshall was a collective endeavor, and owner Jimmie Marshall considered himself proprietor of a small theatrical agency as well as of a hotel, even though the hotel itself had no formal performance space. Performers transformed the dining room into a commercial success, and the Johnsons were so committed to the Marshall's growth that they helped buy the building next door, doubling the hotel's capacity. Within the safe space of the hotel, performers entertained friends and colleagues, celebrated holidays, and participated in a performance culture that revolved around midnight dinners where the "main question talked and wrangled over" was "always that of the manner and means of raising the status of the Negro as a writer, composer, and performer in the New York theater and world of music."[21]

Black theater critics too gathered at the Marshall. More than simply performance reviewers, these critics fully participated in the performance world, both socially and professionally. *New York Age* critic Lester Walton moved to the Marshall when he arrived in New York from St. Louis in 1906, and he worked closely with Ernest Hogan (also a Marshall resident), most notably writing lyrics for his show *Rufus Rastus* (1905–1907). *Indianapolis Freeman* critic Sylvester Russell was so enthralled by the Marshall's social scene that in 1904 he devoted an entire column to reviewing the evening he spent there in the company of Cole and Johnson rather than report on the show he went to New York to see. Russell too had spent several years touring with minstrel troupes and musical revues before retiring from the stage to write his column; he assumed that *Freeman* readers were more interested in the social happenings and character of the offstage performing world than in a white Broadway show that only included songs authored by Cole and the Johnson brothers.[22]

Through the pages of the black press, news of the Marshall and New

York City's Black Bohemia traveled to a national black audience, and the hotel quickly gained a reputation among aspiring African American musicians and performers around the country. Musician James Reese Europe left Washington, D.C., knowing that New York was the mecca for black performers, and as soon as he "could afford to eat in its dining room," he headed to the Marshall. It was there in 1903 that he scored his first major gig.[23] And when the Chicago-based performer Harrison Stewart left the African American–run Pekin Theater, he got in touch with black talent through New York's performance culture based at the hotel. White managers may have frequented the Marshall in the search for black talent as well, but no mention is made in the black press of whites taking part in this social world. In their novels, James Weldon Johnson and Paul Laurence Dunbar both included white characters "slumming," which further suggests that whites occasionally patronized "Black Bohemia," but all accounts describe the hotel as a black-controlled and black-inhabited space.[24]

The informal social world of the Marshall served both as a black employment center and as a place where performers could share knowledge and learn techniques. Harrison Stewart, who had come to "try his luck" in New York in 1907, noted that Ernest Hogan had "always sought to show me things that would be beneficial not only to myself but to all young performers," and that he would "give any of the young performers an opportunity to make good," providing they were sincere. Of "his old friend" George Walker, Stewart explained that he "sat up many a night telling me of the methods used by him to elevate himself to the high position he now holds, which has been an inspiration to me at all times." Looking back from the 1930s, Roi Ottley surmised that "Negro theatrical talent created for itself an atmosphere of congeniality and guildship" that "gave birth and nourishment to new artistic ideas" and made possible a "collective advance" by African Americans in theater.[25]

The Marshall was not the only space for this performing guild; the artists' social world spilled over into a few nearby taverns on West Fifty-third Street. Isaac "Ike" Hines ran an establishment that also celebrated and supported black performers. In 1883 Hines had managed a basement nightspot in Greenwich Village, then the center of black residential life. At the turn of the century, he opened another bar in the West Twenties, and continued to follow the black community's demographic shift to Fifty-third

Street and eventually to Harlem. By moving his saloon, Hines helped sustain a safe public space for African Americans to gather—one that honored black achievement. Often described as a museum of black success stories, Hines's Fifty-third Street location was an "an exclusively professional place on the main floor of a three-story building." Inside, "the windows were draped with lace curtains and the walls were literally covered with photographs or lithographs of every Negro in America who had ever 'done anything.'" Pictures of Frederick Douglass, famous and not-so-famous prize-fighters, and "stage celebrities, down to the newest song-and-dance team" adorned the walls. Hines honored African American achievement as well as facilitated performers' searches for work. Like the Marshall, Hines's establishment became an informal meeting place where artists could network. George Walker praised Hines's commitment to performers, congratulating him and his wife, Carrie, for hanging pictures of "every colored man and woman who has made any sort of mark on the stage."[26]

Another indication that this new generation of black performers had taken over "Black Bohemia" was their ability to transform John B. Nail's saloon, also located on Fifty-third Street, into another hangout for the performing world. Nail lived in Brooklyn among New York City's black elite, and hoped his saloon would earn a reputation as "a place for gentlemen." Most of his Brooklyn neighbors, however, chose to do their entertaining at home, in part because of class etiquette and racial segregation. "The object of the wealthy and educated colored man," explained Nail, "is to be as inconspicuous as possible, so far as white people are concerned. He doesn't want to spend his hours being reminded of the fact that the great mass of his fellow citizens despise him on account of his color." As Willard Gatewood tells us, "Aristocrats of color . . . favored assimilation into the larger society . . . they found most black-owned establishments socially unacceptable" because they "encouraged indiscriminate mixing of all classes." Those elite men who did venture to Manhattan preferred a social world that revolved around the Society of the Sons of New York, a private black club also located on West Fifty-third. Since 1892, it had been "the ambition of every respectable colored man in this city" to belong to this society, a club that maintained its exclusivity by admitting only African American men who had been born and raised in New York.[27]

All of the leading performers had been born outside of New York, so would not have been invited to join the club. But even had such an invitation been extended, it is not clear that they would have accepted. Instead, they transformed Nail's saloon into their own hangout and were much more interested in mingling there, at the Marshall, and at Hines's joint. They were less concerned that the spaces were segregated, or that social classes mixed, than they were enthusiastic about "steppin' out" along with the rest of urban America. The artists' ability to turn Nail's saloon into an acceptable nightspot reveals how much a new sensibility of respectability was taking hold. As the *New York Age* reported, "At any time during the day if you want to locate a Negro performer just 'drop' around to Jack Nail's. If not working you will very likely find the object you search either in the thirst emporium settin' em up, or in the billiard room, playing a 'combination in the corner.'"[28] Nail's place joined that of Hines and the Marshall in redefining the cultural life of New York's black community, making it possible—even stylish and respectable—to take part in America's burgeoning, if segregated, public culture.

Performers like Hogan and Williams hardly represented the majority of African Americans in the country, since in 1900, 90 percent of blacks still lived in the South, and the majority of those eight million people toiled in agriculture at low or no wages. But they did represent the hopes and dreams of new black urban populations. The leading performers themselves hailed from America's growing cities, whether in the North, South, or West, and they paved their way to New York City with performance work. Outside of the South, African Americans were a decidedly urban people with roughly 70 percent of northern and western blacks residing in cities at the start of the twentieth century; the figure would be closer to 80 percent by 1910. Additionally, even though most black southerners still lived in rural regions, post–Civil War migration meant that African American southerners too became more urban; black Americans constituted about 30 percent of the population in major southern cities by 1900. Seventy-two American cities had black populations greater than five thousand; among these, New Orleans claimed more than 77,000 blacks, Baltimore 79,000, and Washington, D.C., 86,000. In Chicago and New York, blacks constituted only about 2 percent of the population, but both cities had black populations numbering around forty to fifty thousand people.[29]

The artists who gathered at the Marshall represented a new generation that had entered adulthood with the rise of Jim Crow. Their experiences differed sharply from that of their parents, many of whom had come of age with the promises of Emancipation and Reconstruction. Will Marion Cook, for example, was born in 1869 on the campus of Howard University where his father was dean of the law school. As a teenager, he studied music at an Oberlin high school, in the Ohio town where both his parents had earned college degrees—after which, with Frederick Douglass's financial backing, he traveled to Berlin to study violin. When Cook reached adulthood, however, hope for full citizenship rights had sharply diminished. He faced a federal government that had turned its back on lynching and had found a place in the Constitution for segregation with the *Plessy* decision in 1896. But he also witnessed an America that celebrated the city as the promise of the future, as well as saw a flood of popular amusements that might just help him find an audience for his music.[30]

Although Cook probably had the most elite family history, other artists too came from relatively privileged backgrounds. George Walker was born in 1873 and raised in the university town of Lawrence, Kansas; his father was a hotel porter, then a better job than most available to African Americans.[31] Bert Williams was born a year later in the Bahamas, and attended high school in northern California. His father had moved his family to Florida and then to California when Williams was a child. Williams circulated various stories about his family background, perhaps in part because his father had fallen on financial hard times. He claimed once that Williams was not the family name and on another occasion that his grandfather had been the Danish consul. Having attended high school in California, Williams had hoped to study engineering at Stanford University, but did not have the money. Instead, he joined a minstrel troupe in San Francisco where he and Walker met shortly before their stint as Dahomeans in the Mid-Winter Carnival.[32] Paul Laurence Dunbar was born in Dayton, Ohio, in 1872 to formerly enslaved parents, and he grew up and graduated from high school in that small midwestern city. Of the Williams and Walker Company's leading ladies, Aida Overton was born in 1880 and raised in Manhattan, beginning her stage career with *Black Patti's Troubadours* at the age of sixteen; and Abbie Mitchell, born in 1884, spent her childhood in both New York City and Baltimore.[33]

Comedian Bob Cole was born in 1868, also to formerly enslaved parents. As a youth, he moved with his family from the university town of Athens, Georgia, to Atlanta, where his father became prominent in Reconstruction politics. Instead of finishing a degree at Atlanta University, Cole headed to a New Jersey resort town to earn money with the musical skills he had learned from his family. The Johnson brothers, James Weldon and J. Rosamond, were born in Jacksonville, Florida—James Weldon in 1871 and Rosamond in 1873—and were raised there. Their family was closer in social status to Cook's, and their mother, a public school teacher and musician, first introduced them to classical music.[34] Born in 1865, Ernest Hogan was the eldest and least formally educated of this cohort. He came from the small city of Bowling Green, Kentucky, and began his theatrical career at the age of twelve in one of the many productions of *Uncle Tom's Cabin*. Of the group, Will Marion Cook and J. Rosamond Johnson had the most formal musical training; Cook with the violinist Joseph Joachim in Berlin and Antonín Dvořák in New York, and Johnson at the New England Conservatory of Music. Although classically trained, Cook and Johnson both joined with actors—many of whom were college-educated themselves—and made careers on the popular stage because no other was open to them.

As a cohort, then, these men and women were the sons and daughters of the black well-to-do. With parents who were lawyers, teachers, and Reconstruction politicians, the group set their sights on making their own mark in a dramatically different era. Faced with the strictures of Jim Crow and the growth of a lively urban culture, these young artists dove into careers on the popular stage, hoping to achieve success, advance the race, and transform black urban life in the process.

The world they created on West Fifty-third Street became a magnet for other young, stage-struck African Americans. While leading performers can be shown to have come from relative privilege, it is far more difficult to trace the backgrounds of the large numbers of performers playing regular vaudeville turns, or making up the choruses of the large black shows. It is clear, however, that African Americans around the country would have known about the availability and nature of performance work. Descriptions of stage life filled the theatrical pages of the black press, and theater troupes regularly printed advertisements seeking actors. One company manager, Tom Logan, confirmed the popularity of the stage and stage work when he wrote to the *Freeman* in 1904 to announce that his advertisement had netted 216 applicants. Usually smaller, lesser-known troupes advertised in the press, although occasionally, leading stage stars announced job openings in their companies. Ernest Hogan placed an ad for a few replacement members for his 1900 summer season; he requested that applicants be "sober and reliable and well behaved" as well as "capable of playing many parts." He listed no wage, but claimed that salary would be "no object to right parties."[35]

A career on the popular stage was a much more attractive option than most jobs available to blacks prior to World War I. Before the demands of war production, urban blacks could at best hope to attain work in the service sector—even in the booming industrial cities of the North and Midwest. The packinghouses of Chicago and textile industries of New York City relied on the labor of vast numbers of European immigrants, who were arriving in numbers close to a million every year. The more fortunate blacks obtained employment as hotel porters and waiters; others worked such jobs as household domestics, day laborers, elevator operators, or laundresses. On occasion, blacks won the better-paid industrial jobs, but usually as strikebreakers rather than as regular employees.

Financial gain was not the only draw of a stage career, especially since the inconsistency of theatrical bookings hardly guaranteed steady wages. Rather, young African Americans found a stage career an attractive option because they could travel, gain recognition, and enjoy modern leisure culture. One black critic explained that touring with a vaudeville troupe quite often meant that "with sometimes not enough to eat and nowhere to sleep, men labored along with their white companions and bosses, happy in their circus life and happy to see the sights of the country and roam around the world." Despite the long hours, hard work, and seasonal nature of employment, performers tended to speak "with pride with the people who generally tell them how much satisfaction they got from the negro portion of the show."[36]

Performance work could even mean travel abroad. Minstrelsy, and subsequently vaudeville, had earned an international audience in the late nineteenth century, most notably in England, Australia, and South Africa. Advertisements like the one from Billy Farrell—who in 1900 was looking for "colored minstrels" to perform with his troupe at the Paris Exposition—were not uncommon.[37] Ernest Hogan had toured Australia in 1899, stopping along the way to perform in Honolulu. Little direct evidence exists explaining performers' experiences abroad or how they viewed the race problem internationally. But Hogan did explain that he had left the United States after his violent encounter in the American South, and reported, "I didn't get myself together again, until I was in Australia with my own company," inferring that distance from American racism had helped in his recovery. Travel abroad no doubt helped shape black performers' responses to Jim Crow.

European tours continued in the early years of the twentieth century and elevated performers' status among both whites and blacks. African American fans loved hearing about their favorite performers' experiences abroad, and white management could market "coon acts" as having international appeal. When the Williams and Walker Company left for London in 1903, they enjoyed a send-off from hundreds of black New Yorkers who waved to them from the dock. The women in the cast graciously accepted farewell gifts "of candy, fruit and flowers" from their admirers. Various incarnations of the company toured the show in England through 1905, and their performances were so popular that a British company issued a series of postcards that marketed the actors' images as "Coon Studies." Cards were mailed within the United States as well as in Europe, and surely helped advertise black performers as international stars, despite the cards' demeaning title. In 1905, Cole and Johnson toured Europe and wrote about their experiences in London, Paris, and Brussels in the *New York Age.* Will Marion Cook too toured Europe in 1905 with a vaudeville entourage known as the Memphis Students. Billy McClain, who had conceptualized *Black America,* liked performing in Europe so much that he left for Paris in 1906 and stayed there until 1913, when he retired from the stage and settled in Tulsa.[38] Certainly the lure of performing increased when travel, exotic places, and the possibility of an appreciative and respectful audience beckoned.

International travel, participation in America's new leisure culture, and accolades for black music and dance all contributed to the development of the black bohemian sensibility, which was centered at the Marshall Hotel. Black performers had, in a sense, created a new urban style, one attractive to young African Americans from around the country. Some evidence that the social life of the Marshall actually signaled a larger changing culture can be found in descriptions of slang used by performers. Vaudevillian Tom Fletcher called it a "professional language" and W. C. Handy called it a "private" vernacular, but they both referred to a type of speech deliberately created to exclude others. Fletcher identified the new lingo as an original and collective American creation that enabled performers to hold conversations that could be understood only by those in the theater or amusement fields. Handy claimed, however, that this "Negro custom" could be traced "all the way back to Africa," and said the language included the words "ofay," used to refer to a white person, and "jigwawk" or "jogo" to refer to an African American. Fletcher recalled that performers "would often revert to this 'professional language' when riding in trains, standing on street corners, at social functions and, of course, in the theater itself and lay people, colored and white, would gather around and listen eagerly, trying to determine what language it was and what country it came from." Outside listeners became puzzled, because "in practice, one could use words from any language, and sometimes in conversation one could hear words in Spanish, Latin, Italian, German and French," and "we would get a great kick when the onlookers would start guessing among themselves." Aside from the few words named by Handy, neither he nor Fletcher offered much description of the content or sound of this language, but they made clear that it was slang that only people "in the know" understood.[39] On one level, its use extended the black political space of the Marshall well beyond New York City, since knowledge of this professional language identified like-minded folks whether in Chicago, Atlanta, Pittsburgh, or Paris; further, it suggests that the culture of West Fifty-third Street was emblematic of a new state of mind for this generation.

If it was hip to join the performers onstage or backstage, it had also become stylish to go to the theater, despite segregated seating. Vaudeville's popularity, along with the urbanity of black performance culture, made going out to see black performers one of the highlights of urban life. Perhaps Paul Laurence Dunbar described this best in *Sport of the Gods* (1902), his novel that was in part about New York City's performing world. Upon arriving in New York City from the rural South, the character Joe announced, "Back home there had been no place much worth going to, except church and one or two people's houses"; it was clear that the young men he so admired in New York were going neither to church nor to a "family visiting."[40] For Joe, New York City—in particular, the vaudeville houses, hotels, and saloons where African American performance culture thrived—was a place to meet cosmopolitan, avant-garde, urbane black folk, a population he yearned to join.

Balcony and Stage

When African American patrons attended vaudeville shows, they did so not just to observe the actors they admired, but also to communicate with them. Vaudeville and "then fledgling musical comedy" were known for playing to the audience, creating an air of intimacy usually absent in legitimate theater. Performers knew their audiences expected such interaction, and, accordingly, the most loved performers "spoke and sang directly to the audience." Bert Williams perfected this aspect of performance, often complying with requests for his well-known songs and sketches. Indeed, once he did not actually have to sing his song as "someone with a very good voice sang it from the wing while Williams pantomimed it." This interaction prompted the *Freeman* critic to comment that Williams "made the audience entertain him" while his partner George Walker made his usual "twenty or twenty-three changes of wardrobe."[41] As critic Mary Cass Canfield explained in 1922, the vaudeville audience "becomes a part of the show and enjoys it." The communication between artist and audience, "however manufactured," she continued, was "central to the way vaudeville won and shaped audiences."[42]

This intimate conversation inspired Canfield to name vaudeville as "community art" and historian Robert Snyder to describe it as a "popular culture community."[43] What neither mentioned, however, was that this "community" was racially segregated. Like neighborhoods and workplaces, race and racial etiquette divided vaudeville's community; African American patrons sat in the balcony in most northern as well as southern theaters. The New York State Penal Code actually legislated against segregation, declaring it "a misdemeanor for any person to exclude from full enjoyment of an inn, tavern, restaurant, public conveyance, theatre or other place of amusement a citizen by reason of race or color." So segregated seating in New York City theaters was more than a de facto practice; it was illegal.[44] Still, segregated seating was the custom at vaudeville houses there and across the country. American vaudeville thus contributed to the growth of two distinct audiences that reflected and reinforced the racially segregated urban environment.

Black vaudevillians responded to white market demand, but in part because of segregated seating, they were actually able to play to white and black audiences at the same time. As long as whites felt secure in the relative privacy of orchestra seating, they flocked to see real African Americans portray white-determined representations of blackness. But African American performers were also able to target a collective black audience, literally and often times figuratively "over the heads" of white patrons seated in the orchestra. White critics and managers frequently commented on this interaction and seemed to embrace it as part of the performance. "It was especially interesting to watch the audience," noted one critic reviewing a 1907 Cole and Johnson production, "for the white people laughed moderately at incidents that made no impression on the Negroes, while the latter shouted in glee at jokes that did not interest the white spectators." Another white critic reviewing Bert Williams's *Mr. Lode of Koal* in 1909 commented that the performers exhibited "no evidence that they are working for their salaries" and attributed the cast's exuberance to the "enthusiastic appreciation of the upstairs spectators."[45] Even though this white critic reinforced existing stereotypes of the "happy darky" with his description of the pure joy found in work, his review also demonstrates a noticeable communication between the performers and the spectators "upstairs"—a space that a white reviewer could observe but not enter. Overtly racist, Helen Green's review of Williams and Walker's *Abyssinia* read: "When Ras shot the moon, and it made a pass at him, the balcony and gallery sent forth a collective screech of delight. Coontown was up there, and every time one of those big words of Messrs. Shipp and Rogers, who wrote the book, came out, they applauded mightily."[46]

Vaudeville's managers paid close attention to audience response since applause determined future bookings, and their reports often relayed similar instances of communication. In 1902, the manager of Keith's Providence house reported that one black act was "very coarse to the more refined people in the audience, although it gets considerable applause from up stairs." When the Watermelon Trust played the Boston house, the manager reported that the act "went big with the back portion of the floor and balconies, but did not make any favorable impression on those in the higher-priced seats." In Philadelphia, the Keith manager reported that the black duo "Black and Jones" was a "highly recommended coon act . . . the singing is only fair, but the comedy introduced into the eccentric dancing catches the gallery."[47] Although these particular managers did not refer to the race of the audiences, Keith houses were segregated and any African American patrons would have sat in the gallery.

While it is easy to document this communication, it is much harder to match it to a particular storyline or joke. Piecing together a plot summary of early-twentieth-century musical comedy is extremely difficult—with or without a script. The scripted plot changed frequently from performance to performance, and often times these "full length" musical comedies more closely resembled a series of thematically related (and sometimes un-related) vaudeville sketches. Further, while white critics commented on the balcony laughter and applause, the jokes themselves were not understood; the black press, by contrast, focused on the performers' successes rather than telling their black readership what was funny.

The coverage of one show, however, does provide a glimpse of what spe-cifically aroused black audience members. One white critic reviewing Wil-liams and Walker's *Bandana Land* (1907–1909) in New York announced: "The mélange drew capacity business, playing to the largest audience of the year over one-half of which was colored. The audience was so noisy that it spoiled the performance for quiet people who wanted to hear it. Many of the best lines were drowned in waves of horse [sic] laughter which swept over the seats occupied by the colored contingent." The white weekly *Brooklyn Eagle* praised this same show, stating that "the touches which portray the life and character of the ordinary Negro arouse quick and hilarious laughter among the colored auditors, pretty good evidence that the authors and actors have told the truth."[48]

The "truth" that Williams and Walker told in *Bandana Land* emerged, in part, from a storyline about African American realtors putting one over on white folks. The comedy team set the show in Georgia and used plantation imagery familiar to early twentieth-century audiences. The plot loosely re-volved around the negotiations of white amusement park owners inter-ested in purchasing an African American–owned tract of land adjoining their property. Bud Jenkins (George Walker) convinced his companion Skunkton Bowser (Bert Williams) to invest recently inherited money in the African American realty corporation that owned this piece of land. The black owners of "Bandana Land" set out to increase the sale's margin of profit by making "themselves as objectionable as possible as neighbors." Preying on white fears of a black-owned, black-controlled public space, the realty corporation opened an African American amusement park and "organized a big noisy negro jubilee" to "raise such Hades that the people bought them out" at an inflated price.[49]

In this one show, Williams and Walker addressed segregated public space, white racist stereotypes, and African American exploitation of stereotype for economic gain—themes that went unmentioned in white reviews. Most white reviewers simply lauded the show for "negro flavor," "picturesque rural scenery," and "naturalness." One reviewer noted that the show provided evidence "of a negro's appreciation of humor, even when the joke is on himself," but showed no understanding that the larger joke was on the white buyers of "Bandana Land." Sometimes a white review included a reprint of the plot synopsis from the playbill, but rarely did the critic comment on it. One such reviewer explained that the plot was of little consequence since the show was musical comedy. Meanwhile, one black critic commended the show for "striking off of real life" and another lauded its "orderly plot and most excellent melody," reporting that "the colored authors have nothing for which they need apologize and have done a good deal which reads a useful lesson to some white librettists and composers."[50] In *Bandana Land*, Williams and Walker repackaged the formulaic plantation myth and resold it to white audiences, but few African Americans would have missed the irony in whites being taken due to their own racism.

If it is difficult to identify differences between white and black responses to plot lines, it is harder still to find individual jokes that may have been missed by white folks. But a few jokes attributed to Bert Williams would most likely have resonated differently with white and black audiences, even if these jokes were not part of a full-length musical comedy plot line. One portrayed characters, presumably black, who could not (or would not) identify watermelons:

> Spruce Bigby was peddling a wagon load of fine, large, perfect watermelons. A flip young fellow, trying to appear smart as he turned one of the melons over, examining it, remarked, "These are powerful small apples you've got here, Uncle." Spruce replied, "Son, you sho mus' be a stranger roun' dese parts 'cause you shows dat you don't know much 'bout fruit. Dem ain't apples. Dem's goose berries."[51]

The flip young fellow was probably a black character, even though he addressed Bigby as "Uncle," a derogatory term when spoken by whites. Bigby then addresses the smart aleck as "son," a term he probably would not use to address a young white man. With this joke, whites may have been secure in witnessing "darky" ignorance, but blacks would have understood the feigned ignorance as a conscious refusal to recognize watermelon and an implicit critique of the stereotype of watermelon-eating "darkies."

Another Williams joke told the story of a mishap at a barbershop. The white patron received a botched cut because he assumed black barbers to be ignorant and unworthy of conversation.

> One of them great, big, I-own-the-earth kind of men, rushed into a barber shop. There was a colored fellow there with an apron on.
>
> Mr. I-own-the-earth: "I want a hair cut and no talk."
>
> "Why the—," commenced the man with the apron.
>
> "No talk I tell you," shouted the big man. "Just a plain hair cut. I've read all the papers and I don't want any news. So get busy."
>
> The man in the apron got busy. When he was through the big man got up and looked in the glass. "Great Caesar!! Is it really true that you barbers can't do your work right unless you talk?"
>
> "I dunno suh," said the man in the apron, quietly, "you'll have to ast the barber, he'll be in pres'nly. I works nex' do' in the bake shop."[52]

No commentary or specific reference to these jokes existed in reviews, but the evidence that black and white audiences responded differently to these performers, even while watching the same performance in the same theater, certainly evokes how Williams's humor must have reverberated in the balcony.

Clearly black vaudevillians occupied an interesting space—one where they had to carefully entertain white audiences without provoking anger or resentment. Aida Overton Walker once explained, "Every little thing we do must be thought out and arranged by Negroes, because they alone know how easy it is for a colored show to offend a white audience." James Weldon Johnson described how this skill evolved into a larger aspect of black life in his 1912 novel, *The Autobiography of an Ex-Colored Man:* "The coloured people of this country know and understand the white people better than the white people know and understand them." The Williams and Walker Company's phenomenal success depended on pushing beyond stereotypes, but only so far as white audiences could accept. Of their Broadway-bound show, *In Dahomey* (1902), the black press reported that this full-length musical comedy was "so nicely told that the prejudiced whites in front are beguiled into a profound interest, even though the characters appear in beautiful gowns and full dress suits."[53] Conscious that they were performing for white managers and white audiences, the Williams and Walker Company carefully weighed how much familiar stereotype they needed to include in order to move beyond the boundaries of minstrelsy, something the black critic fully appreciated. Thrilled by Bert Williams's blackface performance, white audiences did not seem to mind that these black artists were not dressed in the minstrel rags deemed more acceptable and appropriate for black acts. This same show even introduced a song that commented on the white gaze, Will Marion Cook's "Swing Along." The lyrics included the line: "Come along Mandy, come along Sue, White fo'ks a-watchin' an' seein' what yo' do. White fo'ks jealous when you'se walkin' two by two, so swing along chillun, swing along."[54] While "prejudiced whites" may have felt threatened by blacks walkin' two by two in day-to-day life, in the security of their orchestra seating, they were no more than entertained.

Black vaudevillians succeeded in attracting large black audiences as well, proving that their act, although catering to white tastes, did not descend into offensive racist diatribe. As early as 1901 the *Indianapolis Freeman* asked, "If there is always room at the top, how is it, when a theatre is crowded, the gallery is always the first place to fill?" Even when performing with the otherwise all-white Ziegfeld Follies in 1910, Williams continued to attract black audiences. As the *Age* reported, "In every town in which the company has played the colored play-goers have flocked to see the colored comedian." Later still, in 1914, when Bert Williams played a solo turn at Cleveland's Keith house, the manager commented that the "United States census shows that there are about three million dark-skinned humans in this country, and after a close count yesterday, I believe that four of them were absent."[55] This manager had announced Williams's black audience as a "dark cloud" hovering over and then entering the theater, and like several of the white critics, he seemed to regard the large and appreciative black audience as part of the spectacle.

In a very real, if different, sense, the chance to be in a large gathering of African Americans was part of the draw for blacks of going out to see black entertainers. For African Americans, whose access to public space in Jim Crow America was tightly circumscribed, an acclaimed black troupe's performance pretty much guaranteed a night on the town with other blacks intent on seeing the show and enjoying a new (even if short-lived) sense of freedom. One white reporter from Chicago noted that black New Yorkers lived in "widely separated quarters of the town" because their housing was "dependent on the disposition of landlords toward colored tenants." But when Bert Williams performed, it meant "a nightly gathering of the Afro-American clans from all neighborhoods."[56]

Even so, black theatergoers and black performers knew that their theater cachet had limits in the everyday world. When black performers stepped offstage, they had to rely on the hospitality of local black people for accommodations, since exclusion and segregation still governed race relations. Consequently, when black troupes toured regions with no significant black population, they often found it difficult to find places to stay. At one Ohio performance, Will Marion Cook responded to the white audience's applause by berating them for their hypocrisy. "Shut up . . . we don't want your applause," he yelled. "This morning this group of great musicians and myself arrived here. All day long we've sought places to sleep, to eat. Everywhere we went we were turned down because we're Negroes . . . the only rest we've had was the little we could get on trunks and boxes backstage . . . then you come here tonight and have the audacity to applaud our singing." Warren G. Harding, then a local editor and senator from the district, leapt up from the audience and promised to appoint a committee to make sure that the company was "housed in the homes of the best people of the city." Ironically, Cook was neglected in these plans because everyone seemed to have assumed he had already been extended an invite.[57]

Across the country, however, black people rallied around black performers when they came to town. When Williams and Walker arrived in Louisville, Kentucky, in 1901, the "colored professionals" of that city honored them with a "grand musical reception."[58] And in Ogden, Utah, the local "colored society" attended the performance and then held a reception for the Williams and Walker Company that lasted "till the wee small hours, after which all adjourned to the Assembly Club where champagne was indulged in freely." Black performers drew such large crowds in Portland, Oregon, that "reserve seats were sold in the gallery," and they were "much delighted to meet many of their old friends there." While Williams and Walker refused to tour the South, other companies such as the Black Patti

Troubadours and both incarnations of the Cole and Johnson Company regularly toured southern states, receiving enthusiastic responses from African American audiences. Black patrons (only) turned out to see black performers, packing the galleries at a time "when at almost all the theaters the galleries are simply cavernous recesses of empty seats depressing to actors and audiences alike."[59]

Black people turned the gallery itself into an important and empowering meeting place. In his 1902 novel *Sport of the Gods,* Paul Laurence Dunbar, who had been quite active in the theatrical world during his stays in New York City, described how African American patrons transformed balcony seating into both a social gathering and a forum for theater critique. The "large number of coloured people in the audiences," explained Dunbar, seemed to "take a proprietary interest" in the performance. As black audience members walked down the aisle, they discussed the "merits and demerits" of the African American-created show "in much the same tone that the owners would have used had they been wondering whether the entertainment was going to please the people or not." Dunbar further described the experience as one where theater patrons frequently entertained friends in their seats and even went out for drinks between acts. Performers regularly attended and critiqued each other's shows as well, further blurring the lines between performer and audience. At one performance, Bert Williams sat directly behind S. H. Dudley, star of the Smart Set Company, who reported that Williams got "his laugh into action . . . every explosion striking me in the neck and rocking my head like a Gans uppercut," referring to African American lightweight boxing champion Joe Gans.[60]

Often black audiences were bigger than the capacity of the theater, creating another sort of spectacle. In 1901, when Williams and Walker performed with their Sons of Ham Company in Brooklyn, the fire department turned patrons away on one of the "weeks when the black friend and his brother is given a chance to sit even in the boxes and they crowd about the house in droves." Seven years later, theater managers called police to prevent black patrons from entering the theater for a Williams and Walker anniversary event, because two hours before the show every seat in the two upper floors was filled. Williams and Walker were not the only performers who drew capacity crowds. When in 1904 Black Patti's Troubadours played Hot Springs, Arkansas, there "was a terrific crush of women, and at

6:30 PM SRO [standing room only] was being sold ... and at 7:00 PM a women's riot occurred. No more SRO tickets could be sold and an officer was called to clear the lobby, as the crowd continued to increase."[61]

By attracting such large black audiences, African American performers actually created the grounds on which to challenge Jim Crow seating rules. At times, a large crowd thwarted management's efforts to maintain segregated seating. For example, in 1899 in Washington, D.C., "the local theater manager secured extra police to keep the colored people out of the orchestra seats but they did not succeed." At another D.C. theater, the manager complained that his "trials came not just from colored auditors, but also from the management of the company, which insisted that all comers should be permitted in any part of the house." African American reformer Mary Church Terrell once defied segregated seating with six of her friends to see her favorite performer, Bob Cole, in Washington, D.C. She recalled how they entered the theater a few at a time and that most were fair enough to pass. They arranged it so the lightest and darkest women entered together, and all were seated before the show. An usher did approach them before the curtain was raised and asked the darkest woman to leave. But this woman staged her own performance in the aisle and pretended to be a foreigner. In broken English she questioned indignantly, "What you say to me? I buy my ticket, I come to the theatre, I take my seat"—all with what Terrell reported had the "distinctive rising inflection characteristic of the French." In the end, the usher apologized profusely and all of the women stayed for Cole's show. The black press proudly reported other instances of passing, including one report from Albany, New York, where "some of the elite of the colored race ... sat in the most desirable orchestra seats unnoticed" at a performance of the Black Patti Troubadours.[62]

Theater managers used a variety of tactics to try to maintain Jim Crow seating. Philadelphia Keith-house manager H. A. Daniels was so troubled by black audiences that he pleaded with the circuit to stop booking black acts. After one show he wrote, "With lawsuits on our hands, and 'niggers' insisting on boxes and front orchestra seating, I think perhaps Mr. Albee will cut out coon acts in the future. We do not need them, and they draw an element here that we do not want to cater to. Had more trouble to-day on opening, and had to sell front seats to coons, which drives away the regular patrons." One manager boasted that he solved the problem by seating "a couple of stage hands" next to the black patrons who had managed to sit in orchestra seating. The stagehands would cause a disturbance, a policeman would be called in, and all would be taken to the station house.[63]

These theater managers were well aware that large black audiences posed a challenge to segregated seating and thus threatened their ability to attract white patrons. "One of the chief questions discussed before Bert Williams and F. Ziegfeld, Jr. came to terms last spring was the probability of the colored citizens making trouble if an attempt was made to exclude them from the roof." No tickets were sold to blacks for the rooftop show, and few sought admission after discovering that "colored patronage was not desired." Williams and the Follies were also booked for a performance later in the year at the Grand Opera House, where blacks could buy gallery seats. Ziegfeld management agreed to book the company at the opera house during what was considered the worst week in show business—the week before Christmas. They knew that since black audiences had been barred from the summer show, they would attend regardless of the poor timing, and sure enough, black patrons "assembled in large numbers throughout the week."[64]

Although blacks failed to break the color line for the Ziegfeld performance, challenges to segregated seating became a regular part of going to the theater for African Americans. Noting this development, one white columnist commented that if African Americans "set out to assert their legal rights, they could make it uncomfortable and expensive for the managers." And black New Yorkers did turn to the courts, winning two notable cases in 1911. In both, the courts upheld New York State's law banning segregation. In one case, Mrs. Hattie and Dr. Charles Roberts sat in orchestra seating at the New York Theater, but were "compelled to give up their seats on the first floor." Mrs. Roberts sued Joseph Carr, the theatrical manager, for the maximum fine of five hundred dollars, and won a settlement of two hundred. The *Age* reported on the Roberts's victory, but the paper made clear that their case was not the first to be initiated by black patrons. Rather their case was the first launched in several years that had been decided in favor of a black plaintiff.[65]

That same month Louis F. Baldwin won another victory. He had sent a messenger to the New York's Lyric Theater to purchase two tickets for orchestra seating. On the night of the show, he and his date arrived at the theater only to be "shifted from one usher to another, all of whom declined to seat them." After the head usher "sought to take the tickets from

Mr. Baldwin by force, tearing one in half," Baldwin went to the box office to complain to Harry Levy, the theater's manager. Levy plainly stated that "it was not the custom of the Lyric or of any other first class theatre in the City of New York to permit colored people to occupy seats in the orchestra," and he offered to refund Baldwin's money or exchange the tickets for ones in the balcony. Baldwin decided instead to press charges. The court found Levy guilty, but only fined him fifty dollars, the minimum penalty.[66] Despite these victories and the *Age*'s exuberant announcement that managers now had to fear arrest for maintaining segregated seating, Jim Crow stayed a part of first-run theaters into the 1920s. In 1921, the black show *Shuffle Along* did break the color line in seating on Broadway, but even at this show, African American patrons could only sit in a section of the orchestra.[67]

Despite the resiliency of Jim Crow traditions and the inevitable confrontation with white authority, black patrons who went to see their favorite entertainers perform sometimes hoped to simultaneously take part in direct political challenge. In his work on black working-class resistance, Robin D. G. Kelley describes buses as "moving theaters" of daily resistance, in part because individual acts of resistance took place in the presence of an "audience" of passengers and shaped the "collective memory" of that audience. Kelley's metaphor works as well here, where black theater patrons staged challenges to segregated seating in full view of black and white audiences. Any victory, however small, was reported in the theatrical pages of the black press, making these battles a regular part of theater criticism and situating them in a larger struggle over equal access to public facilities. As early as 1902, the *Indianapolis Freeman* printed a cartoon depicting poorly dressed white patrons being admitted to orchestra seating while impeccably dressed black patrons were shut out. And when *New York Age* drama critic Lester Walton was denied orchestra seating in 1908, he complained that it was "strange how much prejudice many white persons have who are in the employ of colored people" and that this white manager was "clearly ignorant as to how influential black newspapers were in the black community."[68]

The press also reported on performers who had challenged discrimination, and expanded its coverage to challenges to segregation in other places of amusement. One of the earliest documented cases was Ernest Hogan's victorious 1900 lawsuit against a steamship company that refused to carry his troupe from Honolulu. He won only $2,250 of the $586,000 sued for, but the case was well-known and highly regarded in theatrical circles. Much later, in another well-publicized case, black patrons desegregated a public beach in New Jersey in 1911. The *Age* reprinted the article from the white press that announced: "Last Monday morning, scores of dusky bathers jumped into the water from all parts of the beach and not a one was molested . . . it is said that the authorities, knowing that the Negroes fully intend to make a test case, fear that legal proceedings would very likely result in the colored people's favor and are, therefore, letting them go where they please." After reporting on the success of this case as well as those of Roberts and Baldwin, Lester Walton issued a call to arms as part of his theatrical comment. He had heard that a young black couple went to the Royal Theater in Brooklyn and were told that they would have to sit in the balcony since orchestra seats were reserved for unescorted ladies only. After settling in the balcony, however, the couple noted several white escorted ladies in the orchestra and realized that they had been Jim Crowed. Walton saw an opportunity to build on the small legal victories, and called on black New Yorkers to "Carry the War into Brooklyn!"[69]

Shaping a Black Public Sphere

That critic Lester Walton publicly called for a war on segregated seating in 1911 shows how much black performers, critics, and audiences had established the performing world as a sphere for struggle. The explosion of commercialized leisure and the demand for black actors had created the conditions for black artists and critics to transform the performing world into a central institution for black urban life, despite the constraints of Jim Crow. Theatrical press coverage reflected the broader political trend of challenging segregation and exclusion in larger society and unveiled the burgeoning black rights struggles in urban areas. During the years between New York City's riot of 1900 and the Roberts and Baldwin lawsuits of 1911, black performers had managed to make it safe for black Americans to gather together in public spaces for their entertainment. They had transformed the hotels and saloons of Black Bohemia into secure spaces where they could nurture each other professionally and politically. They had facilitated communication with their balcony audiences, who were just as successful in turning segregated balcony seating into a place of "sustenance and preservation" that fostered collective response and resistance. In a sense, African Americans had turned the world of popular theater into a black public sphere—a social space that facilitated discussion of public concerns.[70] No formal organization underlay this sphere of interaction, but a new black public culture had emerged out of the informal networks sustained by the Marshall, the theater pages of the black press, and the theater companies themselves.

The world that black performers made, incongruously, resembled that

Cartoon, *Indianapolis Freeman,* January 4, 1902. The white patrons were drawn with caricature consistent with nineteenth-century stereotyped drawings of Irish immigrants.

(General Research and Reference Division, Schomburg Center for Research in Black Culture, The New York Public Library, Astor, Lenox and Tilden Foundations.)

of the black church. African American artists expanded their work far beyond the realm of entertainment just as the black clergy had so often moved beyond a program of spiritual support to provide needed social services and to house political activities. The long history of African Americans transforming religious space into political space had begun as early as Africans set foot on American land. Among enslaved blacks, religious culture supported (and sometimes intentionally masked) political activities. Church affiliation was equally critical in the civil rights struggles of antebellum free blacks, including in their antislavery work. With the demise of Reconstruction and the rise of Jim Crow, the black church was one of the few remaining institutions able to provide any support. African Americans used church buildings as meeting halls, auditoriums, educational and recreational facilities, and employment and social service bureaus. "More effectively than any other institution," historian Evelyn Brooks Higginbotham tells us, the church "stood between individual blacks, on the one hand, and the state with its racially alienating institutions, on the other." Because they were some of the only institutional spaces under African American control, churches assumed a vital role in black public culture as black-controlled democratic space, and essentially constituted a black public sphere.[71]

Although the church continued to nourish African American politics throughout the twentieth century, the rise of a secular leisure culture—one that was quickly capturing the hearts and minds of young African Americans—began to challenge church authority.[72] That the theatrical world might be able to act as a similar mediating institution was not lost on black performers or critics. In 1908, Walton requested "the best elements of the church and the best elements of the stage join hands and effectively preach sermons in their *spheres.*" He called for collaboration of preacher and performer, saying, "In the past, there has been a mighty chasm between the Negro church and the Negro performer, due mainly to the attitude assumed by the former." Ernest Hogan too recognized a similarity and called the stage the "right arm of the church," explaining that religion had always used drama. The "church seized upon the instrumentality of the stage," he said, "to bring home to the people the great lessons of life." Bert Williams likewise argued that the church and the stage both provided forums for education and politics. He asserted, "If we see a thing, we carry the instructive effect for years, whereas we might forget it inside five minutes if we only read it." Activist Ida B. Wells also recognized the cultural shift and supported the establishment of the African American–operated Pekin Theater in Chicago over the strong objection of local clergy. She said "a theater in which we could sit anywhere we chose without any restrictions" would be a boon to race advancement.[73]

The performers clearly understood themselves as race leaders, rather than as simply entertainers. "In the profession there are many intelligent and cultured men and women who are doing much to solve the so-called race problem," declared Aida Overton Walker in 1908. She continued, "It cannot be denied that the stage today is doing great work in the cause of the colored man." George Walker claimed that he and Williams had helped the race in part because of the many jobs they had been able to provide for African Americans. Having started out earning eight dollars a week, he and Williams brought in thousands weekly at the height of their careers. They lived well, but they poured the bulk of their earnings back into their company, paying the actors, writers, musicians, stagehands, and the rest of the personnel who made their company so successful. Walker commented on the large sum, "Figure out how many families that would support. Then look at the many sided talent we are employing and encouraging. Now, do you see us in the light of a race institution?" Critics praised Walker for just this point. The *New York Age* commended him for bringing "about conditions providing positions for colored writers, composers and performers—positions paying large salaries," and declaring him "the commander-in-chief of the colored theatrical forces."[74] Sylvester Russell went further, calling good performers "social heroes," and one Chicago critic went so far as to name Ernest Hogan "one of the less serious exponents of the Niagara Movement."[75] Although a comedian who performed in blackface makeup, Hogan had impressed on this critic that he was working for racial advancement, so much so that the critic aligned him with the precursor of the National Association for the Advancement of Colored People (NAACP).

Secularism was apparent not only in the new leisure culture; the number of secular political organizations also increased as ever more black professionals were drawn to American cities. Many individual artists themselves collaborated with political activists. Paul Laurence Dunbar and Will Marion Cook had worked with Frederick Douglass and Ida Wells at the Chicago World's Fair in 1893. A few years later, Dunbar worked with

W. E. B. Du Bois, along with other intellectuals, in the American Negro Academy, and he became very close friends with Mary Church Terrell, his next-door neighbor in Washington, D.C. James Weldon Johnson, too, who had been so enamored with the Marshall social set and wrote popular songs with his brother and Bob Cole, is actually far better known for his later work with the NAACP. In 1904, black Republican leader Charles W. Anderson had called on Johnson to help him start a "Colored Republican Club" on West Fifty-third Street across from the Marshall, and the men began a political relationship that resulted in federal appointments for both.[76] These sorts of political alliances among artists and activists co-alesced in 1911 when NAACP lawyers represented Louis Baldwin in his case against Harry Levy.

Still, the performers did not follow the lead of activists, and little evidence exists of their particular views on leaders like Booker T. Washington or W. E. B. Du Bois from this era. Rather they were involved in parallel projects—their performing world and that of twentieth-century black political organizations grew up together. In 1895, the year that *Black America* turned a park in Brooklyn into the likeness of a southern plantation, Booker T. Washington took to the stage in Atlanta to deliver his famous speech urging blacks to cast down their buckets, and stating, "No race can prosper till it learns that there is as much dignity in tilling a field as in writing a poem." The following year—the same year that Williams, Walker, and Hogan burst on the vaudeville scene with their "coon" acts—Mary Church Terrell and Ida B. Wells supported the formation of the National Association of Colored Women (NACW). This organization chose as its motto "lifting as we climb," and promoted a program of racial uplift and self-help. In 1903, the Williams and Walker Company took *In Dahomey* to England, and W. E. B. Du Bois publicly denounced Washington's politics in his *Souls of Black Folk*. Two years later, Du Bois met with twenty-nine other political activists in Canada and formed the Niagara Movement, an organization set on implementing its own vision for racial advancement. This group convened annually, growing to a membership of around four hundred by their last meeting in 1908. That year, Williams and Walker addressed Jim Crow on stage in *Bandana Land,* and the following year most of those involved with the Niagara Movement had joined with white activists to form the NAACP.

While disagreements arose among this generation, particularly between the Washington and Du Bois camps, in daily reality, political alliances frequently shifted as an increasingly educated and urban black population responded in varying ways to the rise of Jim Crow. Although Washington disdained vaudeville, he praised Bert Williams and had attended a performance of *Bandana Land*. The Williams and Walker Company had invited him, along with President Roosevelt, to opening night of their 1906 production, *Abyssinia,* "because of the many encouraging letters they have received from both gentlemen." And while there is no direct evidence that Washington ever went to the Marshall—black theater central—one of his clerks attended a Thanksgiving Day celebration there in 1906. And Du Bois actually frequented the hotel by 1911, despite his public critique of commercial amusement.[77]

However much their methods differed, performers and political leaders had similar projects. Both groups were attempting to carve out space in racially segregated America, and in part hoped to use this space to educate white Americans, something Cary Lewis alluded to in a 1908 *Freeman* article. He wrote, "The coming of such talent as Cole and Johnson will leave a higher feeling among the races. Whenever such men as Cole and Johnson, Williams and Walker, [and] Booker T. Washington . . . appear on the stage or platform, it causes such great newspapers as the *Courier Journal, Louisville Herald* . . . to 'sit up and take notice.'" Lewis continued, "The healthy comment awakening the hope of the Negro by such papers is one of the most momentous and most gratifying signs of the times. Cole and Johnson have made a study of sociological problems and have done their part upon the American stage in elevating the race. Three cheers for the standard they have set and the lofty service they are rendering our people."[78]

Rather than any clear program, what these artists created was a new understanding of race relations and its complications for participation of African Americans in modern life. What they represented were the views of a new generation coming of age during Jim Crow. If the black church in the nineteenth century had fostered a collective vision of freedom among African Americans—long free or recently freed—then the rise of the performing world at the dawn of the twentieth century contributed to a sense of "double consciousness" among black Americans, a way of seeing described well by W. E. B. Du Bois in 1903. Du Bois was hardly speaking about the world of popular performers when he wrote *Souls of Black Folk,* but these black entertainers were the African Americans perhaps most hyperconscious of the "twoness" that he described. Whether on- or offstage, they epitomized that "sense of always looking at one's self through the eyes of others, of measuring one's soul by the tape of a world that looks on in amused contempt and pity." So it is no surprise that Paul Laurence Dunbar, ensconced as he was within the performing world, also poignantly described this twoness. His well-known poem begins, "We wear the mask that grins and lies / It hides our cheeks and shades our eyes," and continues in the next stanza: "the world" should "only see us, while we wear the mask."[79] Although set apart from the immediate world of Du Bois, these bohemian artists formulated new understandings of black identity and new presentations of black modernity that dramatically influenced twentieth-century sensibilities.

33333333

The "Coon Craze" and
the Search for Authenticity

A famous culled preacher told his listnin' congregation,
all about de way to act ef dey want to be respected
an become a mighty nation to be hones' fu' a fact,
Dey mus' nebber lie, no nebber,
and mus' not be caught a stealin' any pullets fum de lim'
But an aged deacon got up an' his voice it shook wif feelin'
As dese words he said to him.

Who dat say chicken in dis crowd?

COOK AND DUNBAR,
"WHO DAT SAY CHICKEN IN DIS CROWD?"
1898

S OMETIME IN 1894, the German-trained composer Will Marion Cook
met with Paul Laurence Dunbar to write the libretto for *Clorindy: or,
The Origin of the Cakewalk* and some of the show's songs, including "Who
Dat Say Chicken in Dis Crowd?" notable for the line in which the preacher
takes offense at the stereotype of the chicken-stealing black man, and perhaps for challenging at the same time the presumptiveness of the black
elite in speaking for the entire race.[1] The following day, while Cook was
at the piano playing this rag—what he called his "most Negroid song"—
his Oberlin-educated mother cried, "Will! I've sent you all over the world
to study and become a great musician, and you return such a nigger."
Later, Cook's future teenage bride, Baltimore resident Abbie Mitchell, au-
ditioned for his show during a trip to New York, and when Cook asked her
if she "knew any Negro songs," she replied pertly, "I'm a nice girl. I only
sing classics." Frustrated by her response, Cook played "Darktown Is Out
Tonight" and "Love in a Cottage Is Best," two compositions written for
Clorindy and that would be categorized as "coon" songs. Visibly moved,
Mitchell exulted, "My soul was in my eyes, in my heart, in my voice, as I remained almost too affected to speak coherently . . . to think that this
gruff man could create anything so wonderful!" Cook told her, "That's the
kind of music you should sing, that's Negro music and you're ashamed
of it."[2]

{81}

Cook stands out among the period's black artists as the musician who had both the training and talent for classical composition, but chose instead to write for the popular stage. The tensions he, his mother, and his wife expressed well describe conflicts that black musicians confronted in the 1890s. Cook turned his back on the European classical training his mother cherished, and wrote for the popular stage when he was unable to get his music—what he called "real Negro melodies"—produced in other venues. He had envisioned *Clorindy* as light opera, but could only find a manager willing to produce his show as a variety act with its music sold as "coon songs."

It seems as if the entire history of race relations could be told through the naming of black music. Cook called "Darktown Is Out Tonight" an example of "Negro music," but it reached markets as part of a craze for "coon" songs. His inspiration for its creation were what he called the "real Negro melodies" he had heard black southerners sing. Called slave songs by some, sorrow songs by others, these melodies made up the corpus of sound that inspired (and continues to inspire) black music from spirituals to ragtime, blues to gospel, jazz to hip-hop. These songs could be identified by their use of the note intervals and syncopated rhythms more characteristic of African music; and on occasion, even had lyrics with similar texts. Cook sought to reclaim this music, hearing in it the sounds that might more accurately represent his people. His project, however, and that of any black artist attempting to render authenticity, was a complicated one. White minstrel performers had drawn from slave songs as well to compose the ditties they would sing while caricaturing black Americans on stage, and over the course of the nineteenth century, they had made their interpretations of black song widely popular throughout white America. Thus, when Cook set about selling his interpretations of "real Negro melodies," he confronted the daunting task of marketing them to white and black audiences whose interpretations would be shaped by their experience of minstrelsy's racist imagery.

As Cook struggled to present authentic "Negro song," he had to deal with the biases of whites, most of whom believed that minstrel shows represented some hint of authentic African American life, as well as of blacks, many of whom cringed at any depiction that might be read as stereotype by whites. Against the dominant white perception, African Americans strove for different understandings of authenticity, and their competing claims to black culture often rested on generational, regional, and class differences. Cook broke from the aesthetic and political sensibilities of his parents to join the stage performers and critics who gathered at the Marshall Hotel. He ventured into the modern world of commercial amusement, reinterpreting a black past that his parents' generation had wanted to forget.

Although Cook was to make his career in the world of popular theater, his reflections on his early life experiences reveal his commitment to using "real Negro melodies" for racial advancement. As he neared the end of his life, Cook began an autobiography in which he reflected on pivotal events that shaped his racial identity and race politics. He stressed that though he worked in commercial culture, and wrote songs marketed as "coon" songs, his goals as a black artist were always political as well as aesthetic. His well-educated parents had circulated among D.C.'s elite black leadership when he was very young, but when Cook's father died from tuberculosis in 1879, his mother, Isabel Marion, moved herself and her son to Kansas City, supporting them by teaching school. At the age of twelve, he fought a teacher who tried to whip him with a strap after he repeatedly asked her if Hannibal had been a black man. His mother decided to send him to live with her father in Chattanooga, Tennessee, to "learn discipline." Looking back on this incident years later, Cook attached racial attributes to his stubborn nature, saying his behavior emerged from his mix of "Negro (Kaffir), Indian (Cherokee), and a little English" blood—"all proud, all adventurous, and all resentful of insult." As he explained, this temperament did not further his "being a good Negro and respectfully knowing his place."[3]

Cook left Chattanooga only ten months later, after receiving a most brutal beating from his grandfather, but his travels in the South had a lasting influence on his perception of racial politics. His education had begun as soon as he set foot on the train to Tennessee—what he called the "real South"—when he refused to move to the "smoker" car reserved for African Americans. Because of his youth, the conductor did not force him to move but "cussed him," and of course Cook "cussed him right back." Cook recalled, "Biting my lips until blood trickled down on my woolen shirt, hands clenched until they ached, trembling all over, too frightened to sleep for fear of the Ku Klux—disbanded but quietly reviving—this twelve-year-old boy, not ready to die and less ready for injustice, rode into Chattanooga in a first-class coach, unharmed, but plenty scared." Still defiant, but not wanting to repeat this experience, Cook made sure to buy cigars for his return trip so that he would be sitting in the smoking car to smoke rather than because of his skin color. When the conductor asked, "Ain't you kinder young to be smoking, boy?" the young Will Marion countered, "I ain't too young to be riding in the smoker, am I?" As Cook told it, "the conductor then mumbled something about 'these damned darkies' and continued tearing up tickets."[4]

During his stay in Chattanooga, Cook received another powerful lesson from a thirteen-year-old African American girl named Hattie, whom he had befriended. She associated only with lighter-skinned blacks, said Cook, and "considered herself a blue-blood—like some of those Negroes in Washington who boasted that they were descendants of our First President—and who looked down on Negroes generally." Cook remembered that since "girls were a new experience" he "stomached her prejudice until she asked: 'Do you have any trouble with the niggers in Washington, William?'" Furious, he yelled back, "What are you anyway, a damned fool?"

Cook explained how these experiences brought him a new racial awareness and a new defiance that resulted in half a dozen fights with "white boys who had called me 'nigger!'" In Chattanooga, he turned his energies to chores assigned by his grandfather as well as to surviving the regular beatings he received from him. For escape, he would run off to "the top of Lookout Mountain" to plan his life. On the mountaintop, he decided he would become a musician and "do something about race prejudice." And most important for his career, Cook first heard "real Negro melodies" during this brief stay in Tennessee, feeling "that such music might be the lever by which my people could raise their status."

Drawing on personal connections, Cook's mother arranged for her son's entrance to Oberlin's public high school to study music—a decision that thrilled Cook, who felt he "was going to enter a real school where there wasn't any segregation." But before going to Ohio, Cook acted on the "intensified race consciousness" that he had gained from his southern travels. His father had named him Will Mercer in honor of Oberlin-educated attorney and diplomat John Mercer Langston, a race leader who was known for praising the generosity of his slaveowning father for freeing his mother and providing for his education.[5] Cook, however, upon hearing Langston deliver an address, reported that he "wanted to vomit!" He lamented, "There he was, my father's friend, the great race leader, my namesake, publicly boasting that he got his lovely hair, his tiny feet and hands from his white ancestors!" Cook rushed home to his mother and exclaimed that his "bushy, wiry hair certainly didn't come from any white ancestor," and chose instead to take her middle name to become "Will Marion."

Reflecting in 1938 on this incident, Cook wondered if he had misinterpreted Langston's remarks, but recalled that they "produced the same feeling of revulsion" at the time as did "Hattie's comment about 'niggers.'" He kept the name "Marion" throughout his life, but did name his only son "Mercer," perhaps in response to some lingering doubt about Langston's politics. Still, his reactions clearly demonstrated his anger at African Americans who had themselves internalized racist beliefs. Cook remained convinced during his lifetime that "until the Negro became proud of his African blood, of his African heritage, the race was doomed." Throughout his musical career, whether in classical or popular arts, he struggled to stay true to this proudly nationalist sentiment.

He wrote *Clorindy* shortly after he ended his year studying composition in New York City at the National Conservatory, where Antonín Dvořák served as guest director during the year of the Chicago World's Fair. Cook attended the conservatory along with black vocalist Harry T. Burleigh—an artist who had sung on Colored American Day. Although they chose different musical paths, they remained friends. Cook plunged himself into writing for the popular stage; Burleigh remained more firmly within the world of noncommercial classical music, although he too sang, on occasion, in popular shows. Cook wrote music that became known as ragtime and jazz, while Burleigh privileged spirituals he considered untouched by modern musical styles.

While Cook and Burleigh studied at the conservatory, Dvořák composed his famous "Symphony No. 9 in E minor, op. 95 'From the New World,'" a work powerfully influenced by black song. Reportedly Burleigh's singing, more than Cook's compositions, influenced Dvořák. "I gave him what I knew of Negro songs—no one called them spirituals then," recalled Burleigh, "and he wrote some of my tunes (my people's music) into the New World Symphony." Cook knew that Dvořák preferred Burleigh's singing to his compositions. "Dvořák didn't like me anyway," he said; "Harry T. Burleigh was his pet." Since Dvořák taught composition, Cook studied more formally with him, but felt stifled by the rigid and hierarchical structure of orchestral work. He confessed, "I was barred anyhow from the classes at the National Conservatory of Music, because I wouldn't play my fiddle in the orchestra under Dvořák." Both Cook and Dvořák were known for their feisty temperaments, so it is no surprise that they found it difficult to work together. Reportedly, Cook once smashed his violin on a reporter's desk in anger at a review that praised him as the "greatest Negro violinist." Cook declared that he preferred being known as the "greatest violinist in the world," and left the reporter's office with his splintered violin.[6] Dvořák was equally intimidating; conservatory students said he often made them rework their scores dozens of times, and was even known to throw on the floor pages of a manuscript that displeased him, grinding them under his heel and "punctuating the performance with grunts like unto those of a wild boar."[7] But although Dvořák favored Burleigh's singing, he did recognize and admire Cook's talent. According to Lester Walton, Dvořák said of Cook's work: "Plantation melodies constitute the soul of American music, and this boy may some day be the greatest American composer."[8]

After leaving the conservatory, Cook decided to end his career as a classical violinist and devote himself fully to composing for the stage. He returned to Washington, D.C., and convinced Paul Laurence Dunbar to work with him on *Clorindy*, even though Dunbar was more concerned with being taken seriously as a poet. Along with Cook and Burleigh, Dunbar straddled the worlds of so-called high and popular art forms throughout his career. None of these artists set out to work solely in the popular arts, but rather they found their expressive culture categorized as such, in large part because of their race. Dunbar and Cook certainly enjoyed working on *Clorindy*, however. According to Cook, during their all-night writing session they drank two dozen bottles of beer and a quart of whiskey, and ate steak with onions and peppers. They were so involved in their work (and their drink) that they ate the steak raw because they did not have a stove available in the basement room where they were laboring. Dunbar expressed skepticism about the show, but Cook tried to reassure him, slapping him enthusiastically on the back and saying, "Wait till it gets to New York. You'll see."[9]

The year that Cook and Dunbar wrote *Clorindy*, Burleigh worked as a baritone soloist at St. George's Episcopal Church just west of Stuyvesant Square, no small feat since this fashionable and wealthy church had an all-white congregation. Burleigh remained friends with Cook, and became well-known among the crew at the Marshall. His steady job even enabled him to assist Cook while he struggled to produce *Clorindy*. "I was desperate," recalled Cook. "My feet, with soles worn through, were burnt black by walking on the hot cobblestones of New York streets. I was hungry almost all of the time, except when I could meet Harry Burleigh." Although he "only made a small salary" at St. George's, Burleigh always "had enough to treat me to coffee and crullers at a little dairy called Cushman's." Later, when he finally put *Clorindy* on stage at the Casino Theater Roof Garden, Cook wore clothes borrowed from Burleigh when conducting the orchestra.[10]

While Cook envisioned *Clorindy* as an opera, he had trouble convincing either promoters or critics of this designation. Isidore Witmark, who had signed the contract to publish songs from the show in 1895, told Cook that he "must be crazy to believe that any Broadway audience would listen to Negroes singing Negro opera." In his struggle to bring his show to the stage, Cook reportedly visited theatrical producer George Lederer a number of times. But as Lester Walton later surmised, Lederer seemed to think "a position as elevator-boy was more in the line of the persistent caller."[11] In 1898, when Cook finally won a booking for *Clorindy*, it was for a trial performance at the Casino Roof Garden, which provided after-theater variety shows for Broadway audiences. Since the performance would be late at night and outdoors, little of Dunbar's libretto could be used—its dialogue would not carry well.[12] Rather the truncated show consisted of song and dance numbers; a mélange that resembled variety shows popular at the time.

Even so, *Clorindy* was a huge success, and the opening-night audience brought blackface comedian Ernest Hogan back for ten encores of "Who Dat Say Chicken in Dis Crowd?" While Cook did not achieve his vision of producing a "Negro opera" with *Clorindy*, he did produce an all-black musical variety show for an appreciative Broadway audience. Additionally, with this show, he launched a fruitful career composing for the popular stage—one that earned him praise for writing "real Negro melodies." Commenting on his work in 1908, Lester Walton described Cook as possessing "the happy faculty of writing music out of the ordinary and yet making it characteristically Negro" and as "without a doubt our leading composer." Walton also said of Cook: "In all his compositions he never forgets to impress the public with one thing—that he has written negro music." Reflecting back from the 1930s, James Weldon Johnson surmised that Cook was "the most original genius among all the Negro musicians" and said that Cook believed "the Negro in music and on the stage ought to be a Negro, a genuine Negro" and that "the Negro should eschew 'white' patterns."[13]

Cook's intent was to write "real Negro melodies"; the word "ragtime" was unknown when he and Dunbar sat down to write *Clorindy*. There is no evidence that Cook set out to write ragtime or "coon" songs, and he made no mention of altering the songs themselves for the market. Rather, the publishing industry and popular press affixed the labels categorizing black music. Of Williams and Walker's *Senegambian Carnival*, the *New York Dramatic Mirror* proclaimed in 1898, "The rag-time craze received another boom here last week, when Williams and Walker's big aggregation of colored talent were seen in a sort of black musical comedy in three scenes" and credited Harry Burleigh with leading the "ragtime music with great success." Some black critics did call *Clorindy* a "comic opera," but more typical was this comment by the *Indianapolis Freeman* describing the production as "a good, first-class, rag-time, musical cakewalk," and specifying, "no opera can be written all in rag-time." Cook's music was "Negro music"; as Scott Joplin quipped in 1913, "There has been ragtime music in America ever since the Negro race has been here, but the white people took no notice of it until about twenty years ago."[14]

The popular stage had helped the music become such a success, and "Negro music" made its way from its vaudeville debut to Broadway popularity via white singers like May Irwin. A popular vaudeville actress, Irwin adopted Hogan's song "All Coons Look Alike to Me" in 1896, and quickly became known as a "coon" shouter through her singing of his songs as well as those by Cook and Cole and the Johnson brothers. Black music, and its association with black dance, had become such the rage on Broadway that in 1898, one of the largest white shows, *Yankee Doodle Dandy*, even included a cakewalk finale.[15] Although Broadway stages rarely featured African American performers, their music and dance had found an eager audience.

Still, like the comedy of black vaudevillians, black music, no matter the style, met derision from the dominant culture. Both white and black turn-of-the-century music critics repeatedly attacked ragtime as a "low" form of music—which helps explain why Isabel Marion Cook and Abbie Mitchell were initially so distraught by Cook's compositions. One black critic claimed that the music has done "much to lower the musical taste and standard of the whole musical public, irrespective of color or nation-

ality." A white critic went further, calling the "ragweed of music" a pernicious evil: "In Christian homes, where purity of morals are stressed, ragtime should find no resting place." Jazz pianist Willie "the Lion" Smith
recalled that "when you played in a raggy style, folks would right away
think of the bad words and all the hell-raising they heard about in the red-
light district."[16] As these commentators made all too clear, ragtime em-
bodied many of the anxieties associated with modern culture—raising issues not only of race, but also of class, gender, sexuality, and the rise of im-
morality associated with city life generally. Ragtime remained linked with
ideas of a rough, tawdry, and sexually charged leisure culture even though
the foremost ragtime composers hailed from relatively privileged backgrounds and had been trained in the classical European style. Similar to
Cook, J. Rosamond Johnson had studied at the New England Conservatory of music before writing for the popular stage. Scott Joplin too had
studied classical piano with a German teacher in his hometown in Texas
before he moved to Missouri and became known for his rags.[17]

Despite his European education, Cook demonstrated a proud black
identity and remained deeply committed to furthering the interests of his
race. Still, he composed songs that lent themselves to categorization as
"coon" songs for "coon" shows. Like his fellow stage artists, Cook did not
choose an easy path by incorporating the racist imagery that sold his
songs. His creation and popularization of "Negro melodies" through modern entertainment industries meant compromise, even as he subverted
ruling mythologies of black primitivism and creative capacity. As Tricia
Rose states about late-twentieth-century rap artists, "To participate in and
try to manipulate the terms of mass-mediated culture is a double-edged
sword that cuts both ways—it provides communication channels within
and among largely disparate groups and requires compromise that often
affirms the very structures much of its philosophy seems determined to
undermine."[18] She could easily be writing about late-nineteenth-century
African American popular artists as they took part in the "coon craze."

The Craze for "Coon" Songs

"Coon" songs had officially taken off in 1896 with the publication of Ernest Hogan's "All Coons Look Alike to Me" and Ben Harney's "Mister
Johnson Turn Me Loose," and would remain popular throughout the first
decade of the twentieth century. Hogan was a popular African American

blackface comedian, and Harney was a pianist who may have been an African American passing for white.[19] A song did not necessarily have to contain the word "coon" to be marketed as a "coon" song, and many songs that contained multiple uses of the word were not specifically marketed as such. But the vast majority of "coon" songs used some amount of dialect, syncopation, and reference to black stereotype. Hogan's song "All Coons Look Alike to Me" used all three aspects to recount the woes of a gentleman who had lost his beloved to a more wealthy man. Hogan sang:

> Talk about a coon a having trouble
> I think I have enough of ma own
> Its all about ma Lucy Janey Stubbles
> And she has caused my heart to mourn
> Thar's another coon barber from Virginia
> In soci'ty he's the leader of the day
> And now ma honey gal is gwine to quit me
> Yes she's gone and drove this coon away
> She'd no excuse to turn me loose
> I've been abused, I'm all confused
> Cause these words she did say
>
> All coons look alike to me
> I've got another beau, you see
> And he's just as good to me as you, nig!
> Ever tried to be
> He spends his money free,
> I know we can't agree
> So I don't like you no how
> All coons look alike to me.[20]

The song's popularity inspired musicians, actors, and publishers alike, and although "coon" songs varied widely—particularly between those authored by blacks and by whites—by the end of the first decade of the twentieth century well over six hundred "coon" songs had been produced, selling in the millions of copies.[21]

In fact, it was the popular song craze that elevated the relatively new use of the word "coon" as a racial designation to a mainstay of popular language. The term became widely used so quickly that its use has been described as a "linguistic coup." While it is clear that the word was used as a

Ernest Hogan, ca. 1900.

(Helen Armstead-Johnson Theater Photograph Collection, Photographs and Prints Division, Schomburg Center for Research in Black Culture, The New York Public Library, Astor, Lenox and Tilden Foundations.)

racial epithet in the 1880s and became enmeshed in American culture with the publication of "coon" songs in the 1890s, it is far less apparent how and why this particular term was used to deride blacks. Although the minstrel stage introduced the character "Zip Coon" and made myriad references to "coon-hunting and eating coons," most references to human "coons" were directed at white folks before the Civil War. The word "coon" usually referred to "a white country person, to a sharpster or, in phrases like a *pretty slick coon,* to both." Its use was so prevalent that the Whig party adopted symbols like Davy Crockett's coonskin cap, nailed coonskins to people's doors, and used live raccoons as signs of party loyalty to reach out to rural whites. Whigs then became known as "coons" and Democrats criticized "coongress" and "coonventions." The transformation of the word as a derogatory one for blacks may have derived from the Whigs' nickname as the "Whig Coon Party," because of their slightly more tolerant attitude toward antislavery. Since Reconstruction brought former Whigs along with African Americans to political office in the South, maybe Reconstruction was seen as bringing "coon" rule.[22] A more plausible explanation, however, is that over time the names of minstrel characters simply began to be used offstage to deride African Americans.

Ernest Hogan's account of his decision to use the word in his song further illustrates the pre–"coon craze" ambiguity of the term. He wrote "All Coons Look Alike to Me" after encountering a piano player in Chicago who was depressed because his girlfriend had left him and was singing, "All pimps look alike to me." The tune stuck with Hogan and he changed the lyrics, confiding to his friend and colleague, black vaudevillian Tom Fletcher, that "we have been called every name under the sun, so I added another." He claimed to have chosen this particular word because "the coon is a very smart animal."[23] While the use of "coon" as a racist designation predated Hogan's song, his story does fit with the earlier use of the "slick coon" or "sharpster." It is clear, however, that the use of the term was intimately related to the growth of turn-of-the-century popular amusements, specifically vaudeville theater and sheet music publishing—culture industries that fed white America's craving for caricature and stereotype.

Despite the use of stereotyped imagery, the "coon" craze earned significant support in the black press. Extensive coverage demonstrates that a larger black population joined composers like Hogan and Cook in their hopes in the liberating potential of commercial music, however racist its underpinnings. Black theater critics reported extensively on the popular stage shows that featured "coon" songs, and throughout the pages of the two black weeklies with regular theatrical columns, the *Indianapolis Freeman* and the *New York Age*, there are numerous descriptions from 1896 through the first decade of the twentieth century of Hogan and other black performers as singers of "coon" songs, as practitioners of "coon" comedy, or simply as "coon artists."[24] Rarely did the word "coon" appear with quotation marks during this period. In 1902, when critic Sylvester Russell condemned the use of the word "nigger," he maintained, "There seems to be no objections to the word 'coon' and the word 'darkey' could easily be substituted for 'nigger.'" The *Freeman* announced in 1900 that "colored people turned out in large numbers" to see Bob Cole and Billy Johnson sing "coon ditties" in their show *A Trip to Coontown,* and three months later, the newspaper reported that this same show played to "crowded houses" in Memphis, drawing "representative white and colored citizens." A 1901 review of Williams and Walker's "modern comedy play," the *Sons of Ham,* reported that "these two real coons" would be performing with their "own big organization of fifty people" and that Williams and Walker were "bound to be good in any sort of a coon play." Numerous advertisements for shows as well as reports from smaller African American touring companies appeared on the pages of the black press with names like "Gay Coons from Darktown," "Pan-American Coons," "Coon Hollow Co.," "Hottest Coon in Dixie," and "A 'Honolulu Coon' Co."[25]

The *Indianapolis Freeman* described performers who traveled abroad—like Williams and Walker, Ernest Hogan, and Billy McClain—as "educating the foreigners to 'Coon Comedy.'"[26] When Williams and Walker brought *In Dahomey* to England in 1903, Walker said that he did not think "the King would like Williams and Walker's coon business, but he did," and the black press praised the team for "overcoming the many drawbacks consequent upon the putting together of a real 'coon' comedy."[27] Even the more subdued *Colored American Magazine* included an article by Lester Walton in 1903 that lauded Williams and Walker with producing "the First Coon Show on Broadway."[28] As late as 1908, as dramatic editor of the *New York Age*, Walton argued that these men desired to further the interests of the race and "did not quit and exclaim they knew their place when they were told that coon shows would never do on Broadway." Black audiences at Chicago's African American–run Pekin Theater too were said to have enjoyed performances of cakewalks, ragtime, and "coon songs of the nineties." And Paul Laurence Dunbar's 1902 novel *Sport of the Gods* reveals how enmeshed the language of "coon" songs had become in the American vernacular when his fictional master of ceremonies at the Banner Club announced: "Mr. Meriweather will now favour us with the latest coon song, entitled 'Come back to yo' Baby, Honey.'"[29]

Neither the black nor white press distinguished between these songs and ragtime; any piece of commercial music that referred to black life (stereotypical or not) could earn either designation. Some say the term "ragtime" derived from the music's "ragged" rhythm, or syncopation, where the accent lay on the second beat, followed by a pause. Others suggest that blacks named the music after the practice of flaunting handkerchiefs, or "rags," to signal a dance. Sylvester Russell once credited "a white newspaper critic" for naming ragtime, saying that the reporter "was not aware that he was a discoverer of a new name for comic Negro music."[30] Russell's comment, however, is one of the few made at the time that included any such delineation, and no commentator specified any significant difference between the genres. Rather, "ragtime" appeared frequently to refer to syncopated music generally, as well as to "coon" songs, whether or not they were syncopated, and the terms "rag" and "ragtime" first appeared with regularity around the publication of Hogan's and Harney's "coon" songs in 1896.

Instrumental piano "rags" were no more well defined than song "rags"; everything from a piano arrangement of a "coon" song to the "ragging" of a western classic by changing its rhythmic structure was named at one time or another "ragtime."[31] One advertisement in the *Freeman* conflated these terms completely when it included the lyrics to the "latest coon song craze on the market," titled "A Coon with the Raglan Craze." In a later issue, the song publishers marketed the song as "characteristic ragtime, yet extremely inspiring and catchy—touring far above all previous efforts in ragtime coon songs."[32] Perhaps most tellingly, judges for the "Ragtime Championship of the World Competition" held at Tammany Hall in New York on January 23, 1900, chose Ernest Hogan's foundational "coon song" as the final test. The three pianists who made it to the finals were asked to demonstrate their skill by playing "All Coons Look Alike to Me" for two minutes.[33]

Having little choice but to enter the realm of the "popular" at the end of the nineteenth century, African Americans did participate in the making of the "coon craze," but they attempted to do so on their own terms and to meet their own goals. Significantly, African Americans managed to win audiences without resorting to the use of the most vicious and violent stereotypes in their work. Williams and Walker earned praise for their "clean, well planned show" in which "chicken-stealing and crap games were conspicuous by their absence"—this at a time when white authors portrayed the "coon" character as a violent razor-wielding man who stole chickens and gambled.[34] Moreover, even when using stereotypes, black authors of "coon" songs approached the images differently than did white authors, often shifting the structure of their compositions in ways that allowed them to include commentary on black life. Black songwriters frequently arranged their compositions so that meaningful interplay occurred between verse and chorus. Many black composers used a verse of thirty-two measures, compared to the sixteen measures more common in white-authored songs. The longer verse allowed them to develop a story line, whereas the shorter verse used by white authors drew more attention to the chorus. Moreover, black authors used the word "coon" far less than white authors, and, equally as significant, whites used the word more frequently in the chorus—the part of the song that white audiences would be more likely to remember.[35] Not unlike the physical space of the theater where black performers addressed whites in the orchestra and blacks in the balcony, black songwriters addressed African American audiences with the verse and white publishers and audiences with the chorus.

One of the best examples of this technique appears in Bob Cole and Billy Johnson's "No Coons Allowed!" from their musical comedy *A Trip to Coontown* (1898). The song's lengthy verse tells the story of a "swell gentleman of color" who "saved up all the money he could find." When he took his date to the "finest place that could be found," he "almost went blind when he saw a great big sign up o'er the door which read 'No Coons Allowed.'" The shorter chorus then repeated the phrase "no coons allowed" a few times, and continued, "We don't want no kinky-head kind, so move on darky down the line." While the song's verse told a story about confronting segregated space, the chorus repeated the word "coon" so many times that it likely drowned out the song's rather pointed challenge for most white audiences. The chorus's cry, of course, represented the white voice that the black gentleman was challenging. The song's second verse returned to the story, and told how the protagonist obtained a lawyer who accompanied him to "the courthouse with a crowd."[36] Thus, "No Coons Allowed" included within it a narrative of a black public gathering resisting segregated space—a theme that must have resonated well with black patrons who themselves sometimes challenged Jim Crow seating in the same theaters where these songs were performed.

Although Cook and Dunbar generally wrote verses and choruses of similar length, they too included the interplay of social commentary (in the verse) with stereotyped language (in the chorus) in both "Who Dat Say Chicken in Dis Crowd?" and "Darktown Is Out Tonight." The chorus of the first song replicated the stereotype of chicken-stealing, including the line: "Blame de lan' / let white folks rule it / I'se a lookin fu a pullet."[37] And the chorus of the second song referred to the stereotype of razor-wielding:

> An' there'll be warm coons a-prancin', swell coons a-dancin'
> Tough coons who'll want to fight; so bring long yo' blazahs,
> Fetch out yo' razahs, Darktown is out Tonight!

The verses of both songs, however, told different stories. Both songs presented stories of African American public congregation—an important political goal at the time and one that was achieved when black audiences gathered to watch black performers. "Who Dat Say Chicken in Dis Crowd?" began:

> There was once a great assemblage of the cullud population,
> all the cullud swells was there,
> They had got themselves together to discuss the situation
> and the rumors in the air
> There were speakers there from Georgia
> and some more from Tennessee who were making feathers fly.

This celebration of black participation in public life appeared repeatedly in African American–authored "coon" songs. In her empirical study of one hundred songs categorized as such "coon" songs, archivist Leah Kathleen Cothern found that this celebration of black sociability—what she called "a philosophical and lively appreciation for 'darktown'"—was one of the significant differences between white-authored and black-authored songs.[38] Dunbar and Cook described the safety and joy of a black-controlled public gathering in "Darktown Is Out Tonight."

> Hey dere, Sal, Come on, gal, Jine dis promenade;
> Tek my ahm, What's de harm? Needn't be afraid!
> Dar's ole Dan—Watch dat man, comin' down de line.
> Dat ole coon, Hot-tah'n June, Longin' sweatin' time.
> Howdy do? Hope dat you 'Joy yose'f immense!
> Rekon Bess Got dat dress, Off Miss Lucy's fence.
> Clear de paf! Needn't laf, Dat'll be all right!
> White fo'ks yo' Got no sho'! Dis huh's Darktown night.

With the verse so strongly reveling in the strength of an all-black crowd, the chorus even takes on new meaning. Sung by an all-black cast, it conveyed a veiled threat to whites that African Americans would be in the streets that night, swell, tough, and ready to fight. In a later composition, "Swing Along," Cook reiterated this theme of whites threatened by black crowds: "White fo'ks jealous when you'se walkin' two by two / so swing along chillun', swing along."[39]

Other similar commentary that likely resonated with black audiences appeared in songs from *Clorindy*. In "Darktown Is Out Tonight" the strength in numbers meant that African Americans "needn't laf," a critical distinction at a moment when white audiences refused to accept black performance as anything other than comedic. Additionally, Cook and Dunbar wrote that Bess "borrowed" her dress from "Miss Lucy" for the event, a practice common among laundresses intent on compensating for their low wages.[40] Cook may have been especially familiar with this practice since there is some evidence that his mother—an Oberlin graduate and teacher—may have worked as a laundress.[41] Had Cook's mother labored as a washerwoman, it may have contributed to Cook's developing class consciousness as he observed the workings of D.C.'s black bourgeoisie.

In "Who Dat Say Chicken in Dis Crowd?" Cook and Dunbar critiqued elite pretension. They wrote that "all the cullud swells" had gathered to discuss "the situation and the rumors in the air," and that a "famous culled preacher" told his "listnin' congregation, all about de way to act Ef dey want to be respected an become a mighty nation." The preacher then went on to instruct, "Dey mus' nebber lie, an' mus' not be caught a-stealin' any pullets fum de lim'." The chorus responded by asking, "what's de use of all dis talking," and by declaring, "blame de lan',' let white folks rule it / I'se a lookin' fu a pullet." While on its own the chorus seemed to reinforce white stereotypes of chicken-thieving, as a response to the verse, it suggests a critique of a black elite leadership that spent so much time instructing African Americans how to act that they missed addressing the real problems of land ownership and the hunger that might cause one to steal. The second rendition of the chorus confirms this with the lyric, "What's de use of all dis talkin' Let me hyeah a hen a-skwakin." The song ends with another cry of "Who Dat Say Chicken in Dis Crowd?" Cook and Dunbar never explained in print the reason for the song's title, but in the context of the complete lyric, the title seems to suggest a challenge to those elites who claimed the right to speak for the entire race.

It is not inconceivable that these artists would cloak a political statement in such humor by using the medium of popular song. They did, after all, compose *Clorindy* during a festive all-night drinking session, and they understood unambiguously what Cook's mother and those in her social world thought about the music. As cloaked political dialogue, their lyrics would definitely take on new meaning and provide greater insight to the feelings of a younger generation who had to negotiate nineteenth-century notions of morality and middle-class ideas of respectability. Cook and Dunbar continued to include political commentary in their popular songs, and after *Clorindy,* they teamed up with Williams and Walker to write *In Dahomey.* Dunbar fell ill with tuberculosis and died in 1906, but Cook continued to work with the company on *Abyssinia* and *Bandana Land*—shows that included commentary on black America's relationship to Africa as well as a critique of Jim Crow. For *Bandana Land,* Cook wrote at least one song where the double entendre came from the interplay between the words and music, rather than from the lyric alone. With Williams and Walker Company member Alex Rogers, Cook composed "Any Old Place in Yankee Land Is Good Enough for Me."[42] Rogers's lyrics told of a gentleman who traveled the world over, but who declared that he would only live in "Yankee Land." To clarify the reasons behind this choice, Cook's score included several musical references to "Dixie," the minstrel ditty that had been adopted as the Confederate national anthem. Although Cook and Roger's song did not include any "coon" or "darky" references in the lyric, the music certainly would have resonated with both black and white audiences. Whites may have been left with the impression that the song was celebrating life in America as a whole, while blacks would have undoubtedly understood the song as a rejection of southern racism.

The presence of politically relevant themes, along with the artists' sophisticated understanding of the relationship of white audience demand and their own artistic goals, helps explain how and why so many black critics praised these artists for their songs and shows. Still, a comparison of the praise of black critics with that of whites further illustrates the very different meanings the "coon craze" had for white and black communities. For instance, black critics did not praise white "coon" songwriters or performers. While African American composers Bob Cole and the Johnson brothers wrote for white shows, most famously for performances by May Irwin, the theatrical pages of the black press only covered African American performers and composers. There is no evidence that whites ever sang the more politically relevant songs, but even if they had, it is impossible to imagine a white vocalist singing "No Coons Allowed!" or "Darktown Is Out Tonight" with anywhere near the same intensity and intentionality of an African American vocalist. The songs Cole and Johnson wrote for Irwin were generally devoid of political commentary.

The significant aspect of the "coon" craze for African Americans was the success and artistry of black performers and the ways that the music's popularity helped build the careers of a generation of black stage professionals. Black critics saw how stage success made African Americans more visible and how it helped build professional and social networks. The first regularly published black theater critic, Sylvester Russell, saw his role as integral in building the profession and took pride in being the esteemed critic of "coon comedy." White theater critics "know that coon comedy is young," said Russell, "and as all their time is taken up reviewing the other races, the burden of weeding out the coon comedy garden falls to Russell and the *Freeman.*" Russell had definitely sidestepped white performers when he chose to review Marshall nightlife instead of the white show (with songs authored by Cole and Johnson) that he had traveled to New York to see. He, along with other black critics, approached the "coon" craze as a window of opportunity for professional development, and used the term "coon" only to refer to a type of black entertainment. *Indianapolis Freeman* and *New York Age* readers learned about "coon ditties," "coon plays," "coon business," and "coon comedy." They read about vaudeville acts such as the "Two Real Coons" or read advertisements announcing shows and songs like the "Hottest Coon in Dixie" or "Gay Coons of Darktown." But it was clear from the reviews that the critics were writing about a new type of entertainment, and were measuring the artistry and success of the songwriters and performers. In 1899, when Williams and Walker placed a full-page advertisement in the *Freeman* sending "Holiday Greetings" to black readers from "Two Real Coons," they were clearly two distinguished actors who had made it big with a comedy act. As was typical of reviews in the black press, the images included were portraits of the actors offstage and in formal wear, rather than onstage and in makeup.[43]

The treatment in the white press provides a qualitatively different view. White reviewers typically did not write about "coon" acts as artistically rendered entertainment, but rather as authentic representations of African American life. Typical of white reviews is the comment "Williams is a light colored darkey, and has to use make-up in order to become the black coon that he represents on stage." Another critic surmised that the "chief interest" of Williams and Walker's *In Dahomey* "lies in the fact that very nearly all concerned in it are negroes or coloured people, and that a kind of ethnological purpose seems to run through the whole undertaking." Rarely did white reviewers see beyond the stage types to recognize the African American performers. One white reporter praised Ernest Hogan's *Rufus Rastus,* saying that it was "a big bunch of coon entertainers which means coon songs, coon dances and coon fun as only coons can produce them."[44] White reviewers included accompanying images less frequently, and when they did, they preferred onstage photographs or sometimes drawings of minstrel figures rather than the studio portraits published in black newspapers.

On rare occasions, whites seemed to be sincerely interested in the men behind the stage types. One interview with Bert Williams illuminates why white reviewers, and whites generally, were so drawn to "coon" acts and so wedded to stereotyped imagery, even when they seemed genuinely to appreciate the humanity of African American performers. The exchange also helps explain why black performers imagined that they could use the "coon" craze and their newfound celebrity status to educate white audiences, and, ultimately, advance the race. Not unlike the two white men who had encountered George Walker on a streetcar and had invited him for a drink after questioning him about his flashy clothes, the white reporter asked Williams about his views on racism. Like Walker's admirers, this reporter considered Williams both respectable and familiar enough to ask provocative questions. The Minneapolis newspaper even published Williams's responses, which began with a series of aphorisms about race.

1. The colored man who holds himself detached is happiest.
2. The colored man who tries to get into the white man's class is making a bad mess of it.
3. The colored man with money has it all over the poor white man without money.

Williams continued, "The world says that since some people are white and some are colored there must be a distinction made; a social distinction. I accepted the inevitable. If there are public places that do not want to serve me, well, they are the public places I do not care to patronize." While the reporter included Williams's words, his only comment was that Williams then "smiled, a broad expansive smile, suggestive of southern cotton fields and chickens and watermelon."[45] This interchange offers a rare look at how a white reporter resorted to stereotyped imagery to resolve his own anxieties about changing race relations. Not unlike the men who thought they had befriended George Walker, but still referred to him as a "nigger," this reporter reduced Williams's eloquence, dignity, and protest to a slice of watermelon. Of course, most published comments do not reveal such

Williams and Walker advertisement, *Indianapolis Freeman*, December 30, 1899.

(General Research and Reference Division, Schomburg Center for Research in Black Culture, The New York Public Library, Astor, Lenox and Tilden Foundations.)

give and take, but simply include the assertion that "coons" portrayed "coons" as only "coons" could. These comments suggest, however, a willful ignorance, with the majority of white critics and audiences feeling safe in their belief that the "darky" acts they saw were representations of real life. Most whites so feared the African American presence that they did not want to consider these shows as contrived performances.

Despite such blatant racism, surprisingly little criticism of the "coon" craze appeared in black weeklies. Rather the press and the large theater companies had more of a symbiotic relationship as they supported each other through advertisements and favorable reviews. "Tom the Tattler," who wrote a weekly column filled with snide critique, issued one of the few critiques of the racist and exploitative power of the "coon craze." He noted, "The colored man writes the 'coon' song, the colored singer sings the 'coon' song, the colored race is compelled to stand for the belittling and ignominy of the 'coon' song, but the money from the 'coon' songs flows with ceaseless activity into the white man's pockets." Still, he did not call for an end to writing the songs, but rather lamented that whites, not blacks, reaped the financial profits. It seems that Duke Travers, a pianist, voiced his own frustration with the widespread popularity of "coon" songs. In 1900, as the only black finalist in New York City's Ragtime Championship of the World, Travers declared his unfamiliarity with the required final test song, Hogan's "All Coons Look Alike to Me." Since by the time of the contest the song was one of the most well-known tunes of the day, Travers's declaration of ignorance could be read as a pointed critique of "coon" songs—one that resulted in the judges capitulating and allowing the three contestants to play whatever they pleased.[46]

Most of the published black criticism emanated from African American classical music enthusiasts, although the amount of critique does not come anywhere near the amount of praise published in the black weeklies. The criticism reveals how African Americans debated authenticity in black expressive culture, highlights how their interpretations differed substantially from those published in the white press, and debunks the idea that "coon" songs and ragtime represented the entire race. A small, short-lived periodical, the *Negro Music Journal,* stands out as the black publication most critical of "coon" songs and ragtime. Six years after Hogan's debut of "All Coons Look Alike to Me," black pianist J. Hillary Taylor founded this publication to educate African Americans "towards a correct and intelligent knowledge of the art" of music. Published from September of 1902 through November of 1903, the *Journal* both hailed European composers and celebrated slave songs. Its views on ragtime were well summed up by one reader, who pleaded that the publication "do a little missionary work among us, and help banish this 'rag-time' epidemic."[47] Although the *Journal* ceased publication in November 1903, its editor kept its ideas alive at the Washington Conservatory of Music, a school focused on the study of European classics and founded that autumn.

Even with its relatively harsh criticism of popular song styles, the *Journal* praised the professionalism and talent of musicians who themselves wrote the songs categorized as "coon" songs or ragtime. "Among our violinists who have really accomplished something," wrote one journal correspondent, "I think none comes nearer the great artist than does Mr. Will Marion Cook. Although he has not appeared in public as a violinist for several years, yet we cannot forget his true worth." Cook's "true worth" turned out to be studying at Oberlin, in Berlin, and with Dvořák. Though the *Journal* mentioned that he attracted attention as a composer and praised him as the writer of music for Williams and Walker's "new comic opera," no claim was made that this was "Negro music," or that the songs were being categorized as ragtime or "coon" songs by both the white and black press.[48]

Although Cook based his compositions on the "real Negro melodies" he had heard sung in Tennessee, the *Journal* credited him for his European classical training rather than for his interpretation of slave song. While *Negro Music Journal* writers were also interested in identifying and celebrating black song, they did not want to associate ragtime with authentic black expression. Like W. E. B. Du Bois, who at the same time celebrated what he called sorrow songs in *Souls of Black Folk,* the *Negro Music Journal* wanted to reclaim slave song, seeing in its celebration the salvation of the race, but could not imagine elevating Cook's melodies to this status. "The average 'coon song' of the present day bears not the least relation to . . . *real* Negro melodies," reported one *Journal* author. Rather "real Negro singing was as old as the world, for it has been chanted in the wilds of Africa"; yet could also be found in the "rich and penetrating . . . yet unstudied and natural" singing of the "plantation Negro." He credited black tobacco workers, not performing artists, for singing "real Negro melodies," saying it was "impossible not to forget too, the effect produced in one of the Southern tobacco factories by singing of the Negro employees. Out of the silence there will arise a low, crooning sound, generally in a minor key."[49]

Journal authors praised those black musicians who mastered the "high culture" of European composers from Haydn to Beethoven, and at the same time sought to claim the untutored black voice—the sorrow songs—as "high culture." The authors' celebration of black creativity certainly challenged racist notions of black inferiority, but their inability to conceptualize Cook's music as somehow also authentically black suggests an elitism wary of popular musical categories. Cook had imagined that the music he composed for *Clorindy* would similarly be a lever with which to lift his people. In praising his skills but discrediting his music, the *Negro Music Journal* actually reaffirmed some predominating ideas about intellect, talent, and success, insinuating that somehow formal training made Cook's songs less black. One writer even went so far as to define "real Negro singing" as the result of a "natural" (and biologically based) musicality of black people. He claimed, "There is a peculiar vibrating quality in the Negro voice, due perhaps to a peculiar arrangement of the vocal chords, which is not found in the white race . . . this remarkable quality is lessened by cultivation although it is not entirely removed."[50]

Sylvester Russell debated similar ideas with the British-born black composer Samuel Coleridge Taylor (1875–1912) on the theatrical pages of the *Freeman*. Taylor had become quite popular among black American classical music enthusiasts and was often featured in the *Negro Music Journal*. He too worked with individual artists who had composed or performed ragtime music; he toured with Harry T. Burleigh and composed music for some of Paul Laurence Dunbar's poems. And at least once, Will Marion Cook conducted an orchestra playing Taylor's compositions at Chicago's Pekin Theater.[51] But Taylor denounced "coon" songs as well, calling them the "worst sort of rot." He elaborated, "In the first place, there is no melody and in the second place there is no real Negro character . . . in these 'coon' songs." He further declared, "I will not object to the term 'coon' songs. They may be that, but they are not Negro melodies." Since Taylor was critiquing the craze in 1904, it is difficult to discern what his response may have been to Cook's earlier songs from *Clorindy*, but it is still significant that he heard nothing at all in the songs that referenced black life. Russell took great pains to correct Taylor's assumptions, and explained, "'Coon' songs or rather ragtime music is of the lighter class of true genuine American Negro music" and was "invented but not named by them." Russell attributed the naming of ragtime to a white newspaper critic, but like Cook, Russell argued that ragtime "was originated, by the southern Negroes of America." He called syncopation "an inherited musical gift" that had been "born in the tortures of slavery." Unlike some *Negro Music Journal* writers, Russell understood Cook's melodies to have emerged from the historical experience of slavery rather than from biology, and recognized Cook's music as black, even though informed by other musical styles. Taylor could not understand ragtime, said Russell, "until he visited some low Negro concert hall and saw how naturally it is executed in music, song and dance."[52]

Unlike many black critics and despite ragtime's categorization as "vulgar," Russell willingly claimed the music's black origins. He understood ragtime as one type of authentic black music, even if the music was influenced by the artists' classical training and was funneled through commercial venues like vaudeville stages and dance halls. Taylor, Du Bois, and the *Negro Music Journal* seemed to suggest that the commercialism of ragtime robbed it of its claim as "Negro music." Harry Burleigh later wrote similarly that spirituals had to be "rescued" from the corrupting influence of jazz. The "growing tendency of some of our musicians to utilize the melodies . . . for fox trots, dance numbers and semi-sentimental songs," claimed Burleigh, threatened the musical purity of spirituals. In her study of rap music, Tricia Rose notes a related tendency: "Once a black cultural practice takes a prominent place inside the commodity system, it is no longer considered a black practice" and is "instead a 'popular' practice whose black cultural priorities and distinctively black approaches are either taken for granted as a 'point of origin,' an isolated 'technique,' or rendered invisible." That Cook and Dunbar, along with Williams, Walker, and Hogan worked in commercial entertainment and used racist stereotypes does not necessarily mean their cultural work was primarily about marketing to whites. Even as they urged whites to publish their songs and book their performances, they struggled to reach black audiences and create a more "authentic" black sound. Their approach actually draws attention to the racist underpinnings of categories like high and low culture, and their inventive manipulation of the "coon craze" and of modern musical categories demonstrates a distinctively (and authentically) black approach to composition in a culture saturated with racism.[53]

"Strictly Negro Traits"

Cook and his generation of artists did not just attempt to hook audiences with hokum; they subverted and manipulated stereotypes as they struggled to present black identity. After all, Cook characterized his songs as "Negro" not simply because the lyrics included biting commentary on black life, but also because something about the sound—the syncopated melodies—made them authentically black. Yet the dominant culture's investment in what it considered "real" in the way of African American life made presenting black authenticity in any form terribly complicated. Black artists had to grapple continually with how audiences read any particular trait. Since whites tended to reduce the complexity of black life to one racial dimension, many African Americans feared that whites would misinterpret any part of their experience as fitting a stereotype. Black artists who so dearly wanted to celebrate and claim a collective identity had to negotiate the different fears of black and white audiences. In doing so, they gave voice to a new black sensibility—one adept at navigating a modern world inundated with racism.

In some ways these popular performers were actually less trapped by the dominant culture's stereotypes than were the critics at the *Negro Music Journal*. By actively engaging with stereotyped imagery, they continually reaffirmed that they were not that which they performed. Well aware that they were in the business of entertainment, not ethnology, popular stage artists were cognizant of the multiple ways they played with the concept of "real" black life. Perhaps nowhere was the discussion more layered than with Williams and Walker's debut act, "Two Real Coons." Reflecting on the act ten years later, Walker explained that he and Williams had watched the very popular blackfaced white comedians who billed themselves as "coons," and that they had been "often much amused at seeing white men with black cork on their faces trying to imitate black folks." Vowing that he and Williams would "do all they could to get what they felt belonged to them by the laws of nature," Walker explained that although he played the character of the "swell darky" and Williams the blackface funny man, the duo still labored to introduce "native African characteristics" in their act. While he did not lay out exactly what he meant by these characteristics, he did make clear that the more "natural" he and Williams could be, the better, for as he saw it, "Nothing seemed more absurd than to see a colored man making himself ridiculous in order to portray himself." Naturalness, for Walker, meant representations that were closer to actual daily life and distinct from characteristics interpreted as "native" or "primitive" by white folks. Walker went on to credit his partner with being "the first man that I know of our race to attempt to delineate a 'darky' in a perfectly natural way."[54]

African American critics praised Walker and Williams for this naturalness, claiming that "they don't overdo" and that they had the right idea as to "what the stage darky really should be." One critic wrote in the *Freeman*, "White folks have claimed all along, with some degree of truth, that they can outdo the Negro in the aping of himself, but they now admit that they have stubbed their toes on Williams, who refuses to enter into horseplay or overdo his character." In 1903, Lester Walton assured *Colored American Magazine* readers that both Williams and Hogan were "doing much to elevate the negro on the stage" and that "their impersonations of the 'funny darky' are the best and truest yet given." Some black performers assumed "roles that are unnatural—which never existed," said Walton, and these "false impressions" cause them "to overdo their endeavor to personate their idea of the 'funny darky.'" He concluded that Hogan and Williams "depict life subjects."[55]

When Walton began his weekly theatrical column in the *New York Age* in February of 1908, he further elaborated on what he meant by authenticity, and on how these "natural" depictions could advance the race. His first column appeared just days after Williams and Walker opened *Bandana Land* for a run of eighty-nine shows at New York's Majestic Theater. Through his commentary on this show—what he too at times referred to as a "coon show"—Walton discussed everything from performers' hairstyles to what he named "strictly Negro traits." Stating "our white brethren know very little of us," he asserted that the stage must and could "play no small part in acquainting the white people of the colored man's customs, environment and types." He went on to praise Williams and Walker for including what he called "a little more sentiment and genuine darkey comedy" in *Bandana Land*.[56]

One such moment of thematic authenticity occurred when Skunkton Bowser (Bert Williams) produced a treasured pocket Bible that his mother had given him years before. Bud Jenkins (George Walker) looked at it and exclaimed that his mother also had given him one, which he kept in his trunk. Walton described this "sentiment" as "strictly Negro" and he surmised "that in the colored contingent there were few whose mothers had not given them in early life just such a book to keep and read." In another act Bud Jenkins named the piece of property "Bandana Land" after a bandana handkerchief that reminded him of the days when his mother wore such a head covering. It seems that in Walton's eyes the bandana referenced an image not yet tied to the widespread distribution of Aunt Jemima products. Instead, Walton lauded the inclusion of both the bandana and Bible as a "bit of sentiment" that should have been "appreciated by many in the house"; he explained how glad he was that "the day has come when our big actors have pleasure to introduce in their shows some

(Above) Bert Williams, ca. 1911.

(Photographs and Prints Division, Schomburg
Center for Research in Black Culture, The New York
Public Library, Astor, Lenox and Tilden Foundations.)

(Opposite) Publicity portrait of Bert Williams
in blackface, n.d.

(Photographs and Prints Division, Schomburg Center for
Research in Black Culture, The New York Public Library,
Astor, Lenox and Tilden Foundations.)

little character bits that bring out strictly Negro traits and customs of which the race should be proud."[57]

The *Dramatic Mirror* printed one review of *Bandana Land* that provoked Walton to be even more explicit on the importance of staging authenticity. This white critic had enthusiastically praised the show, but complained that the management permitted "most of the men and nearly all of the women to wear straight hair." While he eventually admitted that "the singing of the straight-haired chorus is just as vigorous as it would be with kinks," he continued to articulate his desire for "authenticity," claiming that the stage types "would be very close to natural if it were not for this hair." Walton published these comments in his own article in the *Age* to complain to the predominantly black readership, "Like most white critics, in fact, white people in general, he has certain set ideas as to just how colored people should look, and when they appear other than what he has in mind, he charges that the members of the chorus wear wigs and are not strictly Negro."[58]

Walton blamed ignorance rather than racism for this critic's blindness, saying that the high praise for the show itself exonerated the critic from prejudice. His concession to ignorance made some sense, since the mass production of hair- and skincare products was a relatively recent phenomenon, making it more possible for ordinary people, white or black, to vary their appearance. Madame C. J. Walker, whose cosmetics firm would take off in the 1910s, earning her millions, had developed the first commercially successful hair straightener in the 1890s, and advertisements for such products appeared widely in the black press at the time. Not only did the presence of these products disrupt white expectations of black appearance, but they made alterations in hairstyle more controversial among African Americans as well. Although in *Bandana Land* actors carefully styled their hair, years earlier, the Williams and Walker Company had specifically mocked African Americans' desire for straighter hair and lighter skin in *In Dahomey* (1902). In that show's opening scene, a character named Dr. Straight was hawking "Straightaline" to straighten hair and "Oblicuticus" to lighten skin—prompting one of the characters to reflect, "I do think the colored race is the biggest set of fools I ever cast my optics against."[59]

If African Americans engaged in a complicated discussion about the relationship between hairstyle and authenticity, whites expressed a simplistic rigidity when it came to their expectations. The white critic reviewing

Bandana Land sheet music cover, Gotham-Attucks Music Company.
(Sheet Music Collection, The John Hay Library, Brown University, Providence, Rhode Island.)

Bandana Land finally "concluded that Williams and Walker had permitted their people to depart from their true and natural type—kinky hair—and wear wigs." It was just "too much for the poor writer," explained Walton, when "he saw over half a hundred colored performers appear on the stage, the men with their hair parted in the middle and combed and plastered in many different ways about their foreheads (and) when he viewed with alarm the women wearing their hair done up in all of the latest styles."[60]

Walton took the *Dramatic Mirror*'s review as further evidence that black performers played a particularly significant role in educating, not just entertaining, white audiences. He explained that when whites saw a light-skinned African American on the street, they might wonder, "Is he or she colored?" and asserted that "daily many colored people with straight hair or fair skin bring about no little discussion in public places." But, as Walton explained it, when white patrons went to see Williams and Walker, they knew that they were seeing an entirely black-acted production, so when they saw an actor "other than one with kinky hair and a flat nose" they would, he hoped, conclude that "there is no one certain type of Negro, but that types are varied." While Lester Walton published his remarks in the black press, his writing style hinted that he hoped the *Dramatic Mirror* critic, and white folks generally, would read and learn from them. He explicitly stated that the black performers intentionally styled their hair, saying that although there were "more straight-haired individuals than ever before," they used "lots of brushing and small applications of oil" for the style.[61]

That black performers intentionally straightened and styled their hair to their liking is not insignificant considering white demand for a particular representation of black life. If whites expected kinky hair, then performers' insistence on straightening their hair was a kind of protest against the stereotype. By presenting themselves in ways that directly contradicted white notions of "real" black life, the cast fulfilled the educational role of the stage laid out by Walton. Indeed *Bandana Land*'s success led Walton to imagine the day when the *Dramatic Mirror* critic would recognize the fiction of black stage characters by discovering that only Bert Williams—who blacked up to play the stage "darky"—wore a wig.[62]

Yet Walton's comments demonstrated his own ambivalence about black hairstyles and status. He had gone to great lengths to explain the many different hairstyles, but he eventually agreed that kinky hair was somehow less desirable. "If the *Dramatic Mirror* knew as much as we do about hair," he wrote, "it would make an additional assertion that nowadays you seldom see colored people with real kinky hair, and that the time is not far off when all possessors of kinky hair will be subjects for the dime museum—they will be so rare."[63] This comment, not unlike some of the claims made by the *Negro Music Journal* about black sound, demonstrates how often African Americans internalized ideas from the dominant culture and how difficult it would continue to be to represent black identity without somehow resurrecting stereotypes.

Like hairstyle, speech carried loaded meanings for black performance. The use of what became known as "Negro dialect" played an enormous role in the "coon" craze, because the overwhelming majority of "coon" songs used some amount of dialect speech. Performing artists' attention to the use of "Negro dialect" reflected similar concerns regarding the depiction of "strictly Negro traits." All these representations of black life and culture had to engage with pervasive stereotypes. Like the intentional changes of hairstyle, black artists alternated their use of dialect with lyrics in "straight" English, in large part to help denote variation and complexity in black life. Many more black composers employed this technique than did white songwriters; whites usually relied solely on dialect, as if to show that they could imagine only one version of black identity.[64] Just as with their song structures, black songwriters varied their use of lyrical language, highlighting their ongoing conversation with assumptions of authenticity or "real" black identity. The Williams and Walker Company used this technique in their major productions, and Dunbar juggled dialect and "straight" English in his poetry and novels, alternating these voices even within a particular piece. By shifting their voice from dialect to "straight" English, black artists emphasized that not all (or any) African Americans spoke that way. Rather, dialect speech signified only one aspect of black culture—an aspect potentially inauthentic, especially when literally translated through the cultural prism of white mainstream society.

While black artists responded to demands of the white market, they also spoke to the particular assumptions about black identity held within black communities, particularly with reference to social class. As Willard Gatewood explains, black elites prided themselves on speaking "flawless English"; they differentiated themselves as a class in part because they were not among "those blacks who sprinkled their conversation with 'dialect' expressions" and who clearly belonged "to the lower class of colored people." Poet Langston Hughes would later similarly characterize one of the pretensions of black elite culture as privileging "frightfully correct English."[65] And George Walker once told a joke based on an alleged exchange between two black actors that well demonstrates this attentiveness to the racial assumptions embedded in styles of speech.

> FIRST BLACK PERFORMER: What's the use of you trying to play Shakespeare; you can't be a white man. Why not be a nigger and a good nigger?
> SECOND BLACK PERFORMER: My dear fellow, I talk English too well to be a Negro.[66]

His joke shows how he recognized that language—"Negro dialect"—both represented black identity and at the same time referenced racist stereotype, so much so that the second performer disavowed his link to the race.

Like Walker and other black artists of the era, Cook paid extraordinarily close attention to the many meanings embedded within styles of speech. In his autobiographical notes, he recorded one particularly ironic incident that occurred while rehearsing the chorus of one of the early shows, most likely *Clorindy*. The chorus's rendition of his music "sounded like a mess," he reported. His score included "very syncopated" rhythms and "peculiar chords," and "worst of all," the lyrics were "all in Dunbar dialect," a style of speech that their choral training had apparently excised from their repertoire. Cook was exasperated. "Here's a paradox!" he cried. "When speaking, these singers, most of them with little or no education, used a dialect that even Dunbar (the Master) could have listened, learned and transcribed— in fact, he did!" But when they sang, "that was different. They used a more perfect English than did Harvard or Yale."[67] As Cook's reminiscence and Walker's joke also make clear, "Negro dialect" carried with it cultural markers not only of race but also of class; performing Shakespeare was read as "white," and speaking "straight" English was read as possessing an elite education.

As with other "strictly Negro traits," dialect speech held significantly different meanings for white and black audiences, as well as within the black community. To whites, it signaled the "darky" character, which they read as authentic. For many blacks, however, it represented uneducated, poor, and southern behavior, an image far too close to the stage "darky" and one that they believed needed to be left behind in order for the race to progress. The young artists disagreed, and asserted that dialect too represented an authentic voice important for them to claim. Just as he had discussed the representations of motherhood from *Bandana Land,* Lester Walton identified dialect speech as a "Negro trait," clarifying, "Most Negroes have heard Negro dialect songs since infancy." Will Marion Cook similarly recounted that he wrote "Swing Along" in dialect while he was feeling homesick in London because the speech style reminded him of home. And Paul Laurence Dunbar went further to claim dialect as black speech by connecting it to ragtime culture generally. In his novel *Sport of the Gods,* the character Skaggs, a white reporter, remarked to Sadness, the African American character who sat alongside him at a bar, "I tell you, Sadness, dancing is the poetry of motion." To which Sadness replied, "And dancing in rag-time is the dialect poetry."[68]

Black artists' use of dialect conveyed a certain representation of black identity to black audiences, and this community—rather than white management—was often the intended audience. Cook and Dunbar, along with many others of their generation, likely used dialect speech to challenge black elite culture as much as to attract white audiences. After all, Will Marion Cook had upset his mother with his "negroid songs," and had bristled at John Mercer Langston's politics and black elite pretension. Dunbar too had an ambivalent relationship with D.C.'s black elite society. After the world's fair, his reputation as a writer had grown and had gained him acceptance into elite society, despite his dark skin and less-than-prestigious family background. Yet although the Washington elite courted Dunbar, society rituals did not impress him. He described Washington as "the most Godforsaken and unliterary town in America," and on another occasion, wrote to his mother that he wished "Washington Negroes would mind their own business."[69] Thus it is hardly a leap to understand these artists' embrace of dialect speech as their own call to authenticity—one that challenged the ideas held by their parents' generation and celebrated those "real Negro melodies" from the South. Cook had rejected his European classical training, choosing instead to compose music rooted in black American culture. Although his songs were marketed as "coon" songs and, as such, played into white racism, Cook's goals, and those of his colleagues, were actually less assimilationist than those of his parents. He attempted to represent and distinguish the black experience through mass-mediated culture, all the while highlighting and celebrating black identity.

Yet even though these artists challenged black elite pretensions, they remained ambivalent about the potential repercussions. George Walker explained his dedication to presenting an authentic view of black life: "The black man's future lies in the development of his faculties—physical and mental—as a Negro." But at the same time, he asserted, "Our poets must stick to Negro dialect to make themselves heard," seemingly inferring that dialect would attract white audiences. Ill with tuberculosis, Paul Laurence Dunbar composed his last poem aloud—and through fits of coughing—in dialect, but he had, by then, also claimed to be exhausted with it. "I am so tired of dialect," he said, explaining that he wrote in dialect to "gain a hearing," but that "now they don't want me to write anything but dialect."[70] Dunbar expressed well the predicament of these artists: on some level, their own strategies to escape racial stereotypes trapped them. They had been so certain that white audiences would eventually recognize their acts as performances, and had hoped to educate whites as to the complexity of black life. At the same time, these black artists remained committed to portraying characteristics that they interpreted as "representative" of the race. But their project proved nearly impossible. Traits such as speech patterns, a mother's gift of a Bible, or certain hairstyles had become so permanently associated with racist stereotypes that whites simply read them as fitting those stereotypes, however and wherever they were presented.

Ragtime Tunes and Sorrow Songs

The black composers and performers who participated in the "coon" craze imagined that they could manipulate stereotyped imagery in ways that would accurately represent black identity in part because it was not immediately clear to them how much mass production would affect distribution of their art. The process of putting their compositions onto paper actually limited these artists' efforts to control their presentation of black identities. When Hogan and Cook wrote their songs, they did so for the popular stage, and imagined their songs sung live by black actors. When actors sang "coon" songs in their shows, they varied the emphasis in their delivery—the tone, the speed, the inflection of words. J. Rosamond Johnson noted that Bob Cole even replaced the word "coons" with "boys" when singing lines from Hogan's foundational song.[71] But once the live songs became published song sheets, the artists lost control over the finished product. Worse, the images chosen by white sheet-music publishers forever marked the songs, virtually erasing the visual power conveyed through nuanced black performance. The publishers reproduced heinous stereotyped imagery on the covers of "All Coons Look Alike to Me" and "Who Dat Say Chicken in Dis Crowd?" and printed the lyrics without the artists' inflections. White consumers enjoyed black song without watching black performers and without the palpable presence of a black audience. Moreover, whites generally preferred to buy songs composed by white artists. This only increased the amount of stereotyped imagery on song sheets as publishers often sought to hide the racial identities of the artists themselves, and to reassure their white customers with familiar imagery.

As the market for "coon" songs grew, white writers rushed to incorporate the word "coon" as often as possible into their songs. It was this proliferation of songs from profit-driven commercial publishers that was most derogatory and that sparked more criticism from African Americans. The dissemination of racial demagoguery through mass-produced song even tempered Sylvester Russell's praise for the music. In 1904 Russell reiterated his 1902 statement that "the Negro race has no objections to the word 'coon' and no objections to the word 'darkey,'" but in 1905 he declared, "Song publishers will have to get their eyes open after awhile. Men who write words for songs can no longer write such mean rot as the words of 'Whistling Coon' and expect respectable publishers to accept it no matter how good the music may be." And in 1907, he directly implored "song publishers" to "kindly oblige the respectable element of the colored race by restricting race insult from comic songs."[72] On this point, Russell agreed with the *Negro Music Journal,* whose editors had stated in 1903 that neither blacks nor whites could "be excused for the part it has played in creating, publishing and distributing this often low and degrading class of music. Publishing houses in all parts of the country have, with a few exceptions, published this music more or less." In 1909, a *Freeman* critic cried "Coon songs must go," writing that for "the last five years the more trash put into a song, the better it sold." He reported, "Coon songs, after the great damage they have done to the American colored man, were now dying out," announcing that the word "coon" was "very offensive to the colored race and made the hair rise on their heads when they heard it." This critic even blamed "colored writers not knowing the harm they were doing, took a stick to break their own heads by writing 'coon' songs."[73]

With their success, Cook and other members of the Williams and

Walker Company broke free temporarily from white publishers in 1904 by founding one of the first black-owned music publishing houses, the Gotham-Attucks Music Company—which was to publish most of the music from *Abyssinia* (1906) and *Bandana Land* (1908). Control over publishing helped these by then well-known artists select acceptable images for the covers and limit or entirely omit offensive lyrics. Both of the later Williams and Walker shows contained fewer "coon" references and relied less on exaggerated dialect. Gotham-Attucks song sheets typically included studio portraits of actors dressed in formal wear rather than stage shots in blackface makeup or caricatured drawings—pictures more closely replicating the image that the black press presented of these artists. By 1905, these artists had gained enough popularity to ensure that their songs would sell without the stereotyped imagery, but even so, Gotham-Attucks still faced financial problems. In 1908, the firm sued a white publishing company that claimed ownership rights to "He's a Cousin of Mine." The judge decided in favor of Gotham-Attucks, but the lawsuit cost money and energy. Run largely by the artists themselves, the company faltered, and a white "song shark" bought it in 1911.[74]

Even when black composers published their own work, distribution was a tricky business. After W. C. Handy managed to publish his "Memphis Blues" in 1912, he shopped it around to various music stores. He stopped at one piano store in Memphis, specifically because its windows displayed the sheet music to "At the Ball" by J. Leubrie Hill, a black composer, as well as music by Cole and Johnson, Scott Joplin, and Williams and Walker. As Handy told it, when the store manager suggested that "his trade wouldn't stand for his selling my song, I pointed out as tactfully as I could that the majority of his musical hits of the moment had come from the Gotham-Attucks Company, a firm of Negro publishers in New York. I'll never forget his smile," recalled Handy. "'Yes,' he said pleasantly. 'I know that—but my customers don't.'"[75] As Handy's comment makes poignantly clear, these black artists had found an audience for their music, but had been unable to earn the recognition they deserved as its creators.

As they faced the very modern dilemmas of distributing their own wares via a racist marketplace, a few of the artists, most notably Ernest Hogan, did express some misgivings. Shortly before his death in 1909, Hogan reportedly told vaudevillian Tom Fletcher, "With nothing but time on my hands now, I often wonder if I was right or wrong." "All Coons Look

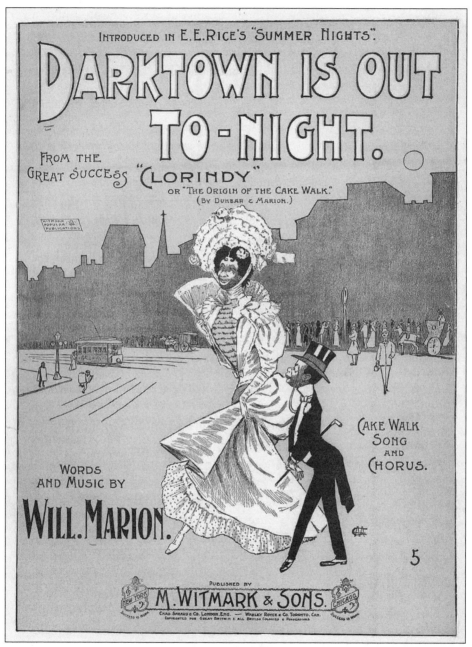

"Darktown Is Out To-Night" sheet music cover, M. Witmark & Sons.
(Sheet Music Collection, The John Hay Library, Brown University, Providence, Rhode Island.)

Alike," he said, "caused a lot of trouble in and out of show business" but it was "also good for show business because at that time money was short in all walks of life. With the publication of that song, a new musical rhythm was given to the people. Its popularity grew and it sold like wild-fire all over the United States and abroad." He also claimed that this "one song opened the way for a lot of colored and white songwriters" who found "the rhythm so great, they stuck to it changing the lyrics, and wrote song hits from my creations without the word 'coon.'" Ragtime had been played "in the back rooms of cafes and other such places," he said, and since ragtime was "played just by ear," the work of ragtime artists "would have been lost to the world if I had not put it on paper."[76] A few years later, W. C. Handy located the origins of his "St. Louis Blues" with the "coon" craze, recounting that the song was about "the wail of a lovesick woman for her lost man," but to tell the story he "resorted to the humorous spirit of the bygone coon songs." Even as he employed the "coon" formula, Handy consciously reflected on the continued tension between stereotype and images of authenticity, explaining that "the question of language was a very real problem" because by 1914 "Negro intellectuals were turning from dialect in poetry." Still, he explained that he chose to write in dialect because it "often implies more than well-chosen English can briefly ex-press" and that "certain words of Negro dialect are more musical and more expressive than pure English."[77]

Although clearly grappling with the results of the creation and distribu-tion of their music, these artists committed themselves to figuring out how to best represent black life with their art. Their efforts distinguished them from their parents, many of whom wanted to distance themselves as much as possible from any cultural expression reminiscent of slavery and equated progress with a European education. The earlier generation had criticized minstrelsy, of course, but they were also less than sanguine about the proliferation of Jubilee choirs that followed the Fisk Singers' rise to fame in 1871. Made up of students from black universities, these choirs performed versions of spirituals reinterpreted through their own European classical training. Although composed of classically trained col-lege students, Jubilee choirs were credited more for performing "simple" melodies than for their musical expertise. Many elite African Americans would have agreed with black Bostonian James Monroe Trotter, a Civil War veteran and music critic, who wrote in 1881 that "notwithstanding their great beauty of melody," these choirs resurrected a "former life of enforced degradation."[78]

Cook and his cohort, however, believed that racial progress lay in recognizing and celebrating black identity, and as such, Cook's struggle to produce "real Negro melodies"—an authentic black voice—had some similarity to W. E. B. Du Bois's own project of identifying and celebrating the sorrow songs as constitutive of the "souls of black folk." In no small way, the exuberant ragtime of Cook's "real Negro melodies" was a counterpart to the soulful stirrings of Du Bois's sorrow songs. The two men possessed similar backgrounds: they were born a year apart, hailed from northern privileged families, studied in Europe, and reported profound—often harrowing—experiences as young men traveling in the American South. With the rise of Jim Crow, they both believed that their political interests lay with the larger black population. They broke from the staunchly assimilationist goals of their parents' generation and sought the authentic spirit and soul of black people.

Although both Cook and Du Bois aspired to bring forth the voice of the black South, they had markedly different understandings about how to identify and interpret black song. In part, their differences reflect their contrasting approaches to the rise of the twentieth-century city and modern leisure culture. Cook's artistic sensibility allowed him to imagine all sorts of possibilities for African Americans in the new urban culture, whereas Du Bois's more conventional intellectual and political journey made him fear how participation in mass public amusements would reflect on blacks generally. Du Bois headed the "talented tenth"—a group of race leaders born between 1855 and 1875 and from mostly northern, urban, college-educated backgrounds. This group included black artists along with activists and intellectuals. Mary Church Terrell, Ida B. Wells, Paul Laurence Dunbar, and James Weldon Johnson were all part of this cohort. But Dunbar, a poet, and Johnson, a writer, were both also central to Cook's work and to the ideas that emanated from the Marshall Hotel. To describe them predominantly through a group that privileged intellectual and political work flattens the cultural context from which their ideas sprang. Their artistic work really constituted a parallel development for this generation, one where the men and women of the popular stage became, in a sense, the artistic arm of race leadership at the turn of the century—a veritable Bohemian Tenth. They struggled to interpret the souls of black folk through modern cultural forms, all the while maintaining a commitment to presenting traits that were "strictly Negro" and demonstrating an incipient black nationalism. The artists' more popular perspective and sharp break from the ideas of the previous generation were not limited to their search for authentic black sound, but would surface even more in the ways they represented Africa on stage—stories that reveal a vision of nationalist identity reflective of their own political imaginations.

"No Place Like Home": Africa on Stage

We's a comin
Ol' Egypts' people
Am a comin
Comin up on high
Fum de Valley
Valley and shadder
Ob de darkness
An' de day am nigh
When he'll call us
Fum out dis wilderness
Ob Trouble
Up into de sky.

COOK AND DUNBAR,
JES LAK WHITE FO'KS,
1900

WILL MARION COOK AND PAUL LAURENCE DUNBAR began their second co-authored script, *Jes Lak White Fo'ks*, with Ethiopianist imagery familiar to nineteenth-century African American audiences.[1] With this show, Cook and Dunbar directly addressed black America's relationship to Africa on the popular stage and launched a project that culminated in their 1902 work on Williams and Walker's *In Dahomey*. Dunbar had become too ill from tuberculosis to keep working, but Cook and the Williams and Walker Company continued their focus on Africa with the 1906 show, *Abyssinia*. While all three shows focused on various aspects of black life, their central narratives addressed black America's relationship to the continent. In *Jes Lak White Fo'ks*, Cook and Dunbar critiqued African American elites who romanticized their relationship to African royalty. In *In Dahomey* the Williams and Walker Company commented on the nineteenth-century colonization movement, and in *Abyssinia* they celebrated Ethiopia for its 1896 victory over Italy.

In many ways, the popular stage provided an ideal venue to explore the ambivalent relationship African Americans had to Africa: the combination of vaudeville skits and musical numbers allowed for a variety of narratives to exist in one show. Since vaudeville was primarily comic, these artists could critique nationalist politics through parody and satire without necessarily making any definitive claims. But their struggle to depict Africa turned out to be as complicated as were their efforts to represent "strictly Negro traits." When they presented their ideas, they had to confront the dominant culture's definitions of Africans and Africa as "primitive," "savage," and the antithesis of civilization. Most whites and more than a few blacks viewed Africa through a lens clouded by social Darwinism, or at the very least, tainted with an ideology that understood the urban industrial European West as definitive of the civilized world. Still, performing artists managed to stage a variety of narratives that not only revealed their own somewhat ambivalent relationship to the continent, but also highlighted their sophisticated engagement with contemporary politics.

Black artists' impetus to depict black America's relationship to Africa was not so different from Cook's desire to interpret the "real Negro melodies" he heard in the American South. Cook had understood that reclaiming his southern roots and grappling with the slave past were necessary for racial progress. His generation saw exploration of their relationship to an African past, present, and future as equally, if not more, important for advancing the race. That these artists represented Africa in diverse ways was in itself significant, if only because these portrayals challenged the monolithic presumptions of Africa as primitive and savage during a moment when European colonialism and American empire building depended on such racial ideology. But the plays' multiple representations of Africa did more than that. They spoke to concerns held dear and debated vociferously in black communities.

The idea and reality of Africa had long played pivotal roles in black America's vision of freedom, and were inextricable from the making of African American identity. Africa's influence over black life had changed over time with generational distance, the promise and failure of freedom at home, European colonialism, and America's own empire building. Facing racial violence, political and social exclusion, and economic marginalization, African Americans were predisposed to "making" themselves American and making America responsive. But America's abysmal failure, and often times blatant unwillingness, to protect black freedom and citizenship at home drove many black Americans to look anew at the continent's role in their own emancipation.

In their stage shows, black performing artists touched on the many new ways their generation looked to their ancestral homeland as well as to the long history of black engagement with the continent. These performing artists took to the popular stage at the same time that emigration to Liberia and the European "scramble for Africa" held the attention of the black press. The West African country formed by American efforts, Liberia, had long held a place in the African American imagination, but the failures of Reconstruction and rise of Jim Crow had rekindled enthusiasm for black emigration there. Meanwhile, European colonial interests were heightening fears that France and Britain were nipping at Liberian borders.[2] Black America's interest in colonial wars further intensified with Ethiopia's triumph over Italy in 1896 and the entry of the United States into its own imperialist wars in Cuba and the Philippines in 1898. Cook, Dunbar, and the Williams and Walker Company touched on all these issues in their shows, but in their first African-themed production, they began their discussion with one of the more enduring sentiments: Ethiopianism.

Jes Lak White Fo'ks (1900)

With a refrain that spoke of "ole Eygpts' people," the opening song of Jes Lak White Fo'ks introduced Africa before the curtains even parted. Ethiopianism derived from the Old Testament passage from the Book of Psalms: "Princes shall come out of Egypt; Ethiopia shall soon stretch forth her hands unto God." By the late eighteenth century, with black conversions to Christianity increasing and slavery still firmly in place, African Americans invoked this passage of deliverance, and likely, the passage itself inspired many an enslaved African to convert. Strengthened by a righteous faith that shaped their political memory, African Americans declared that "the ascendancy of the white race was only temporary, and that the divine providence of history was working to elevate the African peoples." Ethiopianist thought allowed black Americans to reconcile the contradictory biblical images of Egypt as both a land of splendor and a land of oppression. Frequently African Americans merged the images of Egypt and Ethiopia, and conflated Ethiopia with the whole continent. Such thinking, immersed as it was in the Bible, infused most nineteenth-century black nationalism, and in the years before the Civil War the writings and speeches of Maria Stewart, David Walker, and Frederick Douglass included Ethiopian symbolism. Ethiopianism thus played a significant role in the larger black political culture, and although it has been interpreted alternately as a religious, literary, and political movement, it ultimately evolved into what historian William Scott described as an "extended thought-style among black Americans."[3]

By the late nineteenth century, references to Ethiopia were so common that black newspapers, notably the popular weekly *Indianapolis Freeman,* incorporated the biblical phrase in their mastheads. The phrase's popularity suggests that Ethiopianist sentiment more often evoked a sense of national identity, connection with Africa, and the possibility of redemption without necessarily adhering to the tenets of biblical mysticism. Not all leaders who worked for the Christianization and redemption of Africa grounded their beliefs in Ethiopianism, and some writers invoked Ethiopia without perceiving a need to uplift Africans. One of Dunbar's early poems, "Ode to Ethiopia," demonstrates how he used this language to articulate a racial identity and espouse an antiracist politics without placing the narrative within organized Christianity. Dunbar wrote, "Be proud, my Race, in mind and soul; Thy name is writ on Glory's scroll," and he concluded his poem with the line, "And proudly tune their lyres to sing / Of Ethiopia's glory." He used this poem for political purposes, choosing to read it once when he took the podium after a racist speaker and later reciting it for Frederick Douglass.[4]

However central Ethiopianist thought was to black political culture and however seriously Dunbar considered such thinking, he and Cook mixed this sentiment with reference to racist stereotype in *Jes Lak White Fo'ks.* The song's first verse included the lyric "white fol'ks no use tryin / Fu to do us ha'm / Lord's gwine raise his people / High up in his ahm." With the second verse, they spoke of the "Lan whah milk an' honey / Flowin' fresh an' free / chicken and de turkey Waitin dah fu me." The libretto lacked extensive stage directions, and few reviews of this show exist; from the extant text it is difficult to tell just how Cook and Dunbar wanted their reference to Ethiopianist sentiment read. Surely with the inference that revival congregants were praying for a future laden with chicken, they meant to poke some fun at religious devotion, much as they had with "Who Dat Say Chicken in Dis Crowd?" in *Clorindy.* In *Jes Lak White Fo'ks,* Cook and Dunbar continued to mock the revival meeting by concluding the scene with a character named Jube, described as a "boisterous darkey," shouting and singing vigorously, clearly unaware that all the rest had quieted.

It is not difficult to imagine a comedian like Bert Williams or Ernest Hogan turning this particular scene into rollicking critique. Cook actually had hoped that Ernest Hogan would star in *Jes Lak White Fo'ks* since he had previously made *Clorindy* such a success. Because Hogan was already booked for the season, Cook cast the lesser-known actor Irving Jones for the leading role. The show failed to win critical acclaim and played only a short run at the New York Winter Garden in the summer of 1900.[5]

Audiences might have been more enthusiastic had Hogan been starring. But it may well be that by poking fun at such an important aspect of black religious and political culture, Cook and Dunbar limited their show's success by alienating some devout black patrons. White patrons may have been less interested in the show as well, since its title equated African Americans with them.

The mocking of Ethiopianism in *Jes Lak White Fo'ks*, however, fit well with Cook and Dunbar's critique of nineteenth-century black elite pretension. Whether counseling black masses at home or abroad, the black bourgeoisie tended to employ a paternalist ethos and politics of uplift that elevated their own position as chosen religious and political leaders. In commenting on this tendency, the two artists drew on their familiarity with black nationalist ideologies of the 1890s as well as from their personal acquaintances with prolific black nationalist theoreticians like Alexander Crummell. On a visit to London, Dunbar had stayed with Crummell; Dunbar also later accepted his invitation to join the American Negro Academy, an organization Crummell founded in 1897. Born in 1819 of free parents, Crummell became interested in the regeneration of Africa, believing that Christianity would bring West African redemption, and in turn, that the western civilization of Africa was necessary for black American freedom at home. He worked as a missionary in Liberia from 1853 through 1872 and espoused a nationalist ideology popular among missionaries that regarded black Americans as destined to "uplift" Africans by sending its elite to Africa to achieve its regeneration. Accepting western notions of civilization as did Frederick Douglass and others, Crummell and the missionary movement argued that black Americans should work to "lift the African 'from the rudeness of barbarism.'"[6] With its base in black religious organizations—and by extension, black universities—the missionary movement was perhaps the most prominent vehicle for black Americans to connect with Africa in the second half of the nineteenth century, a time when both of these institutions experienced significant growth. Many black Americans heard stories about Africa and Africans through their congregations' support for missionary efforts.

In 1897, at the age of seventy-eight, Crummell brought his missionary impulse home and presided over his American Negro Academy, an organization he envisioned as a domestic counterpart to his work in Liberia. Gathering forty notable black Americans, including the twenty-nine-year-old W. E. B. Du Bois and twenty-five-year-old Dunbar, Crummell hoped this organization would help improve conditions for black Americans in the United States "by the scientific processes of literature, art, and philosophy." Du Bois too hoped that the academy would "be the epitome and expression of the intellect of the black blooded people of America, the exponent of the race ideals of one of the world's great races."[7] Rather than completely support this group, however, Dunbar and Cook wrote an operetta more reflective of discussions they had held with other artists at the Marshall Hotel. For all the attention paid to Africa, argued Cook and Dunbar, many black Americans were acting "jes lak white fo'ks." In their show, an African American man comes into an unexpected sum of money and announces that he intends to buy his way into African royalty. He imagines that such connections will earn him status similar to that of white Americans who heralded their European ancestry.

In vaudeville, characters' names typically offered clues about their personalities. In *Jes Lak White Fo'ks,* Cook and Dunbar named the protagonist "Pompous" Johnson. As the curtains parted, Pompous emerged tugging a chest of gold he had discovered and bragging about how he would use his newfound wealth to achieve his "social aspirations." Pompous announced that when "white men gets rich dem don stay hyeah wha ezybody knows 'em en knows day ain' much. Dey go to Europe." He proclaimed that since William Vanderbilt's daughter had married a duke, he would arrange a "ma'iage of convenience" for his daughter, Mandy, to marry an African prince. As Pompous waited for Prince Ju Ju (also described as "The Cannibal King"), he sang that "to get in high society you need a great reputation" and explained that you "don't cultivate sobriety but rather ostentation."

Pompous bragged that he was going to buy Mandy (played by Abbie Mitchell) a family tree with his fortune. He declared that family trees "er so cheap in Europe dey use 'em fer kindlin wood" and that he would make

Abbie Mitchell, ca. 1910.
(Billy Rose Theater Collection, The New York Public Library for the Performing Arts,
Astor, Lenox and Tilden Foundations.)

sure that Mandy had "a family tree jes' lak white folks." Pompous then presented a drawing of his newly acquired family tree to his friend, Jube, explaining that he descended from a king. When Jube protested, Pompous attested that "dis tree wuz drafted by, the Herald of de Royal Af'o American Fenian Society of de daughters of de Holland dames." Here, Cook mocked white folks' organizations like the Daughters of the American Revolution, along with African American elite obsession with genealogy and tendency to pride themselves on their associational life, whether it was with the Prince Hall Masons or the Society of the Sons of New York. As one black resident of Washington noted, "Colored society has within its bounds clubs galore, clubs for nearly every conceivable object."[8] These organizations usually restricted their membership to those whose lifestyle conformed to a Victorian moral code of gentility; behavior that Cook and Dunbar saw as pompous. The number of black fraternal societies multiplied so rapidly during the late nineteenth and early twentieth centuries that one black journalist claimed African Americans had gone "lodge mad."[9]

Pompous's claim to have been descended from a king mocked the many elite blacks who likewise boasted that their ancestry was tied to a glorified (and often fictional) African past. Black aristocrats tended to claim prominent African ancestors, including numerous princes and chieftains in their family trees. Notably, prominent black nationalists like Alexander Crummell and Bishop Henry McNeal Turner claimed descent from African royalty. According to Crummell, his grandfather was a chief of the Temne people of West Africa and his father was born a prince. Turner claimed descent from an African king, and explained that his free status at birth rested on a British colonial law that forbade the enslavement of African royalty in South Carolina.[10] Cook and Dunbar quite literally described this particular preoccupation with African royalty in the song "Evah Niggah Is a King."

> Evah Niggah is a king
> Royalty is jes de ting
> Ef yo social life's a bungle
> Jes you go back to yo' jungle
> An remember dat yo daddy was a king
> Once it use to be admitted
> Dat the colored man was fervant
> When he said dat he was Washington's

> Mos' loved and trusted servant
> But you see that little story
> Got as stale as soldiers rations
> So now he builds his perpulation
> On his African relations
> An' de very yaller people
> Dey don get into de ring
> An de only blood dats darkey
> Dey go native wid a king.[11]

Cook and Dunbar equated elites who claimed "African relations" with antebellum African Americans who had sought prestige by claiming to have been "Washington's mos' loved and trusted servant." Cook certainly recognized such tendencies from his own family history. His father's friend John Mercer Langston—whose name Cook had defiantly rejected as a teenager—claimed that his mother descended from a "tribe of Indians of close relationship in blood to the famous Pocahontas."[12] For the young Will Marion, Langston's obsession with his own genealogy and "the top stratum of black society" made him the epitome of elite pretension. Langston's intense desire to distance himself from the black masses resembled a desire held by Cook's teenage crush Hattie. She too privileged lighter-skinned blacks and those claiming descent from George Washington. Her "damned fool" question to the thirteen-year-old Cook—whether he had "trouble with the niggers in Washington"—set him on a path that led to "Evah Niggah Is a King."

In *Jes Lak White Fo'k's*, Pompous's daughter, Mandy, contested her father's elitist notions, much as Cook had rejected his own father's friend. Mandy defied her father's desire to be accepted into "high society" through marriage; she refused to marry the African prince. She sang: "Love looks not at estate ah no / T'was folly one should think it so . . . I care not for the world of fools / Love dignifies the soul it rules." When the African prince finally arrived, Pompous found him looking "rather suspicious, seedy and generally dilapidated," then decided that "an honest American Negro was a man who would look after his daughter." Cook wrote that Pompous decided that he was "happier as an ordinary darkey" and decided "to quit acting jes lak white folks." By rejecting her arranged marriage, Cook's Mandy helped convince her father that modern blacks should not aspire to white pretensions by buying claims to African royal ancestry.

With the character of Mandy, Cook and Dunbar introduced the theme of passing, a notably different method of acting like white folks and one far more relevant to a generation growing up under Jim Crow. Drawing on current events, the artists modeled Mandy on Anita Florence Hemmings, the first African American woman to graduate from Vassar College. Hemmings had completed her four years at Vassar by passing as a white woman, and only divulged her racial identity a few days before commencement in 1897. Vassar's administration had decided to keep her racial identity a secret, and allowed Hemmings to graduate to avoid a scandal. This story spread so rapidly in the press that Dunbar read of it in London. He wrote, "Enormous papers of the metropolis, exponents of the opinions of a cosmopolitan city, came out with glaring headlines above sensational columns! And all because a colored young woman, too fair to be recognized as one with African blood, had graduated from Vassar!"[13] In *Jes Lak White Fo'ks,* Dunbar's Mandy sang that she was the "first dark belle who ever went to Vassar" and that "they had never seen my dark papa / and I didn't have to show him." Mandy continued:

> The papers howled and said it was a shame
> And they really thought that I was to blame
> They thought I had played an awful game
> Tho' they had to own that I got there just the same.

Dunbar wrote similarly in his *Tribune* article about Hemmings: "What a reason for dragging a refined woman into unpleasant notoriety! Had she hurt Vassar or her schoolmates? . . . What an evidence of breadth it is in a great institution of learning to even think of taking 'official action' because a pupil who had filled all the requirements of the school, who had been universally respected and loved, was found to have mixed blood. It is utterly childish."[14]

For Dunbar's generation, temporary passing became increasingly common. While Hemmings's story stands out because she managed to make it through four years of college, there is no shortage of stories about African Americans passing to access public facilities. Mary Church Terrell described how she and several friends passed to see Bob Cole perform. And once, when fellow activist Fannie Barrier Williams traveled in first-class accommodations, she answered the conductor's query as to her racial identity by explaining, "Je suis Français"—much as Terrell's darker-skinned friend had responded to the usher at Cole's show. One Williams and

Walker Company member frequented a café where he passed by "jabbering off some French," explaining that whites did not care, "so long as they don't suspect I am an American Negro." Other African Americans passed as Spanish; J. Rosamond Johnson and Bob Cole once relied on Johnson's knowledge of the language to pass as Spanish dignitaries before being "busted" by Irving Jones. By the 1920s, passing had become so common that one Washington theater manager hired a "black doorman to spot and bounce intruders whose racial origins were undetectable by whites."[15] The preponderance of such stories suggests that attempts to pass were a tangible part of daily life. Like references to Ethiopianism, black club life, and claims to an African royal past, Hemmings's story was well-known to black audiences. That passing stories appeared only in black-authored songs of the era is not insignificant. Passing, like the particular representations of Africa, spoke specifically to a black agenda. The theme was so popular that "The Vassar Girl" survived the failed *Jes Lak White Fo'ks* and was interpolated into the Broadway-bound *In Dahomey,* even though it had little connection with the later show's central plot.

Although *Jes Lak White Fo'ks* failed commercially, and closed after a brief run in June 1900, the script outlived these performances. That winter Cook collaborated with Bob Cole and the Johnson brothers to rewrite the show for the following summer season. Renamed *The Cannibal King,* the production starred Cole, J. Rosamond Johnson, Billy Johnson, Ernest Hogan, Aida Walker, and Abbie Mitchell. The show opened August 15, 1901, in New York and toured briefly in Hartford, Connecticut, and Indianapolis, Indiana, in November of that year.[16] This collaboration highlights how much New York's black performers worked together, and suggests that they regularly discussed the politics that Cook and Dunbar addressed in *Jes Lak White Fo'ks.* At the same time, they did not always agree, and political discussions were often heated, particularly those between Cole and Cook. As James Weldon Johnson told it, Cole "strove for the fine artistic effect, regardless of whether it had any direct relation to the Negro," whereas Cook "declared that the Negro should eschew 'white' patterns . . . and that the Negro in music and on the stage ought to be a genuine Negro." The rivalry, however, cannot be fully explained by their different perspectives on the role of black art. Cook taunted Cole for faults in pronunciation and mocked his lack of general education, even though he considered Cole extremely talented. Cook had never forgiven Cole for throwing him off an earlier project with the All Star Stock Company, and was known for a temper so contentious that even Dunbar had trouble with him.[17]

In *The Cannibal King,* Cole significantly revised *Jes Lak White Fo'ks,* and, reportedly, not to Cook's liking. Cole had teamed up with James Weldon and J. Rosamond Johnson to write songs for white performers, and his revisions to this play suggest that he may have been preoccupied with the demands of white audiences.[18] *The Cannibal King* told the story of the farcical efforts of a former black headwaiter at an elite white southern hotel. After suddenly coming into money, the waiter tried to school others in social graces to make them more acceptable to members of high society. No libretto of *The Cannibal King* survives, but the show seemingly omitted the critique of elite obsession with African royal ancestry. Without this theme, *The Cannibal King* more easily fit with the mockery of African American elite pretension made familiar to the dominant culture through the antebellum minstrel character "Zip Coon." Despite the changes, this show too failed to win significant audiences. Cook, however, did not give up on *Jes Lak White Fo'ks,* and he incorporated several of its original songs and themes into the production that brought black musical comedy to Broadway theaters, Williams and Walker's *In Dahomey.*

In Dahomey (1902)

In Dahomey, a full-length musical comedy, centered on the exploits of two southern migrants (played by Williams and Walker) who, upon finding themselves short of money, leave their new home in Boston to join a group of emigrants to West Africa. After the show's opening in Stamford, Connecticut, on September 8, 1902, Williams and Walker took its cast of fifty on tour, earning a booking starting February 18, 1903, at Broadway's New York Theater, where the production ran for fifty-three performances. Williams rejoiced: "If you had any idea how often we've tried for Broadway only to get side-tracked, you'd begin to understand how it hit us." He explained that when "the curtain fell after the first act of 'In Dahomey' and the applause began (not like popping corn, but on a Maxim gun scale)," he did "a breakdown with a pigeon wing on the side (and came near being caught doing it as the curtain went up)." His excitement must have been obvious as he scraped and shook from one foot to the other, fluttering his arms and whispering to no one in particular: "We're here! We've landed . . . maybe the reason we were so long in finding Broadway was because we never thought of looking for it 'In Dahomey.'"[19]

For Williams and Walker, *In Dahomey*'s success meant more than just arriving on Broadway. Rather, with this show, they turned their vaudeville duo—their "coon" act—into a cultural phenomenon that transformed the American popular stage by making full-length black musical comedy marketable. That they accomplished this feat alongside their goal of staging their own representations of Africa made their achievement all the more gratifying. After the Broadway run, Williams and Walker took the show across the Atlantic, leaving New York for London in April 1903. There they performed to great acclaim at the Shaftesbury Theater and Buckingham Palace. Traveling abroad won them an international audience, and brought them more prestige when they returned home. After their London tour, the Williams and Walker Company performed across the United States, and *In Dahomey* ran for over one thousand performances before closing permanently in 1905.[20]

To produce this show, Williams and Walker drew from the crew of black artists that converged at New York City's Marshall Hotel in the late 1890s. While there, the vaudeville pair met playwright Jesse Shipp, who wrote *In Dahomey*'s libretto. Like many of the other black artists, Shipp performed his way to New York. In Cincinnati, while working for a laundry, he performed with local minstrel troupes, but soon left for Chicago to join Sam T. Jack's *Creole Show* at the world's fair. As a member of this cast, Shipp met Bob Cole, and, after this show, he helped Cole write *A Trip to Coontown* (1898).[21] Shipp's talent for writing inspired him to continue working on full-length shows as opposed to the various short skits common in vaudeville. With the unprecedented success of *In Dahomey,* Shipp stayed with the Williams and Walker Company, writing the librettos for *Abyssinia* (1906) and *Bandana Land* (1907–1909).[22]

For *In Dahomey*, Shipp made the mishaps of the Dahomey Colonization Society the central plot device. While the three-act production integrated several other topics pertinent to contemporary black political culture, the main story revolved around this group of emigrants. Produced in 1902, the show drew on contemporary discussions about emigration, and more specifically, Bishop Henry McNeal Turner's exploits. Shipp probably had heard Turner speak in Chicago at the fair, and even if not, he surely knew of the speeches Turner had made there. Black critic J. Harry Jackson reported in his review, "The opera tells the story of two young men who have more brains than money and who join a syndicate for the development of Dahomey, (à la Bishop Turner)."[23]

Born in 1834 of free but impoverished parents, Turner became an itinerant preacher at the age of nineteen, and eventually earned an appointment as a bishop with the African Methodist Episcopal (AME) Church. Initially inspired to support emigration by a speech that Alexander Crummell gave in 1862, Turner postponed his newfound interests while he served as a Union army chaplain, worked with the Freedman's Bureau, and acted as a delegate to the 1867 Georgia Constitutional Convention. When white supremacists again dominated southern politics, Turner combined his political aspirations with his religious devotion and became dedicated to sending black missionaries to Africa. For Turner, emigration and the mission movement were inseparable, and after his first visits to Sierra Leone and Liberia in the early 1890s, he returned to the United States "ready to move heaven and earth" for emigration.[24]

Turner's pleas for emigration found a willing audience as increasing

numbers of African Americans confronted the failures of Reconstruction and the triumph of Jim Crow. The people most interested in emigration during this era were poor, rural African Americans, those with the fewest options in America. They hoped that Turner would guide them to freedom and prosperity in West Africa. While only an estimated one thousand African Americans sailed to Liberia between 1890 and World War I, thousands of others participated in Turner's movement by writing letters, helping fellow emigrants, supporting their congregation's mission movements, and reading Turner's *Voice of Missions,* a tract he published from 1893 through 1899. Through his publications and speeches, knowledge of and interest in Turner and emigration spread among many thousands of others who did not directly participate.[25] Major black newspapers commented on and critiqued all these events, making Turner's activities, and the topic of emigration generally, central to black political culture. Williams and Walker's *In Dahomey* certainly reflected these interests, and arguably, encouraged further discussion.

While many black southerners heeded Turner's call, many northern-born and privileged African Americans criticized his efforts, particularly

Scene from act 2 of Williams and Walker's *In Dahomey,* 1902.

(Helen Armstead-Johnson Theater Photograph Collection, Photographs and Prints Division, Schomburg Center for Research in Black Culture, The New York Public Library, Astor, Lenox and Tilden Foundations.)

his affiliation with the American Colonization Society, a group founded by racist whites set on removing black peoples from the United States. *New York Age* editor T. Thomas Fortune called Turner the "agent, the hired man, the oiled advocate of a white man's corporation" and wrote, "I wish I could take a bludgeon and smash the head of that American Colonization Society flat, oh so flat." Frederick Douglass and Booker T. Washington also criticized Turner; they considered emigration the wrong path. Even Alexander Crummell, whose missionary work had earlier so inspired Turner, turned away from Africa by the end of his life.[26] The critique of emigration was in part a response to the late-nineteenth-century European partitioning of the continent. In 1907 a cartoon in the *Indianapolis Freeman* pictured Turner in a small boat as he confronted an Africa run by France, England, Germany, and Holland. The caption read, "The Bishop Undoubtedly Forgets That the Dark Continent Is Well Occupied."[27]

Still, many other African Americans, like bluesman W. C. Handy, supported emigrants as they encountered them firsthand. Handy described one group "bound for Africa" who had passed in front of his house when he was a young boy. "A quaint crowd of Negroes had left their homes in the snow," he recalled; they had "little more for their journey than the clothes on their backs." Profoundly troubled by the emigrants' poverty, Handy offered a barefoot young boy some socks and shoes.[28] This incident affected him so deeply that he included it in his autobiography written many years later. In 1895, too, several thousand Georgians, both black and white, showed up on a Savannah pier to watch the departure of one steamship of emigrants.[29] Many other African Americans, including performers, probably witnessed similar events, and spread the lure and lore of Turner's groups.

Handy's story poignantly touches on another issue that became increasingly publicized by the black press; that is, the poverty of the actual emigrants and the inability of Turner to ensure that they would survive the journey. Turner painted an idealized picture of Africa, claiming that the land was rich, with abundant water as well as "fruits of every beauty." But several emigrants reported otherwise in letters published by various black newspapers. One emigrant wrote to his mother: "Something to eat is scarce over here . . . I have been glad enough to get one meal of dry rice a day, and nothing in it but salt and water."[30]

If Turner could not guarantee safe passage or a fruitful existence, scam artists made matters far worse by using the American Colonization Society's name to prey on the desperation of black southerners hoping to escape rural poverty and the injustices of Jim Crow. One notable travesty involved two hundred Oklahomans, over half of them children. These Oklahomans traveled to New York in March of 1892 believing that the American Colonization Society would provide travel to Liberia. With no passage available and no money, these emigrants wandered around cold and wet in the city until a Methodist mission provided shelter. While some eventually made it to Liberia, the majority either returned to Oklahoma or stayed in New York. On another occasion in Arkansas, two anonymous preachers collected thousands of dollars, spent three thousand dollars to charter a train, and then sent four hundred African Americans to Brunswick, Georgia, to meet a nonexistent ship. Widely publicized and condemned by the black press, these scandals provoked several black leaders to cast doubt on Turner's emigration schemes.[31]

Despite these critiques, would-be emigrants continued to seek greater freedom in the Jim Crow era of political disfranchisement, economic marginalization, and social segregation. "Anywhere but here" seemed to be the credo as African Americans moved when they could; some left the South for the North and West, others left rural areas for southern cities, and still others looked toward Africa. Black Americans were not the only ones on the move; many West Indians also fled the regions where they and their families had been enslaved. Bert Williams himself had been born in the Bahamas, and his family made their way to California, in the hope of finding more freedom in the United States. Williams and many of the other leading artists continued to move as they strove to make their careers. The Chicago World's Fair and America's new urban culture seemed to promise increased opportunity, and they left their small towns for the northern cities of Chicago and New York. Certainly during this era native-born whites and European immigrants too sought opportunity in America's burgeoning cities, but the movement of peoples of African descent was distinctive because of the particular problems blacks confronted as they traveled. The stage shows, particularly those of the Williams and Walker Company, commented not only on Turner and African emigration, but also on the experiences of migration from South to North and West in the United States.

George Walker, who hailed from Lawrence, Kansas, was well aware of black Tennesseans' exodus to Kansas shortly after Emancipation. Not satisfied with the possibilities available in Lawrence, Walker set out alone from Kansas as a performer with medicine shows before arriving in Chicago. His father, Jerry Nashville, who had been a well-respected hotel porter in Lawrence, had also been on the move, leaving George and his mother to live in Denver, Colorado. The elder Walker's relocation to Denver—in part to become president of the Colorado Colonization Society of Liberia, Africa—likely further influenced Walker's desire to discuss emigration in his work. Although there was less interest in emigration among African Americans in the western states, Denver emerged as a prominent center that continued to promote emigration as late as 1910.[32] Such a family history surely kept George grappling with the connections for black Americans among home, nation, and freedom.

Although Walker stayed emotionally close to his mother, even purchasing a house for her in Kansas in 1907, no evidence exists that he kept in contact with his father. In fact, two biographical sketches suggest that Walker and his father had a difficult relationship during his childhood. A white reporter wrote that while Nash Walker was "one of the best known colored men that ever lived in the university town," his son George used to be "regarded as one of the most worthless little 'niggers' that ever lived in Lawrence." This reporter's condemnation does not help illuminate George Walker's youthful experiences, but it does suggest that he and his father were at odds. Another reporter explained that George Walker turned to men other than his father for mentoring, becoming popular among the business community as well as with college boys who accepted him as their mascot.[33] It is likely that George Walker's personal connection with the nineteenth-century movement for colonization intensified his interest in this aspect of black politics. His estrangement from his father may have actually further influenced his desire to lampoon the practices of colonization societies in *In Dahomey*.

The show began with Williams and Walker playing the characters Shylock Homestead and Rareback Pinkerton, two unemployed African American men who hit rough times after migrating to Boston from the south. Times were so bad for Shylock that he first appears on stage beating a drum for the Salvation Army to keep from starving. Homestead and Pinkerton are soon hired as private detectives to travel to Gatorville, Florida, to locate a silver casket lost by the president of the Dahomey Colonization

Society, Cicero Lightfoot. Shipp foreshadowed Homestead and Pinkerton's jobs by referencing the Pinkerton National Detective Agency, which had become well-known for providing strike-breaking detectives during the 1892 Homestead Strike (a bloody clash at the Carnegie Steel Works in Homestead, Pennsylvania). Similarly, the Williams and Walker Company chose Lightfoot as the name of the president of the colonization society to reference a real person and a notorious event in emigration history. In the 1890s, Reverend J. P. F. Lightfoot perpetrated one of the many emigration scams that garnered national attention. In eastern Arkansas, an estimated three thousand African Americans paid Lightfoot three dollars each, and when some of his contributors realized Lightfoot had swindled them, they killed him. Several newspapers, including the *New York Times,* reported the event.[34]

In the stage show, the quest for the silver box takes Shylock and Rareback to Africa with the Dahomey Colonization Society. Once in Dahomey, all of the emigrants except Shylock and Rareback are taken prisoner after having a misunderstanding with the king. The protagonists, who had little desire to go to Africa in the first place, had brought three barrels of whiskey to the king, since they knew that in Dahomey a gift of whiskey was a sign of appreciation. In thanks for their present, the king awards them governorships, and from their new position of power, they arrange for the members of the Dahomey Colonization Society to be released by giving the king another barrel of whiskey. In the finale, the colonists honor the two corrupt detectives and proclaim, "There's no place like home."[35] One character announces, "Things have been misrepresented and I for one should go back to where I come from." Mrs. Lightfoot, the wife of the colonization society president, admits: "My ambition brought me over here and if ever I get back, my house will be big enough to hold me and my ambitions." Given the history of failed emigration schemes, well-published testimony from disgruntled emigrants, and the grandiose promises of emigrationists, these sentiments were most likely warmly received by African American audiences in 1903. As the *New York Times* review of *In Dahomey* announced, "The Negroes in the audience were in heaven."[36]

The Williams and Walker Company did not just lampoon Turner's colonization efforts; it also commented on larger imperialist ventures of the time. As the United States waged its war against Spain in Cuba in 1898 and then fought in the Philippines for many more years, pro- and anti-imperialist debates filled the pages of the American press. Social Darwinism prevailed in these debates, with most arguing that Filipinos were a "savage" people incapable of self-government. But such arguments over a civilizing mission resonated for many black Americans with their own missionary efforts in Africa. Alexander Crummell and most nineteenth-century black nationalists promoted some sort of "civilizing" mission as an integral component of emigration. Turner continued in this tradition and in his *Voice of Missions* urged black American missionaries to "break the bonds of superstition, chains of ignorance, to dispel the black clouds of idolatry . . . to illuminate the inhabitants of that despised, forsaken, outraged and neglected land." Yet with the European partitioning of Africa and America's imperial ambitions, some of the younger generation questioned whether black Americans should participate and "take up the white man's burden" in that continent.[37]

The characters in *In Dahomey* reflect this ambivalence as Shipp painted a picture of a group of African Americans who believed that they would be able to take over Dahomey and introduce "civilization." One member of the fictional colonization society, Mose, claims that in Dahomey, "it never snows so you don't need no clothes such as the people wear here, and who knows but what you can get a few franchises from the king to start street cars, 'letric lights, and saloons to running." As debates were waged on the pages of American papers between pro- and anti-imperialists, so they appeared on the popular stage. In *In Dahomey,* the anti-imperialist appears in the guise of a postman named Stampfield who steps out of a door of "the intelligence office." He asks the pro-imperialist Mose what he would do if the "natives don't take kindly to the new order of things and refuse to be electric lighted, salooned, and otherwise fixed up with blessings of civilization. Suppose—they look upon you as intruders and instead of receiving you with open arms (*pause*) make war on you?" Mose responds that the colonization society would "arrange with dem gentlemen like Uncle Sam did with the Indians" and would "kick the stuffin' out of dem and put them on a reservation." Countering the idea that Africans needed or wanted western "civilizing," the Williams and Walker ensemble commented on the brutal reality behind the politics of the "white man's burden."[38]

By representing Africans as uninterested in westernization, however, Williams and Walker raised the possibility that perhaps Africans could not be "civilized"—a belief that surfaced in debates over the role of the conti-

Bert Williams and George Walker as Shylock Homestead and
Rareback Pinkerton in *In Dahomey*, ca. 1903.

(Photographs and Prints Division, Schomburg Center for Research in Black Culture,
The New York Public Library, Astor, Lenox and Tilden Foundations.)

nent in black liberation. Stampfield earlier told Mose that he would "find the colored population of Dahomey quite as much a source of annoyance as the colored population of this country," and exclaimed, "Your exalted opinion of the ideal life to be found in a barbarous country is beyond my comprehension." These contradictions show that rather than present a clear political position, *In Dahomey* reflected then-current debates over emigration, annexation of the Philippine Islands, and even the benefits of a consumer society. In a song, the company lightened their critique, singing that "on Broadway in Dahomey" they would serve "giraffe highballs and real coke-nut wine" and would "see on sides of rocks and hills" signs that said "use Carter's Little Liver pills."

Williams and Walker were not the only entertainers addressing the volatile issues of emigration to Africa. Ernest Hogan too departed from his usual short vaudeville skits to produce *The Oysterman* (1907), a show whose central narrative involved a colonization swindle. Like George Walker, Hogan had direct personal connections to Africa. His grandfather had been educated by a wealthy southern family to go to the continent as a missionary. Once there, he married an African woman who became Hogan's grandmother. While little evidence exists regarding Hogan's early years and his relationship with his missionary grandfather and African grandmother, he did write and perform a one-act vaudeville comedy called the "Missionary Man" that in 1901 the *Indianapolis Freeman* called "the most prominent thing presented in vaudeville by colored actors."[39] Hogan followed this act with *The Oysterman*, a full-length production about travel to Africa.

In the play, Hogan played the protagonist, the "Oysterman," who began life as a worker on a Mississippi levee, but left for Baltimore to make his way in the oyster business. Similar to *In Dahomey,* Hogan's main character was already migrating north before becoming involved with emigration to Africa. But unlike Shylock and Rareback, the Oysterman lived a life of luxurious ease until he met a swindler who persuaded him to buy stock in a colonization society. Hogan's Oysterman never made it to the continent. En route to Africa, provisions ran short, and he realized that he had been swindled. This too touched on one of the significant failures of emigration supported by the American Colonization Society. Numerous irate emigrants returned to the United States reporting that the society had failed to provide sufficient rations for their journey or for their first months in Liberia.[40]

Rather than solely comment on failed emigration efforts, *The Oysterman* focused on black business and diplomatic interests in Africa. *The Oysterman* was produced in 1907, five years after Williams and Walker's widely popular *In Dahomey*. By then, Hogan would have been risking audience boredom by merely resurrecting the emigration theme. For *The Oysterman* he likely drew on the experiences of William H. Ellis, an African American man who had become well-known in black communities for his visit to Ethiopia in 1903 to meet its emperor, Menelik II. The Oysterman did not promote emigration like Turner (or Lightfoot), and he was not impoverished like most actual emigrants (or Shylock and Homestead). Rather, he had left Mississippi and become a successful businessman in Baltimore, far more closely resembling Ellis, who had migrated from Texas to make his fortune in New York City. The businesses differed, of course. Hogan's character triumphed in the oyster business, while Ellis had earned his money working for Henry H. Hotchkiss, the gun millionaire.

Both Hogan's fictional character and Ellis were successful businessmen, and both traveled to Africa motivated more by business interests informed by the age of imperial expansion than by the goals of nineteenth-century emigrationists. A swindler won the Oysterman over by convincing him that "it would be a glorious climax if he were to go to Dahomey and be crowned king of that country."[41] In real life, in 1903, the press had claimed that Ellis had "hoped to be 'Abyssini's King,'" after he won notoriety for seeking appointment as the U.S. representative responsible for establishing commercial relations with Ethiopia. As the only African country to defeat European colonizers, Ethiopia already held a prominent place in black political culture, and, as a black man, Ellis felt he was best positioned to represent the United States in negotiating trade with the African nation. He reported that he met the Ethiopian "crown prince" Ras Makonnen in London in 1902, and that Makonnen had invited him to visit his country to meet with Menelik. Serious about his quest, Ellis set about learning everything he could about the country. In late December 1902, he reportedly spent nearly three thousand dollars at a New York bookseller on books about Ethiopia's history. When the State Department overlooked Ellis as consul and instead choose a white man, Robert P. Skinner, Ellis wrote "letters of complaint to the *New York Times,* the *Baltimore Sun* and the *Washington Post,* along with lesser known white newspapers and all the major black ones." Eventually, he made a few trips of his own to Ethiopia. The first, late in 1903, he funded personally, traveling with the Haitian consul

Benito Sylvain. For the second, in June of 1904, he was invited to accompany Kent J. Loomis, the brother of the assistant secretary of state, who had been appointed as the official U.S. representative responsible for delivering the signed trade agreement to the Ethiopian king.[42]

Ellis's story took a bizarre turn during his travels with Loomis—one that *The Oysterman* would resurrect. Sometime during the first leg of the journey, somewhere between New York and England, Loomis disappeared from the ship. A week later his body washed ashore in France. While American papers reported that Loomis had been a known alcoholic, they did not exonerate Ellis from complicity in his disappearance because Ellis's ambitions were so widely known. Ellis actually continued on to Ethiopia and delivered the trade agreement, apparently unaware of the recovery of Loomis's body or the stories circulating about him back home.[43]

Reference to this story appeared in Hogan's show when after the Oysterman sets sail for Africa with the swindler, he realizes that he's been taken, and throws the culprit overboard. While Ellis eventually made it to Ethiopia, the Oysterman never arrives there. Rather he lands on an island, discovers gems and gold, takes possession of the island community, elects himself king, and becomes wealthier than before. This too referred to the real-life Ellis, who had earlier reported that Menelik had granted him all the diamond mines in Ethiopia and some quarter-million acres of land, where he hoped to experiment with cotton cultivation. He had let it be known that he intended to "obtain a concession of land and colonize American Negroes in the Negus' domains in Africa."[44]

Other African Americans expressed interests similar to those of William Ellis. One earlier case, that of John Lewis Waller, the African American U.S. consul to Madagascar, earned front-page news in the black press in 1895 and 1896. This particular story so captivated comedian Bob Cole that he kept a scrapbook from 1895 through 1898 that contained clippings about Waller rather than about his own stage work. As consul, Waller had actively struggled to resist French control of the island, and after his term expired, he received a land concession from the government of Madagascar, where he hoped to set up a land development partnership with African Americans and the Malagasy. The French, however, wanted him gone: they arrested him and sentenced him to twenty-five years in a French prison. The French rightly assessed that Waller's race would prevent the United States from working too hard to help him; he spent two years imprisoned in deplorable conditions before the U.S. State Department procured his release. The black press portrayed Waller as a martyr against white racism at home and European imperialism abroad.[45]

That Bob Cole kept a scrapbook detailing Waller's case attests to the avid interest this cohort of performers paid to contemporary politics, and certainly hints at the sorts of discussions that transpired at the Marshall Hotel in the late 1890s. As the characters in *In Dahomey* made clear, discussions about emigration, missionary activity, and imperialism were ongoing. While no clear consensus emerged from the group, the artists did alter their ideas in response to their discussion of contemporary events. Changes in the lyrics of songs appearing in both *Jes Lak White Fo'ks* and in *In Dahomey* best exemplify this. Shipp had drawn on the earlier script by Cook and Dunbar, and included several of its songs and plot lines. He interpolated the narrative about a man coming into unexpected money and hoping to purchase "royal ancestors" as well as the virtually unchanged song "The Vassar Girl." The ensemble also included the song "Evah Niggah Is a King" in *In Dahomey*, but this song was radically transformed for the later show. Most obviously, the word "niggah" was omitted and the song's title and chorus became "Evah Dahkey Is a King," a change that reflected black artists' desire to limit the worst of language used in "coon" songs. Sheet music included in the score of *In Dahomey* lists Cook's brother as composer and E. P. Moran and Paul Laurence Dunbar as lyricists rather than Cook and Dunbar alone.

More significant is the shift in theme from one that critiqued an African American elite who sought and bought prestige in African genealogy to one that heralded Africa as a nation and a homeland.

> Ev'ry dahkey has a lineage
> Dat de white fo'ks can't compete wid,
> An' a title such as duke or earl why we wouldn't wipe our feet wid;
> For a kingdom is our station, an' we's each a rightful ruler,
> When we's crowned we don't wear satins,
> kase de way we dress is cooler.
> But our power's just as mighty,
> Nevah judge kings by deir clothes;
> you could nevah tell a porter
> Wid a ring stuck through his nose.
> Scriptures say dat Ham was de first black man,

Ham's de father of our nation,
All de black fo'ks to dis very day b'longs right in de Ham creation.
Ham he was a king in ancient days, an' he reigned in all his glory.
Den ef we is all de Sons of ham, nachelly dat tells de story.
So! White fo'ks what's got dahkey servants,
Try an' give dem ev'ry ting;
an' doan nevah speak insulting
Fur dat coon may be a king.[46]

Instead of placing African Americans who sought status through African lineage on a par with those who had similarly looked toward their owner's or boss's social position, this 1902 version embraces African heritage. Rather than critiquing a black elite for claiming royal ancestry, the younger generation embraced all black Americans as potentially descended from African royalty. Bert Williams, known as a voracious reader who stayed up nights "wrestling with the philosophers," once said similarly that after reading John Ogilby's *Africa,* he "could prove that every Pullman porter was the descendant of a king."[47] With *In Dahomey,* the collaborative efforts of the Williams and Walker Company began to move from Cook and Dunbar's heavy-handed critique of African American elite pretension and the schemes of emigrationists. The company both questioned western imperialism and focused on representing Africans in a more positive light—themes that would emerge more fully in their 1906 production, *Abyssinia.*

Abyssinia (1906)

With the incredible success of *In Dahomey,* the Williams and Walker ensemble launched *Abyssinia,* an even more extravagant (and decidedly more reverent) full-length musical comedy focused on black America's relationship with Africa. This show opened in New York City at Broadway's Majestic Theater on February 21, 1906, and although it never gained the kind of attention lavished on *In Dahomey,* it toured for the rest of the year. Like *In Dahomey,* the Williams and Walker Company based *Abyssinia* on actual events, but in this show, they presented a very different picture of Africa. They depicted a fully developed African nation and a cadre of African American travelers uninterested in "colonizing" or "civilizing" the already developed Abyssinia.[48] They also shifted the location from West Africa, which was associated with the slave trade, Liberia, and the American Colonization Society, to the kingdom of Ethiopia, the only African country to emerge victorious from Europe's late-nineteenth-century scramble to colonize Africa. Under Menelik II, Abyssinians had defeated Italian troops in 1896 to remain an independent nation during the West's massive imperial expansion. This victory added an image of a powerful modern Ethiopian present to the long tradition of Ethiopianism that heralded a mythical Ethiopian past.

The Ethiopian victory became an important symbol of black self-determination and came to represent African resistance to white European imperialism. That a black leader of an African country could conquer a purveyor of European "civilization" proved a potent symbol for people of African descent around the world. The black American pulpit and press both dwelled at length on Menelik's victory. The *Cleveland Gazette* editorialized: "King Menelik is proving himself more than a match for civilization's trained and skilled warriors, with all their improved machinery of war. More power to him!" And editor George Knox congratulated Menelik in the *Freeman*, "They hit 'em hard in Abyssinia." The story of triumph made its way through black communities and was so powerful that it survived several generations. One journalist alleged to have heard of the Ethiopian victory as a young boy recalling, "Of course, we all knew about Menelik's defeat of the Italian army in 1896."[49]

Menelik's victory gave the company the confidence and ability to undertake a project that represented Africa and Africans more accurately and more powerfully. The play also reflected ongoing debates among black intellectuals over the nature of East and West Africans. Frederick Douglass had privileged Egyptians and Ethiopians as originators of civilization itself, and as somehow representative of all of Africa. Alexander Crummell, who spent many years in Liberia, by contrast expressed more interest in what he described as the nobility of the indigenous people of West Africa, a population in need of uplift but untouched by the degradation of American slavery. With the East African nation's victory, the black press congratulated Menelik, and the Williams and Walker Company honored Ethiopians with respectful portrayals. Earlier, they had earned some criticism for their depictions of the West African Dahomeans, especially from Sylvester Russell, who had written, "There is no literary merit to be found in a band of American Negroes taking a trip to Dahomey merely to bluff the people around." He "reminded" Williams and Walker that they "belonged to an oppressed race" themselves, and requested that Jesse Shipp "scratch his head and write the third act over again." For the company's representation of Ethiopia, however, Russell only had praise.[50]

With *Abyssinia,* the Williams and Walker Company incorporated images of both mythical Egypt and contemporary Ethiopia on their letterhead and sheet music covers. The letterhead sported beautifully rendered color drawings of desert scenes with camels, and the sheet music included a new company trademark of a "design with pyramids, sphinx, palm-tree, and sun." The image of an Ethiopian coin with Menelik's likeness adorned one piece of music. By the time this show opened, the Gotham and Attucks music publishing companies had merged, and the black-owned publishing house—affiliated with Williams and Walker—chose its own imagery.[51] They wanted to stress Ethiopia as a black kingdom in part because they clearly recognized that whites too saw the Ethiopian victory in racial terms, although with a decidedly different spin. Some whites were so distressed when African troops defeated European colonizers that they attempted to redefine Ethiopians as nonblacks. U.S. Consul Robert Skinner even "circulated a rumor that Menelik had insisted that he was Caucasian."[52]

For their representation of the country, the Williams and Walker Company stayed true to the historical record, naming the king Menelik and the capital Addis Ababa. They used several Abyssinian words in the script such as Ras (prince), Tej (the national intoxicant), and Es-shi (all right), publishing translations of these words in the show's programs. Shipp's Abyssinian characters seemed sophisticated and knowledgeable as they accurately discussed the politics and history of their country. The fictional chief justice, named Tegulet, reported that "the future welfare of Abyssinia demands that we place a check on the aggressive policy of all Nations," and indeed, between 1896 and 1906, the historical Menelik negotiated with Great Britain, France, and Russia to secure the boundaries of Ethiopia to its present size. Tegulet then changed the discussion to order the soldiers to look out for a rebel named Yarabu who was responsible for an uprising in response to "too much taxes levied by the Government." While this particular uprising seems to have been fictional, conflicts over taxation were frequent, since from the time of Ethiopia's victory over the Italians, Menelik sought to change the nation's reliance on a system of tribute to one of taxation.[53]

The company represented African Americans as holding new views about their relationship to the continent, and by extension, about their own origins, identity, and imagined homeland. Most notably, unlike the Dahomey

Colonization Society, the fictional African American travelers in Abyssinia meant to tour Africa, not settle there; they hoped to learn from the Abyssinians rather than bring them western civilization. Like Ernest Hogan, Williams and Walker likely drew from William Ellis's well-publicized travels in 1903 and 1904. *Abyssinia* actually appeared on stage the year before *The Oysterman,* but clearly, these leading artists conceived of these shows around the same time. Hogan had been inspired to comment on the Loomis drowning, while Williams and Walker were more interested in Ellis's actual experiences in East Africa and his meeting with Menelik. Ellis's tours were well-known since he wrote multiple letters to various newspapers as well as several letters to Andrew Carnegie in search of funding. He had returned from his first trip with glowing reports of his encounter with Menelik, maintaining that the Ethiopian king said that he and all his "chiefs and subjects thank you, so when you and all Americans come to visit, we will accept you in love."[54] Although those in *Abyssinia*'s American caravan were to find danger as well as pleasure in Ethiopia, Williams and Walker eventually concluded the show with a similar sentiment as the American travelers embraced their "newfound friends," the Abyssinians.

Abyssinia's fictional caravan ventured to Ethiopia after having traveled in Europe. Rastus Johnson (called "Ras" and played by George Walker) and his friend Jasmine Jenkins (called "Jas" and played by Bert Williams) led the group consisting of Ras's aunt and other members of a Baptist congregation from Kansas. Ras had won fifteen thousand dollars in the Louisiana lottery, and with his winnings, he paid off a nine-hundred-dollar mortgage on some land in Kansas and used the rest of the money to take the church members on a tour of Europe. While in Europe, oil was discovered on his land in Kansas and he came into even more money. With these additional funds, he took his church group to Africa.

Ras wanted to go to Africa to pursue his lifelong interest in astronomy, a science that not only examined the stars, but also, he believed, could control the weather. It was "on the Continent where the first authoritative school of astronomy had its birth, the Alexandrian school," he explains to Jas, "if what I learned of a disciple of this school of astronomy at Cairo be true, I shall be able to bring about any weather condition I desire, which of course will be a great benefit to Kansas." There is an element of humor here in that Ras thinks he can actually control the weather, but importantly, the company here mocked Americans rather than Africans. Rather than bringing "civilization" and science to Abyssinia, Ras hoped to learn something from Africans.

Although honoring Abyssinians, the company did not lose focus on commenting on American race relations. In this scene about astronomy, Ras pontificates about science and philosophy, while Jas, hungry after a day of walking, pleads repeatedly for Ras to give him one of the crackers he was carrying. Ras refuses several times, telling Jas that he "must learn to withstand temptation" and quoting Shakespeare to make his point. An exasperated Jas turns to the audience to ask, "Did you ever see a man stick so tight to a cracker?" This reference built on the theme earlier expressed in "Who Dat Say Chicken in Dis Crowd?" and critiqued Ras as adhering too closely to a white man's philosophy to notice the real problems of hunger. The scene ends with Ras finally giving Jas the crackers as they hear a chicken crowing. Jas exits and returns with the chicken, saying, "I'd a knowed that voice in the middle of the Red Sea, Rastus Johnson."[55]

The company continued to stress the caravan members' American identities by orchestrating several plot turns where characters had to state explicitly their national origins, sometimes under threat of death or dismemberment. At one point, Ras was mistaken for an African prince due to his name, an incident that gave Walker the opportunity to sing a song called "Rastus Johnson from U.S.A.":

> I'm just plain Rastus Johnson from U.S.A.
> I'm traveling 'round to see the sights and throw some coin away,
> I don't know my ancestry, I'se just born down in Tennessee,
> Thank you, just Rastus Johnson from U.S.A.

He explained that when in Paris, "a man once said . . . you'se Coon African" to which Ras "screamed . . . no sir I'll have you understand . . . I'm just plain Rastus Johnson from U.S.A." And later, Jas commented that the only kingdom Ras came from was that of "Wilson County, Kansas." Rastus Johnson's migration thus represented that of the "Exodusters," African Americans who had left Tennessee for hope of a better life in Kansas after Reconstruction.[56]

Vaudeville, an art form that combined a myriad of references, allowed Williams and Walker to easily mix together Bishop Turner's efforts, the Homestead Strike, emigration scandals, U.S. imperialism, and even the *Wizard of Oz*'s concluding sentiment "there is no place like home" in *In Dahomey*. In *Abyssinia* the references to Kansas came just as readily from

Walker's family history as they did from the 1900 children's book by L. Frank Baum. On one level the reference to the "Exodusters" deepened the commentary on the role of migration, movement, and search for a place to call home in the black struggle for freedom. But Kansas was also the home that Dorothy so dreamed of flying away from, and it was a twister that brought her "over the rainbow." Referred to as a "cyclone" in the stage show that opened in 1902, the storm scene lasted twenty minutes and reaped rave reviews.[57] So it is probably not a coincidence that Walker's character had traveled to Ethiopia with hopes of learning how to change the weather back in Kansas. Perhaps he could then summon a weather pattern that would carry his people home. Or perhaps the artists wanted to suggest that dreams of emigration were as ephemeral as Dorothy's trip to the Emerald City.

In *Abyssinia* the company pushed the question of origins still further with the character of Cally Parker, who spoke about her relationship with the American South. "Aunt Cally," as she was called, proclaimed that she had only agreed to join the caravan because Ras had promised that she would see Jerusalem, her religious home. She was actually uninterested in traveling to Africa, and was eager to return home to Kansas to tell her friends that she had seen the holy city. Frustrated with travel in Abyssinia, she stated that she wished she were "right back where I come from— either there or down in Dixie where I was born." When her preacher, Elder Flower, asked her to confirm that she was indeed from the South, she was directed in the libretto to reply sarcastically, "Yes, from the South where all the rest of you come form 'riginally." Aunt Cally's proud claim of her origins in the American South was significant. Like Ras's earlier song, this statement of origin set her apart from both the claims to African royal ancestry by the black elite (as presented in *Jes Lak White Fo'ks*) and the dreams of settling on the continent by emigrants of the Dahomey Colonization Society. Further, Aunt Cally emphasized her origins in the American South, indeed showing resentment that so many northern blacks denied their own ties to the South and slave past.

Even though the African American characters in *Abyssinia* proudly declared their American identity, they did not do so at the expense of Abyssinian characters. In this show, the Williams and Walker Company portrayed vast differences between the two societies, but for the most part, drew equal attention to the peculiarities and failings of the American and Abyssinian cultures. Moreover, at several points in the script, Americans met with greater insult. In the case of religion, the company juxtaposed the pretensions of the Baptist congregation with the devotion of a Muslim population in Ethiopia. Though Menelik himself was Christian, Islam predominated in several regions of Ethiopia, and in Williams and Walker's fictional Ethiopia, the chorus sang "We chosen of Mohammed bow to Allah, Ever Blest, Whose glory is reflected by the sun." Later in the script, the company also wrote that Menelik and his soldiers greeted each other by saying "Salaam, Allah." Not only did the company present positive portrayals of Islam; they also openly mocked the rules and regulations of the Baptist congregation.[58] When one devout church member, Miss Primly, "caught" her niece, Serena, kneeling with Muslims, she loudly proclaimed her aversion to the religion saying, "Is there any way in the world I'll ever be able to keep you looking respectable? Down on your knees singing with these heathens." By naming her "Miss Primly" the company made clear her character. Earlier in the script, she had yelled that someone should kindly tell her why they were "fritting away" their time and "ruining their complexions in the sizzling atmosphere." Later, she sang an entire song entitled "Don't" in which she stated she would "teach these poor benighted people the value of the little word." Here, the company pushed the discussion begun in *In Dahomey* from questioning whether Africans really wanted western civilization to one suggesting that the Ethiopians were, although different, perhaps more civilized than the Baptist congregation.

One other scene mocked Americans rather than Africans. It occurred in the marketplace and depicted Abyssinian women selling their wares while gleefully gossiping about how they took advantage of the African American travelers. One woman, Miram, told her friend Ulissa that she sold "a string of beads worth four Piastres in the market here, for twelve" and "a pair of bracelets worth three salts" to a "very fat woman who couldn't wear them, for Two Dollars and added a couple of Piastres, just to make her believe she had a bargain." Ulissa responded that Miram would be "arrested for high-way robbery," but Miram insisted that the Americans were so gullible that Ulissa should hike her prices by 75 percent. Their observations became increasingly absurd, but really no more ridiculous than some of the American "anthropological" narratives about Africans as presented at world's fairs. Miram explained that overweight American women "go days at a time without food and allow themselves to be fastened in cages over tanks of hot water, in order to melt the fat, so that they can become

Bert and Lottie Williams in *Abyssinia,* ca. 1906.

(Billy Rose Theater Collection, The New York Public Library for
the Performing Arts, Astor, Lenox and Tilden Foundations.)

thin" and that "the thin ones stay in bed and eat oats, the same kind of oats horses eat, also some strange kind of nuts made of grapes." Additionally, "after they reach the age of twenty-five years, they don't have any more birthdays for three years, and then they are only twenty-six years old, and when by this process, twenty-eight years have been reached, no more birth-days are celebrated, isn't it funny?" Of American men, Miram observed that those "with an income of Ten thousand a year are always in debt and in consequence, lead miserable lives, while others raise a family of ten children on Ten Dollars a week and are happy." Miram poked fun at American behavior in ways sure to get laughter out of both black and white audiences. More, this portrayal could provoke laughter and at the same time represent African women as sophisticated enough to take advantage of American consumers.

The plot of *Abyssinia* takes its dramatic turn when Ras is again mistaken for African. This time, however, Bolassa, an Abyssinian soldier, mistakes him for Yarabu, the rebel leader whom Menelik had ordered delivered dead or alive. Ras's very life then depends on actually being able to prove that he is American. His arrest is made all the more dramatic when in the commotion, Jas too is arrested as he is caught holding a vase he had not yet purchased from a vendor. Both men are taken to Menelik's palace for sentencing.

Abyssinia's climactic scene occurs when Menelik sentences Ras and Jas. Here, Williams and Walker staged a powerful African king in his court commanding his troops and determining the fate of foreigners. Stage Menelik vows to send Yarabu "back to the Arusa Division . . . a piece at a time," declaring that "leniency in similar cases in the past, has been mistaken as fear on my part." With his own hand he would "feed his body to the Hyenas, as a warning to any and all who shall attempt to defy the mandates of Menelik, the second King of Kings of Ethiopia." Fortunately, Ras is quickly saved from Menelik's edict, as the soldier Bolassa admits that he had made a mistake and reports that Yarabu had already been killed. Jas, however, was not so lucky. As his alleged crime was theft, he was sentenced to have his hand chopped off. This sentence too reflected historical events; Menelik had explained that he did "not wish people who work to have to feed thieves" and that "mutilated, wandering, and abandoned" convicts would "walk to the end of their lives as an example of punishment." Of the western powers, only the treaty with the United States at that time included a stipulation that travelers would be tried under Ethiopian law.[59] Ras and Jas then witnessed Menelik condemn an Abyssinian prisoner also convicted of theft to have his right hand severed.

The climactic scene of *Abyssinia* then consisted of Bert Williams playing Jas, the wrongfully accused condemned man. Jas has to wait for the sound of the gong while Menelik listens to the testimony of the market women who had accused Jas of theft. If there were four strokes of the gong, Jas would be set free. If he heard only three strokes, he would lose his hand. Without saying a word, Williams portrayed Jas waiting for the ringing of this bell that would determine his fate. Will Marion Cook remembered: "Within five seconds, Bert had run the whole gamut of emotion."[60] The gong struck three times, paused for a moment, and then rang a fourth. Jas was set free and allowed to rejoin the American caravan.

While clearly these artists addressed contemporary politics and a black agenda, they also worked in a medium that needed audience applause and laughter. Still, in this climactic scene of *Abyssinia,* Williams portrayed a wrongfully accused prisoner in an era when two to three black men were reported lynched every week. In addition, the company portrayed an African king who punished criminals with bodily mutilation—a sentence that again reflected the horrors of lynching as well as fit with a dominant culture that viewed Africans as "savage" and "primitive." The company had earlier in the script commented on the theme of savagery when Abyssinian soldiers sang "Jolly Jungle Boys," a song that announced Menelik as "king of savages" and themselves as "happy, snappy chappies, savage through and through." As this song makes abundantly clear, these themes were presented on the musical comedy stage by star vaudevillians, a style of performance that allowed for such contradictions to exist in one show. The comic "Jolly Jungle Boys" poked fun at stereotypes even as the ferocity of Menelik and his soldiers seemed, in part, to uphold them.

Williams and Walker may have left the scripts behind to interpolate their well-worn comic routines even as they sought to bring contemporary issues to the stage. This seems entirely plausible in the third act of *In Dahomey,* where Williams and Walker had earned criticism for mocking Africans. It is difficult to be sure how much their buffoonery reflected their ideas about Africans, since their main goal, particularly at the shows' finales, would have been to make audiences laugh. More, *Abyssinia*'s climactic scene was the perfect vehicle for Williams. As he waited for the sound of the four gongs, he could play his down-on-his-luck "Jonah Man" for all it was worth.

After Jas is acquitted, the entire cast, including the characters of Menelik and Empress Taytu, came together for *Abyssinia*'s finale of song and dance. Entitled "Good Bye Ethiopia," the song announced that the Americans got "a cablegram from home" that said "the time has come when we must go back." The Williams and Walker Company sang:

> Good-bye good-bye Ethiopia we may come back some day,
> You have been good to us, your land would do for us
> But we can no longer stay
> Good luck, good luck to our new found friends,
> To keep your friendship we will try,
> We all wish you success, may you ever progress,
> Ethiopia, good-bye.

This image differed significantly from that of the finale of *In Dahomey*. At the end of that play, emigrants who had originally hoped to settle in Dahomey yearned to return home to the United States. In *Abyssinia*, the members of the caravan, who never sought lives in Abyssinia, were sure that their home was America, but they made clear that Ethiopians were their "new found friends" and that they considered Ethiopia part of their newly "imagined home" and nation.

"Civilization" in Black and White

In contrast to *In Dahomey*, *Abyssinia* contained little dialect and buffoonery, with only the characters of Aunt Cally and Jasmine Jenkins speaking in dialect or directly incorporating traits that could be read as racial stereotype. This presentation earned praise from black critics, with Sylvester Russell saying that he "always contended that 'Abyssinia' was a play of the Negro race and should have succeeded on its progressive merits." Moreover, his review revealed that some images of the majesty of Ethiopia planned for the production never made it to the stage: "The public had never seen it in all its original beauty, because after the first week a cruel manager had ordered it chopped to pieces."[61] Carle Browne Cooke too reported in his *Freeman* review, "*Abyssinia* is indeed a Negro play to be proud of . . . for this production possesses all the elements requisite to any comic opera and far superior in theme, beauty and genuine originality of composition to . . . any of the late so-called successes now biding for a hearing by Metropolitan patrons."[62]

Despite the praise of black critics, *Abyssinia* did not succeed as well as *In Dahomey,* in large part because white audiences remained indifferent to any serious presentation by African Americans. Numerous white critics actually claimed that this show about independent Ethiopia was too "white." One critic announced that "the piece failed to make any considerable impression owing chiefly to the fact that it was a white man's show acted by colored men, whereas to be entirely successful, it should have been a colored men's show acted by themselves." Another proclaimed that the show was "a product from beginning to end of Afro-American enterprise and ability, but unfortunately for the piece the inspiration was largely Caucasian."[63] For white critics, it did not matter that *Abyssinia* was entirely produced by African Americans and addressed the independent nation of Ethiopia.

Blinded by the stereotypes dominating the popular stage, these critics' sentiments exemplified how much race defined cultural realms and how much turn-of-the-century definitions of "civilization" remained embedded in these same racist definitions. For instance, theater critic Alan Dale argued that Williams and Walker tried to be more "legitimate" than a "whiter troupe would have dared to be . . . *Abyssinia* was a 'coon show' in name only," he wrote. "In reality, it was a most serious near-grand opera, for which we were totally unprepared." Another reviewer critical that *Abyssinia* was "too-white" explained that as long as a black actor played the "happy-go-lucky fellow who can rattle a pair of bones, pick a banjo, and laugh so heartily that everyone within earshot must laugh too," he was "a capital entertainer."[64] These comments starkly expose how the dominant culture viewed even this show as "white" because it did not conform to white-determined racial stereotypes. Rather, white culture craved representations of what another critic called the "barbaric splendor of middle Africa, the simple melodies and characteristic dances of the colored race, and the laughing rollicking humor of the black man."[65] Once black performers stepped outside the racial stereotypes and aspired to a sense of selfhood and independence, white society refused to see them, and in fact, could not recognize them.

That the Williams and Walker Company conceived of *Abyssinia* under these conditions shows how rooted was the black agenda in a long history of connection with Africa—and how this agenda challenged a dominant culture infected with social Darwinism. As African Americans confronted American imperial expansion and debated the roles of black American soldiers in America's wars of expansion, they necessarily placed these discussions alongside the history of enslavement and their experience of Jim Crow. They measured citizenship struggles against Ethiopianist theories and emigrationist practice. And they exulted in Ethiopia's victory at a time when America reigned triumphant in the Philippines—a war waged to bring "democracy" to people considered savage.

Many artists and intellectuals who came of age during the era of empire and Jim Crow challenged nineteenth-century rhetoric about "primitive" Africans and the white man's burden—for example, the Williams and Walker Company onstage with *Abyssinia* and W. E. B. Du Bois in print in his 1897 American Negro Academy paper "The Conservation of the Races." Du Bois dismissed the idea that racial and national distinction was the result of "differences of blood, color and cranial measurements," and asserted that differences were, rather, rooted in history.[66] Du Bois too chose to celebrate Ethiopian nationhood on stage; five years after Williams and Walker's *Abyssinia,* he produced *The Star of Ethiopia* (1911), a pageant that hailed the independent nation as a civilized one.

Emblematic of a generation of African Americans, these more pro-black perspectives exposed the development of a new sense of national identity as black people resisted repressive ideas rampant in American culture. Even the narrative of passing implicitly critiqued belief in racial hierarchies, highlighting how much race was not biologically determined but socially decided. Phrenology, too, troubled and fascinated Bert Williams—a prolific reader who included Darwin's *Origin of the Species* on a reading list in his datebook. Ernest Hogan even wrote a song for Williams called "The Phrenologist Coon." And Williams was clearly mocking belief in the pseudo-science when he sang Hogan's lyrics. "If a coon has an egg-shaped head / Means chickens he will steal . . . If his head's shaped like a razor, you can bet that coon will cut . . . In ethnology, I'se the thing. I can tell you what you are by the feeling of your bump."[67]

Although the artists clearly rejected dominant beliefs, they expressed some ambivalence in their approach to Africa just as they had to "strictly Negro traits." Representations of Africa carried with them loaded mean-

Alex Rogers, Aida Overton Walker, and Bert Williams in *Abyssinia,* ca. 1906, New York.
(Photographs and Prints Division, Schomburg Center for Research in Black Culture,
The New York Public Library, Astor, Lenox and Tilden Foundations.)

ings, and presented African Americans with the dilemma of deciding
whether it was more beneficial to identify with the continent or to distance themselves from it. On the one hand many black artists—not unlike
nationalists Henry McNeal Turner and Alexander Crummell—sought to
celebrate African society and people, but on the other, they often privileged western definitions of progress. George Walker once asserted "our
civilization is little beyond its infancy" and that "a few hundred of years
ago we were savages."[68] Critic Sylvester Russell, who so liked *Abyssinia,* had
written that black music in America was much better than "the music of
Africa," which was "more crude and hardly up to modern civilization."[69]

Although absent of explicit Christianity, such comments seemed to echo the missionary impulses of Crummell and Turner as well as views by other nineteenth-century leaders like Frederick Douglass. Using such language as part of his celebration of African Americans at the world's fair, Douglass exhorted, "Look at the progress the Negro has made in thirty years! We have come up out of Dahomey into this. Measure the Negro. But not by the standard of the splendid civilization of the Caucasian. Bend down and measure him from the depths out of which he has risen."[70]

While still ambivalent about the role of Africa in black freedom struggles, these artists clearly distanced themselves from a nineteenth-century civilizationist mission of uplifting Africans, and instead attached themselves to an ideology that celebrated African peoples along with black culture. Black artists elevated Ethiopians, along with black imperialists like William Ellis and John Waller, over missionaries and European colonialists. Like these black entrepreneurs, commercial artists believed their own capitalist ventures would advance the race as well as celebrate black transnational connection and black expression. As such, the popular shows represented a new strain in black political culture and a new generation's thought on Africa; they foretold of a twentieth-century sensibility taking hold among African Americans that challenged social Darwinist thought and let go of Victorian social constraints. Ruptured from nineteenth-century religious belief, this sensibility enabled artists to help lead their generation in the presentation of a civilized and respectable black identity—an identity made in the sphere of public amusements and exhibiting modern conceptualizations of race as politically, socially, and culturally determined.

5555555

Morals, Manners,
and Stage Life

Parson Brown, one Sunday morning was givin' good advice.
He warned his congregation to refrain from sin and vice.
He drew a fire-y picture bout the devil down below,
and said, fo'ks quit your sinnin', or here you're bound to go.
Hell is full of vampire wimmin, whiskey, gin and dice.
Satan, tell em to get thee and prepare thou for paradise.

Mose Jackson jumped up from his chair and said:
Father, is that true?
If hell is full of what you said, well then let me say to you:
If what you said is the positive truth,
Oh Death Where is thy Sting?

CLARENCE STOUT,
"OH DEATH, WHERE IS THY STING?"
CA. 1916

B ERT WILLIAMS made Clarence Stout's "Oh Death, Where Is Thy Sting?"
famous by recording it with Columbia Records in 1916.[1] The song's
lyrics targeted issues prevalent in turn-of-the-century America. One line
in particular captures the spirit of the comic song: "With booze and
wimmin down below, Mr. Devil and I will just put on a show." The new
popularity of a secular leisure culture—complete with alcohol, gambling,
and sexual temptation—challenged the church's authority over private life,
flew in the face of Victorian beliefs on the proper place of women in public
life, and more broadly, refigured nineteenth-century notions regarding private and public spheres. The new leisure environments facilitated changes
in standards of propriety—changes that were perhaps most apparent in the
new sexual mores and gender roles exhibited among stage performers.
Women populated vaudeville's theaters both as performers and audience
members—a tendency that granted a modicum of respectability to the new
form of popular theater, but did not immediately legitimize theatrical
spectacle or condone the "vampire wimmin" as respectable. Rather, performers themselves helped shape twentieth-century amusements into a respectable activity.

It is from within this sphere of theatrical culture that African American popular artists contested prescribed gender roles and delimiting ideas of Jim Crow to create a freer, more expansive notion of being in the world. The new fluidity of gender roles held dramatically different meanings for black Americans, who had long confronted the dominant culture's fears of black sexuality—fears that white America attempted to diminish with Sambo and mammy stereotypes. White assumptions about black sexuality had prompted many African Americans to adopt strict religious and Victorian moral codes as a way of establishing themselves as respectable citizens, and young African Americans had to navigate white racism as well as the Victorian propriety of the black bourgeoisie as they made their own way in America's burgeoning cities.

Black popular artists helped transform stage life and helped lead the way to acceptance of public amusements in middle-class life. This generation of performers was a rebellious group of young artists who disdained middle-class proscriptions for respectability and developed their own ideas of what it meant to be both modern and black. They carefully mediated a world filled with the promise of modern life and, at the same time, fraught with racially dictated notions of what constituted modern propriety. In doing so, they redefined the boundaries of respectability, challenging white norms as well as beliefs held by black middle-class leaders.

Many black professionals joined with established church officials and others who worried that ragtime, vaudeville, and musical comedy would hurt their efforts to overturn racial stereotypes, since such celebrations of black humor, song, dance, and sensibility were generally interpreted as "low-brow" entertainment. These representatives of the black middle class instead professed a politics of racial uplift—an ideology that focused on shaping morals and manners (as much as on protesting and working to improve social welfare) as a means for racial advancement. In 1896, the clubwomen of the National Association of Colored Women (NACW) chose "lifting as we climb" as their motto—a signature that well described a politics in which manners and morality played as important a role as did economics for establishing middle-class status. Black professionals knew that white America looked at each individual African American as representative of the race, and so they urged all to pay extraordinarily close attention to personal behavior and self-presentation—what historian

Willard Gatewood named "street manners." Most subscribers to uplift politics hoped that a presentation of respectability would help blacks in their quest for full citizenship rights, in part by convincing the dominant culture of their humanity and civility. For most, this politics of respectability had little room for popular amusements, and most proponents of racial uplift categorized such diversions as disrespectable.[2]

W. E. B. Du Bois addressed this issue in his 1897 essay "The Problem of Amusement," expressing grave fears that the new urban culture would bring down the race. He even foreshadowed the themes of "Oh Death, Where Is Thy Sting?" when he announced that he was not surprised "to find in the feverish life of a great city, hundreds of Negro boys and girls who have listened for a lifetime to the warning, 'Don't do this or you'll go to hell,'" and who then "took the bit between their teeth and said, 'Well, let's go to hell.'"[3] Like other proponents of uplift, he saw the modern city as rife with possibilities for sin, degradation, illness, and the downfall of the race. Such fears echoed those of white reformers as well as other African Americans; white reformer Jane Addams went so far as to argue that amusement parks such as Coney Island should be razed and replaced with serene and uplifting parks. Reformers saw the policing of leisure culture and the cleaning-up of urban environments as critical to social progress. Years later, Detroit Urban League director Forrester B. Washington well summed up these sentiments, explaining, "You cannot do much for a man spiritually until you have given him a healthy and wholesome physical environment . . . you cannot grow lilies in ash-barrels."[4]

However much Du Bois, Addams, and others wanted to "clean up" the city and erase the new leisure culture, most realized that not much could be done to halt the draw of public amusements. Du Bois saw that the church had lost some of its authority over young people, and held little hope that the "Negro church," contemptuous as it was of "most modern amusements," would adapt to meet young peoples' new desires.[5] He joined Addams and a generation of Progressive-era reformers who acknowledged the appeal of leisure activities, and decided that the problem of amusement could not be left to entertainment entrepreneurs. Du Bois continued to address leisure culture over the next decade, and he put the problem of amusement on the agenda of a series of conferences he later held at Atlanta University. Reports to the conference on "Morals and Manners among Negro Americans" in 1913 included many complaints of the prevalence of "unwholesome" amusements around the country. Conference attendees categorized dance halls and theaters as "unwholesome" spaces, and classified churches, parks, and designated playgrounds as "wholesome" ones. One report from Connecticut confirmed Du Bois's early fears, and reported that the "YMCA and churches are seeking to furnish wholesome amusement, but the masses are not attracted."[6]

Wholesome amusement often meant sex-segregated or chaperoned amusements because reformers especially feared the ways that modern leisure culture encouraged men and women to socialize together. In his 1897 essay, Du Bois expressed special concern for young people between the ages of fourteen and eighteen because the "crucial consideration at this age of life is really the proper social intercourse of the sexes." He even said that ignoring this question "compels us to plead guilty to the shameful fact that sexual impurity among Negro men and Negro women of America is the crying disgrace of the American republic."[7] To address changing sexual mores, Du Bois proposed the hosting of chaperoned dances and supervised billiard rooms to attract black youth away from commercial dance halls and saloons, much as Jane Addams had held social gatherings for working-class European immigrants at Hull House. Neither attempt could compete with modern culture's expanding array of amusements.

However much black reform efforts may have resembled those of white reformers, as Du Bois well realized, Jim Crow and the overwhelming prevalence of racist stereotypes presented African Americans with racially specific problems. Since segregation excluded African Americans from "the public amusement of most great cities" and left the church as the "chief purveyor of amusement to the colored people," Du Bois stipulated that black leaders needed to be ever more mindful of the attraction that saloons and dance halls held for black youth. While he did not mention it specifically, the added problem of residential segregation and subsequent location of vice districts meant that African American communities had to be particularly vigilant about monitoring leisure in their neighborhoods.[8]

Black women faced even greater race-specific problems, since they confronted a dominant culture that characterized them as promiscuous and inherently immoral. Even black songwriter Clarence Stout characterized women who entered saloons as "vampire wimmin" in "Oh Death, Where

Is Thy Sting?" With the increased presence of women in public life, reformers paid particular attention to the public image of black women. The NACW expressed the idea that "a race can rise no higher than its women," and argued that African Americans needed to uplift women if they wanted to uplift the race. Du Bois too believed that the "uplifting of the Negro people" depended on the "development of strong manhood and pure womanhood," and in many ways, he, along with other promoters of "uplift," tried to present an African American "respectability" through their policing of gender relations.[9]

All of these concerns weighed heavily on performing artists. Troupes made up of young men and women performed to segregated audiences, and often became "representative" African Americans for whites. As black actor Harry Brown explained, black performers were "living in a white man's country and work for a living in a white man's theater, and the white manager hasn't got time to find out who among the colored performers are ladies and gentlemen. If a few are bad and fighters, why they must all be, and the white manager acts accordingly."[10] This visibility made the black middle class especially attentive to the public behavior of black performers and particularly concerned with how the increasingly visible performance culture reflected on the race; specifically, how whites perceived African Americans at play. As early as 1896, a pamphlet entitled *The Negro in Etiquette: A Novelty* specifically denounced "the use of too much cologne, the cakewalk and ragtime, and the chewing of gum." A *Freeman* critic echoed this point when he editorialized against blacks who "make a habit of running after every excursion in sight for the mere sake of going—who drink bad liquor and misbehave themselves generally" and claimed that "these Sunday orgies which take place in full view of white people who look upon the proceedings with a mixture of amusement and disgust, do not help us upward." In 1900, a black critic worried that the "majority of our performers" were "rapt in ignorance and lethargy," and warned that it was a "rank injustice to a race struggling for a name and place to be thus handicapped by such persons being foisted in the public eye." That same year, another *Freeman* columnist equated performance work with increased criminal activity, proclaiming that the "respectable colored people of Chicago should rise and rush this fast growing monster." Changing sexual mores were central to this "monster"; John Hope wrote to his wife, Atlanta reformer Lugenia Burns, that the ragtime dancing he observed was as "sensuous, alluring and degrading as that voluptuous music to which the Arab women rendered the *danse du ventre* in the streets of Cairo," an event he must have witnessed at the world's fair midway.[11]

Whereas Du Bois laid out his fears regarding the growth of a modern leisure culture, his contemporaries Williams, Walker, and Cook dove into the fray. Many of the most prominent African American performers and theater critics actually argued that the popular stage, complete with ragtime, cakewalking, and vaudevillian comedy, provided a vehicle for the presentation of respectability of both men and women. One *Indianapolis Freeman* theater critic wrote that "a well-behaved, well-disciplined company in its peregrinations does the race more substantial good than all the sermons, editorials, and such things that can be written." This columnist hailed the Tennessean Jubilee singers, a group that performed both standards and "coon" songs, as a company that made "for the elevation of the race" and that "every time the colored race produces a lady or gentleman the race problem is just so much nearer solution."[12] Critic Sylvester Russell explained, "Actors have a large scope of territory in the genteel picnic of the world," and further argued that African Americans should hail the realm of popular theater because its benefits far outweighed those of another popular form of entertainment—prizefighting. "Williams and Walker," reported Russell, "now shine in the royal 600 class, while the highest station of a prize fighter is a barroom banquet."[13]

Faced with an urban landscape that was transforming notions of work and play, public and private, and secular and sacred, this generation of artists helped create the shift in middle-class sensibility as they themselves carefully negotiated their involvement in the entertainment industry. Many of these artists straddled the world of popular and classical culture. Cook, although classically trained, composed for the popular stage, and Paul Laurence Dunbar wrote verse both in straight English and in dialect, along with his lyrics for Cook's "coon" songs. James Weldon Johnson, too, had been so drawn to the cultural styles of New York City's performers that he enthusiastically joined his brother J. Rosamond Johnson and Bob Cole to write songs for the popular stage. But during the same era, he also wrote a poem that his brother put to music, "Lift Every Voice and Sing," a song that would eventually be subtitled the "Negro national anthem." Quite the opposite of "Oh Death, Where Is Thy Sting?" Johnson ended his poem with the lines:

> Shadowed beneath Thy hand,
> May we forever stand.
> True to our God,
> True to our native land.[14]

Johnson joined the NAACP in 1915, and is best known for his writing and political activities during the years of the Harlem Renaissance. But he spent his early years in New York City enamored with the popular stage and exploring the possibilities of commercial culture—a world he described in detail in his 1912 novel *The Autobiography of An Ex-Colored Man*.[15]

These artists transformed the vaudeville stage and became so popular that middle-class African Americans increasingly discarded their Victorian dismay of theater to attend their performances. The shared cultural worlds of performers and audience members encouraged new codes of respectability that accepted previously condemned behaviors. The black professional classes did not shun commercial amusements, but neither did they entirely embrace the new public culture. Rather they monitored black participation in public amusements, adapting some of the new cultural styles and censuring others. Even clubwomen involved with the NACW ventured out to public entertainment. Many clubwomen did not always practice what they preached, and "understood," as historian Deborah Gray White explains, "that if their private lives were examined along with the public, they would not pass their own very rigid test of perfect black womanhood."[16] NACW founder Mary Church Terrell, who maintained a friendship with Paul Laurence Dunbar, reveled in her forays into popular amusement. Not only did she attend the performances of popular vaudevillians, but she also reported that she enjoyed her visit to the 1893 world's fair, remembering that "the Midway Plaisance with all its original denizens and dancers was something new under the sun, and many perfect ladies who went there to see them perform came away shocked."[17] Other African American elites joined Terrell in her enthusiasm for amusements, and once the *Freeman* announced that Terrell occupied a box with the "crème de la crème of Washington's colored society" to see Ernest Hogan. Among this group was "Governor" Pinchback who, along with Terrell, "appeared to enjoy Mr. Hogan's performance immensely."[18] That Oberlin-educated Terrell, along with other established members of Washington's elite society, enjoyed such excursions reveals how much African Americans had adopted a new sensibility—one that included a secular and public leisure culture, and one where women might take the lead both onstage and off.

Nice Girls Don't Sing Ragtime (or Do They?)

In Paul Laurence Dunbar's 1902 novel *Sport of the Gods,* the young black female character named Kit wanted to sing on the popular stage when she arrived in New York from the rural South. After auditioning, Kit "flew home with joyous heart to tell her mother of her good prospects" and cried, "Oh, ma, ma, Miss Hattie thinks I'll do to go on the stage. Ain't it grand?" Far more troubled than excited, her mother responded, "I do' know as it'll be so gran'. F'om what I see of dem stage people dey don't seem to 'mount to much." But Kit would not be dissuaded and quickly informed her mother, "Nowadays everybody thinks stage people respectable up here."[19] This exchange captures the fluid notions of respectability and women's involvement in popular theater that circulated in turn-of-the-century urban culture, notions that had troubled Abbie Mitchell at the outset of her career. The twelve-year-old Mitchell had explained during her audition for her soon-to-be husband, Will Marion Cook, that "decent colored girls did not sing coon songs or ragtime."[20] Despite her misgivings, Mitchell enthusiastically accepted the role Cook offered her after hearing him sing his songs. She married Cook in 1900, a practice not uncommon in the late nineteenth century, when many women married between the ages of twelve and fifteen.[21] Mitchell went on to star in vaudeville and musical comedy, eventually, in 1910, becoming the first African American woman to perform a solo vaudeville act at New York's Majestic Theater.[22]

By the early years of the twentieth century, women had claimed full participation in public life—a development that led to new fears about the intermingling of men and women during leisure activities. Performing troupes, as some of the most visible African Americans, found themselves increasingly scrutinized for their relaxed mores. One black critic proclaimed that "as a rule with Negroes, talent is coupled with ignorance and all its concomitants," and reported that he was "utterly dumbfounded" at the "deportment on our public streets" of two female members of the chorus of a leading attraction. He described their language as "ribald" and "composed of the ghoulest slang imaginable" and argued that they "left a lurid streak behind them" as they entered an establishment that "would probably rival hell for iniquity."[23]

Black female performers, like Abbie Mitchell, challenged conventions of gender and class to sing ragtime tunes. Many middle-class critics criticized their public exposure, but some praised their efforts and claimed that the performing world actually provided a respectable venue for women. Mitchell, and the other black women of the popular stage, helped effect the change that led to this acceptance. By 1902, the same year that Dunbar published *Sport of the Gods,* a *Freeman* columnist defended black actresses and vehemently criticized the "still widespread superstition as to the inherent and universal wickedness of stage people and particularly of the chorus girls," or as the paper sarcastically commented, "those wicked chorus girls." This columnist described a New York company manager upset with a local resident pleading to offer religious instruction to black female company members. The concerned resident had written the company: "Since so many of the girls in the company live in Boston and therefore have no regular church to attend in New York, a number of us wish to hold a bible class meeting on Sunday afternoon . . . and wish to know if you will let us use the stage for that purpose."[24] Despite his complaints to the sympathetic *Freeman,* the company manager relented, allowing local residents to use the stage for bible study for the female performers.

Two years later, theater critic Sylvester Russell directly addressed stage women with his article, "Should Respectable Girls Adopt the Stage?" claiming that a "pure, respectable girl" who knew how to "put her foot down to the actors" could be successful in show business. Rather than painting show girls as innocent victims of managers' machinations or as "vampire wimmin," Russell argued that a successful female performer "must not be timid" and must know when "to declare herself as the mistress of her own respectability." He also warned, "It is not a good plan for young girls to adopt the stage without first finding out whether they are really endowed with all the qualities that go to make a public woman successful." Rather than seeing show women as responsible for an actor's "ruin," Russell blamed male lust, and instructed show girls to be "bold as a lion" and "ferociously assault any man . . . who insists on trying to molest them." He noted that writers had been generous in "giving out stories of actresses of ill-repute" but never had they "recited that man was the worst cause of it all." To enable their rise in show business, Russell encouraged female performers to use "men as stepping stones" to advance their careers and then "bid them good-bye."[25]

By the time that Russell wrote this piece, black women had performed prominently on stage for well over a decade. The first female chorus appeared in Sam T. Jack's *Creole Show*, which had premiered to a Massachusetts audience in 1890 and had earned national fame during the show's lengthy run during the 1893 Chicago World's Fair. This white-managed show toured through 1897 and spawned John Isham's *Octoroons*, as well as the careers of several performers, including vaudevillians Bob Cole and Billy Johnson. Achieving fame during the world's fair, this show included what would become essential ingredients of the modern stage— the urban setting and the female chorus. Equally as important, Dora Dean and Charles Johnson made their debut as a dance team, and they quickly earned national fame for their version of the cakewalk. They became known as the best-dressed dance team on the American stage: they were the first, white or black, to wear evening clothes on the stage, and they gave public dancing a novel air of respectability.[26] In the 1890s, opera singer Sissieretta Jones led one of the most successful international touring companies— and the only one headed by a woman—the Black Patti Troubadours. Aida Overton Walker toured with this troupe, and Bob Cole too wrote and performed with the Troubadours for a short time before he left to form his own stock company and present the first successful full-length black musical comedy, *A Trip to Coontown*, in 1898. As much as the African American performing world continued to be dominated by men, one of the defining characteristics of the modern stage was the large number of women on stage. These women challenged nineteenth-century gender conventions and helped create new middle-class and working-class identities—or variants of a "New Woman."[27]

Images of just such a new independent woman abound in the lyrics of several songs. As early as 1900, in Cook and Dunbar's *Jes Lak White Fo'ks*, Abbie Mitchell played "Mandy," singing how she "just returned from Vassar," and had passed as white to become the first black woman to graduate from this college. As mentioned earlier, Mitchell's portrayal celebrated on-stage how the real-life Anita Hemmings had earned a bachelor's degree

Aida Overton Walker, ca. 1900.
(Helen Armstead-Johnson Theater Photograph Collection, Photographs and Prints Division, Schomburg Center for Research in Black Culture, The New York Public Library, Astor, Lenox and Tilden Foundations.)

during a time when few black women could escape the drudgery of domestic work. In "He's a Cousin of Mine" (1906), the female protagonist manages relationships with two different men by telling each one that the other is a "cousin." And in *The Policy Players* (1899–1900), Aida Walker sang the song by Williams and Walker "I Don't Want No Cheap Man," which challenged society's expectations of chaste, pure, and submissive women, and both supported and critiqued tendencies in uplift politics.

> Miss Simpson had always been considered de finest gal in town,
> She was de envy of all de coons dat lived for miles around.
> Last week, Bill Johnson took her out to see de minstrels at de hall,
> He bought de seats in de gallery, and she didn't like that at all.
> She said, "I don't like no cheap man
> Dat spends his money on de 'stalments plan;
> Dat's de reason I always carry with me
> 'Nuf money for what I want.
> . . . You's a cheap man, and you won't do!

Miss Simpson's self-sufficiency fit well with and likely influenced Russell's definitions of respectability and his insistence that stage women should use men as "stepping stones." Her disdain for her date's finances actually resembled black female reformers' prescriptions for thrift—advice dispensed in speeches with titles like "Don't Live on the Installment Plan."[28] Walker, though, did not critique spending money on amusements as did many black reformers, but rather disparaged Miss Simpson's escort for paying for cheaper seats, and like Sylvester Russell, she envisioned the theater as a respectable venue for women. Moreover, although Miss Simpson blamed her companion for buying seats in the gallery, Walker likely intended the comment, in part, as an indirect attack on segregated seating. A direct attack on racism was unacceptable on stage, but this covert critique showed a black woman taking the lead in redefining what was permissible to say and still remain respectable.

In the next Williams and Walker show, *Sons of Ham* (1900), Aida Walker sang "Miss Hannah from Savannah," a song written by an associate of Williams and Walker, Cecil Mack (also known as Richard C. McPherson), who published many songs with the Gotham-Attucks music publishing house. This song recounts the story of a black female migrant from the South who announced her family credentials to northern black society. She sang:

My name's Miss Hannah from Savannah,
Ah wants all you folks to understand-ah;
Ahm some de blue-blood ob de land-ah,
I'se Miss Hannah from Savannah!

Hannah appears as a fiercely independent black woman ready to take on the northern society that she imagined would belittle her southern background at a time when northern blacks often derided southern migrants, particularly female migrants, as unkempt. With Hannah, Walker may as well have meant to critique black reform efforts that in the name of protecting black female migrants from vice, often disparaged public amusements as less than respectable. Walker had performed at fundraisers for just such a reform organization associated with the White Rose Mission, led by clubwoman Victoria Earle Matthews.[29] In her song, however, her character Hannah steps into public spaces unmarried and ready to participate in northern urban life on her own terms. As with "I Don't Like No Cheap Man," this song uses the designation "Miss," which reinforced Hannah's independence as a "New Woman" and contested the dominant culture's denial of titles to black folk. It may have also been meant as an implicit critique of the pretensions of some northern black elites.[30]

While black women like Aida Walker publicly challenged both race and gender oppression, they confronted dramatically different constrictions on their self-expression than did white women. For the most part, the virtue of white women remained unquestioned, while most whites refused to believe that virtue resided in any black woman. Black women devised a variety of strategies to resist sexual vulnerability and negotiate the hazards of modern urban life; for instance, they launched the reform efforts policing public amusements and developed a "culture of dissemblance"— a public performance that hid their inner lives from public scrutiny and shielded them emotionally and physically.[31] By presenting powerful images of independent black women onstage, black performing women like Aida Walker and Abbie Mitchell contested sexual stereotyping and offered a vision of black "New Womanhood." In doing so, they raised their own status as artists and achieved a new level of respectability for stage life.

Walker's challenge to conventions of gender and race coalesced with her staging of Salome, the seductive veiled dancer from the biblical tale.

"Salomania" hit vaudeville stages after the Metropolitan Opera House's board of directors closed Richard Strauss's opera about the dancer after only one night in January of 1907 due to its "moral stench." Strauss based his Salome on a play by Oscar Wilde that had earlier been banned in England, and portrayed her as sexual seductress at a time when Americans still refused to embrace such a story as high art. As the story goes, Salome, the virgin princess of Judaea, agrees to dance for her stepfather, King Herod, in return for the head of John the Baptist, a man who had wronged her and her mother. The dance concludes with Salome acting out "a sexual encounter with the head, kissing it and declaring her love to it." Vaudeville's impresarios recognized that American audiences would be enticed by such a story, and so they brought Salome to their theaters, advertising the dance by playing to America's appetite for the risqué. "She is bad . . . that is a great element in her attraction," said one critic. One of the most famous Salome dancers, Gertrude Hoffman, even orchestrated her own arrest on indecency charges as a way to sell tickets.[32]

Aida Walker knew that such marketing of sexual lasciviousness took on an entirely different tone for black women. Perhaps self-possessed white New Women could act out a public sexuality, but black New Women needed to exhibit wholesomeness, grace, and beauty. Walker transformed Salome into just such an image for black women. Because the character originated as so-called high art with the work of Wilde and Strauss, Walker believed that her performance of the dance would help lift the artistry of black female performers from the comedy of vaudeville to the drama of opera. Her 1908 premiere of the dance in a production of *Bandana Land* earned praise from white critics, testifying to her success. One critic called her Salome "poetry in motion"; another named her the "Mllm. Genee of her race," referring to a classically trained Danish ballerina known for graceful movement; and yet another critic commended Walker for "acting" the role of Salome as well as dancing it.[33] Walker transformed the role of a highly sexualized dancer—one that titillated whites when white women danced—into a dramatic achievement.

Although Walker won praise for her classic performance of "Salome" as part of a black musical comedy, when she performed the same dance as a solo dancer at Hammerstein's Victoria Theater in 1912, she was ridiculed. "Salomania" had, in effect, "domesticated" *Salome,* earning the "Dance of the Seven Veils" designation as a classical dance and opening the doors of

Oscar Hammerstein's opera house to a revival of the Strauss opera in the spring of 1909. Hammerstein and his son, Willie, had seen Walker perform the dance in *Bandana Land,* and invited her to perform this newly ordained classical dance at their theater. Although white critics had praised Walker's performance on the all-black stage, most of them rejected her inclusion as part of a "higher class" attraction. One critic announced that "a Salome of color" was "a direct smash in the face of convention." Of Walker's 1912 performance at Hammerstein's, another critic wrote, "Ada Overton Walker's single-handed 'Salome' was funny," and that the music was "all wrong." Instead of the "heavy classic stuff . . . the bunch should have been playing Robert E. Lee."[34] These white critics missed the irony that the dance had earned more legitimate status because of the vaudeville-induced "Salomania," and arguably, because of Walker's magnificent performance in *Bandana Land.*

Ever conscious of the gaze of whites, Aida Walker, and the Williams and Walker Company, had carefully orchestrated her performance in *Bandana Land* so that it would not upset white patrons. Bert Williams followed her performance with a burlesque of the dance, one incorporating enough racial stereotype to distract white audiences from Walker's serious performance. White male vaudevillians too performed comedic Salomes, but likely the Williams and Walker Company understood that Bert Williams's two-minute performance would alleviate whites' anxieties after Walker's classical dance. Williams stripped off his shoes, danced in his stocking feet, adjusted a cheese cloth skirt, and knelt at a watermelon used to represent the head of John the Baptist.[35] This sketch—and Williams's skill—likely reassured white audiences that African Americans were naturally comedic buffoons despite Walker's obvious artistry.

If they still had not earned the respect they deserved from white audiences, black female performers had achieved a high level of respectability for women in the profession among African Americans. By the time of Walker's 1912 Salome, both middle- and working-class African Americans considered stage careers both viable and respectable. The experience of one female vaudeville team in particular shows how middle-class families resolved issues of morals, manners, and respectability when modern public culture beckoned to the young and talented. The Whitman Sisters made their professional debut in the 1890s while accompanying their Wilberforce-educated father on an evangelical tour. Throughout the first decade of the twentieth century, these four daughters of a Kansas minister performed nationally and became among the highest paid performers on the black vaudeville circuit. Though they grew up in a privileged middle-class religious family, the Whitman Sisters borrowed liberally from the dances and music of working-class people. Their act was not always greeted with enthusiasm by middle-class audiences. Atlanta's Lyceum theater canceled their engagement because they failed to meet its standards as a "higher class of attraction." Some African Americans even chastised the girls for disrespecting their father's ministry, and one report claimed that Albany Whitman disowned his own daughters for their career choice. Yet there is also evidence that he left his daughters an estate worth sixty thousand dollars and that their mother served as their manager in the early days.[36] More likely, the Whitmans, like many African American professional families, sought to publicly distance themselves from working-class black cultural pursuits to reinforce their own respectability. Privately, however, African American middle-class families frequently supported and encouraged participation in black cultural forms originating in working-class populations. After all, it was Albany Whitman who taught his daughters the "double shuffle," insisting that it was "just for exercise."[37]

Faced with a growing performance culture that encouraged the participation of women as performers and audience members, many black middle-class critics expressed fears that performing women would reinforce racist assumptions of black female promiscuity. But black women's success on the popular stage forced the critics to reassess the public role of women and their own politics of respectability. By taking to the stage, black female performers had helped transform the public space of the theater into a respectable one for women. Some African Americans concerned with racial uplift similarly focused on managing public and private space as much as on living up to the morals and manners laid out by reformers. "Respectable" black middle-class women could partake in "questionable" cultural pursuits if they were in a location deemed appropriate. For example, the esteemed and "austere" Richmond businesswoman Maggie Lena Walker "built a second story porch overhanging Leigh Street so she could engage in street life even while maintaining a respectable distance from the street." She maintained her own image of respectability by "semi-privately" enjoying public amusement. And in the "arena of the church"

Aida Overton Walker as Salome,
ca. 1911.

(Photographs and Prints Division, Schomburg
Center for Research in Black Culture, The New
York Public Library, Astor, Lenox and Tilden
Foundations.)

even "cakewalks were a respectable activity." It was "the public visibility of working-class activities that often made them threatening to a middle class increasingly worried about image as a sign of progress and a means of obtaining rights."[38] Black participation in commercial culture brought with it an attenuated focus on the presentation of black lives both on and off the stage—a gaze that black performers had to address during a period when long-held assumptions about private and public space were being challenged.

The Burden of Representing the Race

> We do not by any means wish to make you inmates of an asylum, nor
> do we wish at this time to seem to attack your deportment or behavior,
> but, knowing that the bond of prejudice is drawn so tightly about us,
> and that the eye that sees everything we colored folks do is ever ready to
> magnify and multiply many times over the value of the most innocent
> deed committed by us, we write you this letter to warn you to so con-
> duct yourself that your manner and mode of life will disarm all criti-
> cism and place you above reproach.[39]

Thus began Williams and Walker's booklet to their company members explaining the rules and regulations of employment. Bert Williams told the
white press, "I don't suppose there is a theatrical company in the world
which is so strictly disciplined as is ours. We can't afford to let our people
do anything wrong—it would spoil all our efforts to build up a decent reputation." Keeping the benefit of the entire company in mind, Williams
and Walker fined company members who broke the rules and pooled the
money collected "for the immediate use of members of the company who
may be in need of assistance." Their prologue to the rules with its emphasis on how carefully whites scrutinized black behavior—"ready to magnify
and multiply many times over" even the "most innocent deed"—suggests
that Williams and Walker sought to represent the company well in front of
white audiences offstage as well as on, rather than actually reform company members' behavior. Their pamphlet seems to criticize the act of being seen misbehaving more than the actual misbehavior. The company's
attention to audience response resembles a tendency in ideologies of racial
uplift. For example, in their pamphlet directed at southern migrants, the
Detroit Urban League instructed "DON'T carry on loud conversations or
use vulgar or obscene language on the street cars, streets, or in public
places. Remember this hurts us as a race . . . DON'T go about the streets or
on the street car in bungalow aprons . . . DON'T sit in front of your house
or around Belle Isle or public places with your shoes off." Likewise, the national organization's Chicago office warned, "Don't use vile language in
public places . . . Don't act discourteously to other people in public places
. . . Don't make yourself a public nuisance."[40] With instructions like these,
it was not always clear that promoters of an African American respectabil-

ity actually sought to make African Americans "respectable" in their private lives. Rather, many middle-class blacks seemingly expressed greater interest in staging respectability for public display. Regarding the theatrical profession, one *Freeman* columnist despaired that only "a few members of the profession know how to deport themselves in public."[41]

That Williams and Walker were more concerned with monitoring company behavior to ensure respectable public presentation than with policing the company members' private lives is supported in part by Williams's own participation in saloon culture. One year after explaining these company rules to a white reporter, Detroit police arrested Williams along with fourteen company members for gambling. The local press announced, "Dusky actor star is caught in raid of crap game by police" at John Holly's saloon at five o'clock in the morning. However much Williams sought to present a flawless public image, he enjoyed a great deal of camaraderie with company members participating in a lively world filled with "whiskey, gin, and dice." Once this private behavior became public, Williams tried to hide his participation by giving his name as James Johnson, but local police recognized him from billboards and so reportedly entered both names on the arrest form. All those arrested, including Williams, were kept in a cell overnight, but Williams attempted to keep his image clean and gave a statement denying that he was actually shooting craps.[42] African American editors did not publish this story and carefully upheld public images of Williams and Walker as respectable middle-class black men.

Theater critic Sylvester Russell too commented on offstage socializing, but like Williams and Walker, he recommended monitoring one's social life, rather than forbidding participation in urban nightlife. He targeted saloons, commenting that such clubs should have a "moral influence." "A club barroom must not cause actors to become loud and unruly," said Russell. "The indisposition of a single blackguard should not be tolerated by those who are present for a moment and by all hands should be quickly and quietly ousted and given over to the police if he return."[43] An active participant in saloon culture himself, Paul Laurence Dunbar too grappled with the pleasures, dangers, and critiques of bar life in his novel *Sport of the Gods*. Dunbar's novel includes a wide variety of perspectives on the potential dangers of the saloon, and makes clear that this aspect of offstage life, while enticing, presented both possibilities and dangers for aspiring performers; his descriptions bring to the fore how much this generation obsessed over negotiating the racial politics of new urban spaces. Dunbar described his fictional hangout for the performing world, "The Banner Club," as being a "substitute—poor, it must be confessed—to many youths for the home life which is so lacking among certain classes in New York," and as a "social cesspool, generating a poisonous miasma and reeking with the stench of decayed and rotten moralities." At the same time, he seemed to mock middle-class reformers when he described them as those "who for an earnest hour sermonized" on the "the pernicious influence of the city on untrained negroes," claiming that "it was better and nobler for them to sing to God across the Southern fields than to dance for rowdies in the Northern halls." His own ambivalence about city life emerges as he celebrated the camaraderie of Banner Club patrons but made clear that this life brought about the downfall of one of his migrant protagonists. Interestingly, in the novel only the young woman Kit—who had been determined to prove the respectability of stage life to her mother—survived in the urban North; her brother went to prison and their parents returned to the South.[44] However much Dunbar presented ambivalence about the possibilities and problems in city life in this 1902 novel, he spent much time working and socializing in New York City during those years.

Especially concerned about deportment, Sylvester Russell heralded the popular stage as a place to make real "ladies and gentlemen," regularly extending his role as critic of theatrical performances to comment on the social behaviors of actors. Like his commentary on the saloon, however, he did not condemn vaudeville, but rather scrutinized performers' behavior, seeking to lift the profession to a level he deemed "respectable." "You never can tell who wants to belittle you," cautioned Russell. "There are people in supposed respectable circles who will invite you just to hear you sing and for the satisfaction of saying they know you. They will even find out as much of your business as they can including the standard of your character, say nothing of their own inferiority and then be ready to turn you out by a sly excuse that it would be impossible to accommodate you or feed you."[45] When he wrote an article ostensibly offering theatrical advice to men considering stage careers, Russell included very little information about the theatrical profession, focusing instead on physical cleanliness and deportment. He informed "stage struck boys" that "young men who travel should adopt the habit of taking a cold soap and water bath every night" because "you can't bathe too often." While he included one short statement recommending that aspiring performers learn to read music, he spent more than a third of his article discussing personal hygiene, telling young men, "Underclothes could be worn two weeks by a man whose skin is perfectly clean." Boys were informed that "some actors never take a bath at all", and that Russell had seen "crust and dirt on their neck and arms one inch thick." He warned boys that "the lazy filthy man with a crusty coat of dirt on his hide, who sits hugging the stove half frozen to death in the winter time is a fit subject for diseases that will land him in the pest house."[46]

On one level, this commentary highlights concerns about real dangers like tuberculosis then rampant in poor urban neighborhoods. Dunbar succumbed to the disease in 1906, so it is no surprise that tuberculosis might be on the minds of theater critics. Along with a focus on deportment, black theater critics and social reformers addressed legitimate worries over health, substandard housing, and vice through uplift politics— problems either ignored or criminalized by white reformers.[47] Yet, while Russell's commentary on cleanliness resembled ideologies of racial uplift, and he too likely hoped to ameliorate social problems, he aimed to secure the respectability of popular amusements rather than to denounce black participation in them.

The frequent travel that accompanied the theatrical profession compounded the problems of ensuring "respectable" private behavior of performers, since life on the road inherently challenged the conventional separation of private and public spaces. Casts of fifty or sixty men and women spent months together playing at theaters throughout the Midwest and West, and, less frequently, in the South. Jim Crow conditions made train travel difficult and scrambling for friendly accommodations a necessity. Daily insult was common. Tom Fletcher recalled that on one tour, the actors began to come to the train's dining tables with aprons made of oilcloth, because the engineer would purposely back up so hard that their coffee would be knocked into their laps.[48] A few of the more successful companies facilitated their troupes' transport by purchasing their own rail cars, but even so, train etiquette became a favorite topic of theater critics. One critic admonished managers to prohibit "gambling, crap-shooting and expectorating" on trains and stipulated that "bathrooms should be properly provided and all respectable performers should look forward to cleanliness."[49] In addition, because there had been some incidents of actors shooting at each other, another critic warned, "If minstrel men are not yet civilized it will be best for managers not to allow any weapons on the cars."[50] Again, theater critics' rhetoric echoed that of social reformers. For instance, in her "Traveler's Friend" pamphlet, Baptist leader Nannie Burroughs instructed, "Don't stick your head out of the window at every station . . . don't talk so loud to your friends who may be on the platform that a person a block away may hear you."[51]

Moreover, train travel highlighted—and arguably accelerated—changing sexual mores. Nineteenth-century elite sensibility stipulated that to be a gentleman, a man must obey all the "rules of polite society," especially in the presence of women, and must eschew all "vulgar expressions" and "avoid intoxication." To be considered a lady, women must "exhibit dignity and a self-respect that would prevent any violation of the prevailing sexual code."[52] For these elites, unmarried men and women traveling together by train would never be considered "ladies" and "gentlemen." Theater critics necessarily attended to these changes that so troubled a middle class invested in presenting a black respectability. Sylvester Russell warned male performers to stay away from "foolish girls of every nationality who admire actors." In part, he worried about the real danger that accompanied black actors dating local women, and warned "jealous fellows of every nationality who watch these girls, not to protect them exactly, but to see that they do not get familiar with stage actors." Yet Russell also wanted performers to uphold a certain image, and he cautioned that if "Mr. Actor" became familiar with local girls, at best he would lose his job, and at worst he would not only disgrace the company and himself, but the race.[53] While he had informed women to be "mistresses of their own respectability," he saw no such role for young men and instructed boys to avoid the performing world and undertake a business, a peculiar comment for a theater critic. Men who chose stage life were admonished to have "good manners," not to smoke or drink, and not to commit adultery.[54] Given this context, it is possible that Russell's additional suggestion that boys bathe daily with cold water to avoid catching a cold doubled as advice to limit the sexual promiscuity that accompanied road trips.

Marriage became the favored solution to promiscuous socializing in the new leisure environments. Russell often spoke of marriage, once writing, "While nearly all white critics agree that actors and actresses should never marry, I do not regard it applicable to colored performers."[55] He charged,

"All young, successful comedians should marry early" and "should choose the healthiest and most talented women they can find, in or out of the profession; one who would not object to raising a family." He advised "stage struck boys" to "keep away from women as long as you can," but he stipulated, "don't be a bachelor." Most important, urged Russell, was to avoid living "in adultery with an actress posing as your wife." He criticized one man who married a "respectable" woman after having lived for fifteen years with an actress, condemning him for not marrying the actress who "would have made the man the best wife if he had condescended to marry her." Another critic in the *Freeman* noted his pleasure that more black performers were getting married, because marriage countered the perception that the profession contained many "morally rotten members" and that showmen were "humanity's garbage . . . unfit to even pass along the street where virtue resides."[56]

More than simply promoting marriage as a path to respectability, Russell expressed a belief in "good" breeding by stating that "the greatest performers of the future should be the off-springs of our greatest actors."[57] Again Russell echoed the beliefs of many black elites, who prized social rituals like weddings and parties as manifestations of "good breeding," a term that appeared often in the "musings of aristocrats of color."[58] Yet his goal remained uplifting theatrical work rather than preaching morality. And in spite of these recommendations, Will Marion Cook and Abbie Mitchell were the only couple among the leading stage pairs to have children. On October 21, 1900, the thirty-one-year-old Cook married the fourteen-year-old Mitchell—seven months after the birth of their daughter, Marion Abigail.[59] On March 30, 1903, their son, Mercer Cook, was born, and four years later, the Cooks divorced.

Unfortunately, the Cook marriage did not dissolve quietly or privately. In August of 1905, while Mitchell rehearsed for a show with Ernest Hogan's company, Cook entered his wife's dressing room and slashed her stage clothes along with her golden-hued slippers. Cook was angry with her because she had refused to turn over forty dollars of her earnings to his brother. She reported, "I did not mind giving my earnings to Will—I always had—but it made so small of me to have his brother step into our family." Mitchell chose to be the mistress of her own respectability in this instance, explaining: "We were married in Washington when I was very young and he always treated me like a baby. Now, I am a woman and I refuse to be bullied."[60] Notably, stories of their stormy relationship appeared in white newspapers, but stayed out of the black press. Similarly, stories of Paul Laurence Dunbar's notoriously violent courtship and marriage to Alice Ruth Moore stayed out of the black press. He had a drinking problem and had repeatedly physically abused Moore, once threatening to kill her.[61] Yet few black journalists were willing to tarnish the images of their respectable and successful stage performers with stories of their troubled personal lives.

Bert and Lottie Williams had no children of their own but did care for Lottie's nieces after the death of her sister. George and Aida Walker had no children; nor did Bob Cole and Stella Wiley or Ernest Hogan and Mattie Wilkes. Cole and Wiley divorced, and Wilkes left Hogan during the run of *Rufus Rastas* for a vaudeville tour of Europe.[62] Cole, Hogan, and Walker died of illnesses related to infection with syphilis, further suggesting that performers did not regard sexual fidelity in marriage as an important part of performing culture.[63] Reputedly, Walker's affairs were legendary; it was rumored, for example, that Eva Tanguay, a white singer and dancer known for her parodic interpretation of "Salome," would welcome Walker into her dressing room during the one vaudeville tour for which they shared a billing.[64] These performers' personal lives hardly conformed to the picture of aristocrats of color who "prized marital stability and considered divorce a 'terrible something.'"[65] Nor did these stage stars heed Sylvester Russell's suggestions for middle-class respectability. Rather, in *Abyssinia,* the Williams and Walker Company mocked some of the requirements for respectability through the character of Miss Primly. In her song "Don't," she admonished, "Don't kiss beware and if you're asked be sure to say 'I won't' / They say there's eighty-thousand microbes on each kiss so don't."[66]

Black performers had to pay some attention to their offstage life, however. A white press increasingly obsessed with celebrities' private lives worked hard to air these performers' personal problems to white audiences hungry for a view across the color line. While such interest attests to the fame that black performers achieved, the scrutiny that came with celebrity status proved particularly troublesome for black Americans set on challenging stereotypes. One reporter noted that Aida Walker "abruptly" left the tour of *Abyssinia* in Chicago to return to New York. While George Walker reported that his wife had taken ill and needed rest, the reporter speculated, "Why Mrs. Walker should take such an unceremonious leave in the midst of a profitable engagement in which she was a big drawing card, Walker does not explain, but he insisted that there was no cloud on his matrimonial horizon." This reporter insisted that there was "some slight jar between the Walkers, and that the soubrette had taken herself off without standing on ceremony and to the chagrin of the management."[67] Aida Walker died in 1914 from kidney failure at the age of thirty-four, so it may well be that she had suffered a long-term illness. A stage life filled with travel, rehearsals, and performances took a toll on many performers, and under one later headline, "The Pace That Kills—A Moral," a reporter wrote about George Walker's death: "While the *Star* does not, on general principles, approve of stretching the Fourteenth Amendment to the extent of permitting colored players to appear in the same theaters simultaneously with white players, it cannot refrain from expressing regret that George Walker, of the colored theatrical team of Williams and Walker has succumbed to the pace that kills." The *Star* reported that Walker "should serve as an example of too much success, too much popularity. When the firm of Williams and Walker was merely a money-making firm of stage 'mokes,' the two men went their way sensibly and carefully and sanely. Then came greater success; and with greater success came the pace that kills."[68] The critic thus condemned Williams and Walker for their success, suggesting that they had stepped dangerously across the color line by headlining at theaters and playing on Broadway, as well as by enjoying the money they earned by partaking in the revels of urban leisure. Walker died of complications due to syphilis, so the reporter may have meant the "pace that kills" to refer to both the actor's rise to fame and his offstage socializing. The critic's assessment makes all too clear the necessity of Williams and Walker's pamphlet of rules for company members' behavior offstage. Importantly they, along with Russell and other theater critics, took just as seriously society's overt—and unspoken—rules for onstage performances.

The Legitimate Standard

The discussion of respectability onstage surfaced most noticeably in the quest for "legitimacy." Sylvester Russell wrote most directly about legitimacy, but his comments reflect the sentiments of other black theater critics and some performers equally concerned with elevating their art form. Russell's particular obsession with setting standards stemmed from his long career as a singer and journalist before he began his *Freeman* stint as theater critic, and arguably from his childhood experiences in New Jersey, where he had grown up in an otherwise all-white neighborhood. He had toured with the Black Patti Troubadours, stage managed for the *Creole Show*, joined an interracial troupe touring *Uncle Tom's Cabin*, and sung at several summer resorts. Between performance opportunities, Russell worked as a mess boy on a boat, as a barber (which he detested), and as a valet for white students at Brown University. When touring Ohio at the time of the Chicago World's Fair, Russell began his journalism career with the *Youngstown Free Speech*, after which he decided to write about the stage. Drawing on his many experiences, he formulated what he called "the Legitimate Standard" and stipulated that performers should follow his guidelines "for their own good, for the benefit of the coming generation, and for a glorious achievement for the race whom they represent."[69]

The use of dialect, stereotype, or blackface never explicitly entered discussions about legitimacy for Russell. Along with other black critics, he continued to refer to shows as "coon" comedy throughout the first decade of the twentieth century, and celebrated performers like Bert Williams— who performed in blackface makeup for his entire career—as legitimate. The use of stereotyped imagery was so widespread that its categorical dismissal would only have been possible by denying commercial culture's feasibility as a tool for race progress and financial gain. While the previous generation may have been comfortable denouncing popular amusements, twentieth-century black professionals weighed more carefully the benefits (and costs) of engaging in them in their quest for respectability and legitimacy. The different way that black theater critics measured productions and performers for legitimacy not only unveils how critics dealt with dominant black imagery, but further demonstrates how much theater criticism mirrored uplift politics.

In theatrical circles, the term "legitimate theater" referred to dramatic presentations that generally followed one plot to its conclusion, did not encourage audience participation, and omitted vulgar material. Since vaudeville included a variety of sketches—"something for everyone"—it did not immediately gain legitimate status, but vaudeville impresarios had intentionally "cleaned-up" their acts in hopes of elevating this form of theater. Bawdy jokes that thrilled burlesque audiences were unacceptable in vaudeville, because theater managers sold their shows as suitable for the entire family. Musical comedies fell between drama and vaudeville, for they revolved around a central plot, but still included unrelated sketches and rarely followed a clear narrative line. These newer forms of theater challenged nineteenth-century standards of legitimacy. While vaudeville would never conform to the standard of one plot, B. F. Keith and other promoters had elevated vaudeville and comedic performance to a respectable form of amusement. Similarly, black vaudevillians like Bert Williams and George Walker achieved a level of legitimacy by bringing black musical comedy to Broadway. Both the black and white press praised Williams, Walker, Cole, and Johnson for their "clean and legitimate comedy," and for providing "clean well-planned shows," when they performed their own shows and starred on the Keith circuit.[70] The *New York Mirror* singled out Bert Williams for particular praise: "The Williams fun is clean and legitimate and one cannot remember the time when Bert Williams lent his ability to a questionable joke or a vulgar story. It is unnecessary to add here that there are but few white comedians of whom one can say the same thing."[71]

Although both black and white newspapers published discussions of what kinds of theater were "legitimate," the word did not have the same meaning for both communities. For white critics, vaudeville and musical comedy gained some credit as respectable, but white management refused to book black dramas, because most white critics and audiences could only imagine laughing at, not taking seriously, black performers. Williams and Walker produced clean and legitimate comedy, but even so, they only earned bookings on vaudeville and musical comedy stages. Certain aspects of dramatic theater were completely off-limits for African Americans, as Aida Walker discovered when she performed "Salome" as legitimate classical dance. White racist expectation, for example, made it nearly impossible for African Americans to depict romantic love onstage. As early as 1901, Russell declared, "What these new modern comedy plays want is two or three good strong love scenes with clever women," and he later despaired that in *In Dahomey*, "a love scene is conspicuous by its absence." But presenting a love scene on the black stage proved exceptionally difficult, and in 1906 Russell was still writing that "love must find a way in Negro comedy."[72] James Weldon Johnson later described this dilemma. "If anything approaching a love duet was introduced in a musical comedy, it had to be broadly burlesqued. The reason behind this taboo lay in the belief that a love scene between two Negroes could not strike a white audience except as ridiculous."[73] George Walker had also commented, "The colored man's love affairs are like his ragtime music and his dialect poems. No matter how carefully written they must not be otherwise than amusing."[74] When Cole and Johnson managed to include such a scene in their show *The Shoofly Regiment* (1905–1907), Russell described it as "the one Negro show that gives an opportunity to show to the incredulous white that the Negro has ability and talent to produce a play, teeming with music, humor and an interesting love story."[75] Still, white audiences clamored for stereotypes and refused to accept the legitimacy—and the humanity—of black love portrayed on the stage.

Just as they had criticized Williams and Walker's *Abyssinia,* white critics generally interpreted black performers' departures from feigned stereotypes and moves toward "serious" drama as attempts to be "white." For example, along with nearly breaking the taboo against romantic love, Cole and Johnson limited the amount of singing and dancing in their second show *The Red Moon* (1908–1909). White critics panned this show as "too white" and thus uninteresting as black musical comedy.[76] One white critic wrote that when African American performers "begin mimicking the manners and striving after the attainments of white folk they fall far short of their model, and become merely tiresome." Another criticized Cole and Johnson as "a colored company that tries too hard to get away from its color." This critic asked: "Why gild the lily or whitewash the kitchen stove?"[77] Lester Walton responded by lambasting the Schubert organization for not giving much publicity to *The Red Moon* because the show did not contain enough "niggerisms" in it.[78] And he blamed managers who would only hire black acts that included a "plantation scene, do plenty of buck-dancing, and sing a few old-time Negro songs."[79] Black performer Salem Tutt Whitney likewise testified that when a show omitted references to stereotypes, white theater managers would not book it. When Whitney presented his show to white managers for acceptance, "the answer was always the same: 'Very good, but white people will not accept it. They want to hear colored people sing and see them dance.'"[80]

Despite their attempts to pigeonhole black expressive culture stylistically, white critics ironically often congratulated Bert Williams for "whiteness" whenever he met their standards of respectability. Whites who worked with him in the 1910s in the Ziegfeld Follies called him "the whitest black man I know," the "Black man with the White heart,'" and "a *black*

Bob Cole and J. Rosamond Johnson in *The Red Moon,* ca. 1909.
(Helen Armstead-Johnson Theater Photograph Collection, Photographs and Prints Division,Schomburg Center for
Research in Black Culture, The New York Public Library, Astor, Lenox and Tilden Foundations.)

white man."[81] Once when a reporter asked him if he wished he had been born white, Williams responded negatively, but informed the reporter that he did find being black an "inconvenience."[82] In commending Williams for his treatment of his company one white interviewer commented: "Few, if any white managements are so 'white' in handling their people as are these colored comedians." He then asked Williams if "all great negroes did not have white blood in their veins." The interviewer reported Williams's disgust: "'White blood make a black man any smarter!' shouted Williams, 'I guess not! Why, what kind of white blood do we get! The very worst and lowest and meanest there is. And when a man with some of this in his veins becomes famous do you say the bad white blood did it?'"[83]

While performers' struggles for legitimacy—and the black struggle for respectability—did not signal a desire to be white, it can be read as a desire to be seen as "not black," as blackness was then conceived in the dominant culture. As African Americans struggled for legitimacy onstage and respectability offstage, they faced the dilemma of seeking respectable status in a dominant society that understood class status through a lens of racism. Racial hierarchies left black performers with the insurmountable problem of presenting a respectable black identity in a culture that wanted to see everything black as laughable, and everything respectable as white. Juggling the imagery—and the racialized class perceptions embedded within it—presented a formidable challenge. Bert Williams recounted a real event that he would never enact, because it conformed far too closely to racist stereotype. He witnessed a group of razor-wielding black soldiers steal a chicken, and stated that in this instance "nature exaggerated art."[84] Although he found the real-life incident funny, he knew it would anger some black critics. While Williams offered this story as an extreme example, he, and the artists of his generation, had to master the art of skillful negotiation. As he and Walker once commented, "The colored theatre 'goer,' taken collectively, only wants to see when he attends a Negro show such characters as remind him of 'white folks,' while on the other hand white patrons only want to see him portray the antebellum 'darkey.'"[85]

Thus, black theater critics developed their own standards of legitimacy to elevate black arts. As Russell explained, while "the common element of white people . . . care nothing about the boundary lines of coon comedy or anything else that colored actors may do so long as they get lots of fun . . . we have got to establish these precedents ourselves and those in comedy, who do not, will be creatures of criticism."[86] Russell sought to highlight the differences between the buffoonery of minstrelsy and the legitimate comedy of black musical productions, as well as to measure performers both for their style of costume and for the nature of their communication with audiences. Of the leading comedians, Bob Cole and Bert Williams usually passed Russell's test of legitimacy, but Ernest Hogan more often earned criticism as "illegitimate." Williams, Russell announced, "knows how to dress for comedy, and that is everything." Russell sometimes praised Hogan for his costume and noted that in Newark, Hogan "wore a red legitimate comedy suit and later in the play he wore one of green; both of these suits were of excellent legitimate comedy design." But when Hogan "appeared at the Star theater in New York," Russell lamented, "he gave us minstrel rags and variety stage garments . . . the bad judgment of Hogan and McClain has reduced the legitimate bearing of the show to a vaudeville farce." At another point Russell berated Hogan for having his character, "the rich Mr. Bullion," dressed "like a ragtime coon from Memphis."[87] That Russell selected a southern locale to criticize Hogan's character reveals an important part of his search of a legitimate standard, and in many ways, reflects tendencies within the larger black middle-class project of racial uplift—tendencies that became much more pronounced as the number of southern migrants increased. For example, in 1917 the Detroit Urban League established the Dress Well clubs "to create a better impression of the Negro by attention to dress, personal appearance and public behavior." One Urban League pamphlet instructed southern migrants to "TRY to dress neatly at all times, but don't be a dude or wear flashy clothes. They are as undesirable and as harmful as unclean clothes."[88] In ways similar to the black middle-class quest for respectability, Russell's standard of legitimacy reflected and reinforced class and regional differences. As he sought to distinguish musical comedy performers from minstrel imagery, Russell assigned some of those attributes to southern African Americans, and in doing so, revealed his own biases.

Sylvester Russell's other standard for legitimacy concerned the performer's relation to his black audiences. Performers did not always issue subtle appeals for laughter from the balcony, and Russell categorized any performance where an actor spoke directly to the audience—especially the balcony audience—as "illegitimate." After watching the Smart Set Company, often a vehicle for Ernest Hogan, Russell commented: "The greatest exhibition of ignorance is for an actor to stubbornly ignore the recognized criticism of one man, to play to the gallery rather than to receive the legitimate applause of several millions of the best people of the white race who must approve of it, and for the advancement of a black oppressed race, who look to him for race advancement." Russell wrote that the show was "considered legitimate in playing in legitimate houses," but that the production included many actors who insisted on playing their parts illegitimately. He announced that the actors were "glad enough to be legitimate," and that they knew "nought to talk to the people over the footlights, and answer the gallery boys in the bargain."[89] Russell actually liked Hogan's comedy better than that of Williams, but he could not tolerate what he called Hogan's "utter disregard of legitimate methods of acting in a comedy performance." Russell explained, "Whether his continual practice of making extemporaneous speeches has been deliberate or rendered illegitimate by the weakness of accepting of a jolly from the gods of the gallery is hard to decide."[90]

Such disdain for communication with the gallery can be seen as an attempt by black critics to set themselves apart from gallery patrons. Russell even stated that "the common people" accepted the Smart Set's tendency to address the audience and noted that this tactic helped make "the hit of the evening with the people in the gallery."[91] Though he did not delineate standards like Russell, Lester Walton occasionally included comments in his reviews that reflected his own desire to differentiate himself from the larger black audience. When Walton went to the Williams and Walker show *Bandana Land* at Broadway's Majestic Theater, he went prepared to "tear it into pieces" in his review, but ended up praising the performance while criticizing his fellow audience members. "I found myself enjoying the show as much as some of the fellow members of my race who insisted in making their presence known as well as themselves obnoxious to those seated near them by their unsuppressed laughter and merriment."[92] Russell's and Walton's attempts to control audience behavior resembled a politics of uplift present in late-nineteenth-century black churches. Because white observers sometimes referred to the antiphonal nature of many black congregations as unrefined, some black ministers sought to reduce communication by ending the practice of lining out hymns, thus allowing only literate parishioners to participate. A more controlled service may have achieved a more "refined" status, but it limited the "verbal and nonverbal interaction between minister and prayer, speaker and congrega-tion," and hampered the "active participation of everyone in the worship service" in the collective experience of ritual, music, and prayer.[93] Arguably, black patrons watching black actors experienced the antiphonal nature of vaudeville in similar ways.

Yet Russell and Walton had reason for concern. While white audiences enjoyed hearing black laughter from the gallery, they usually considered it to be little more than part of the show. Often, white critics referred to bal-cony audiences as "thunderstorms" or "dark clouds"—ominous, yet as part of the show, rendered safe.[94] For the most part, African American patrons' applause authenticated African American stage performances for white audience members. By criticizing performers for their pleas to the "gods of the gallery," Russell showed that he saw the relationship with white audi-ences critical to black performers' success. He may not have understood (or, perhaps, may not have wanted to admit) how much the white audi-ences also enjoyed witnessing the communication of the stage and gallery, since this enjoyment was based on their racist assumptions. Because Rus-sell made reference in the black press to the "legitimate applause of several millions of the best people of the white race," it is unlikely that he sought to challenge racism with his recommendations.

Black theater critics confronted a dilemma not unlike that facing black reformers: the search for respectability encouraged them to distance them-selves from the same larger black population that they hoped to uplift. Racial uplift challenged social Darwinist beliefs by asserting that behav-ior could be changed, but at the same time, reformers often redeployed power relations by categorizing working-class or southern behavior as "too black," that is, too close to stereotypes and in need of reform. Often, as Evelyn Brooks Higginbotham tells us, the rhetoric of racial uplift "sounded uncannily similar to the racist arguments they strove to re-fute." This certainly was the case when Margaret Washington addressed the NACW, announcing that she looked with "disfavor upon ragtime mu-sic and vaudeville tendencies . . . [knowing] too well that the play of these things upon the already *over-developed emotions* of the race is alarmingly harmful."[95] By distancing themselves from the larger black population, and often from leisure activities deemed "too black" like ragtime music and dance, middle-class proponents of racial uplift actually reinforced the prevailing ideology of racial hierarchy. Russell's criticism of Hogan for dressing his character as a "ragtime coon from Memphis" reflects this tendency.

Black performers, however, had a different method of distancing themselves from dominant black imagery. They played "darky" roles, but they made clear they were not that which they performed; instead they presented themselves as salaried actors benefiting from the new leisure culture—in short, as skilled professionals. Black theater critics followed their lead, embracing them as professionals and not criticizing their continued use of blackface or of their onstage "darky" antics. Rather, black critics commented on their dress and deportment, and faithfully sought to lift the popular stage to reputable status. Black performers and critics mirrored uplift politics' concern for public display—a concern that took on heightened importance with the rise of a public sphere that placed greater emphasis on self-presentation. Although black artists had yet to earn solid praise from whites for true artistry, they had attracted the attention of black professionals. The twentieth-century black middle class continued to battle over respectability and public amusement, but black performers and critics had managed to make stage life an acceptable sphere for determining and shaping middle-class status. In doing so, they reshaped gender roles, shifting the boundaries between public and private space, and tempered religious influences, reconfiguring the focus on morals and manners.

6666666666

Black Bohemia Moves to Harlem

Each time I attend a performance of the Clef Club Symphony
Orchestra, I leave Manhattan Casino more deeply impressed
with the idea that some day the organization is going to make
the devotees of music in New York sit up and take notice,
irrespective of whether they be colored or white; for there is
really some class to the Clef Club.

LESTER WALTON,
NEW YORK AGE,
1911

I N July of 1908 Bert Williams, James Reese Europe, Lester Walton,
and J. Rosamond Johnson were among those who gathered at George
Walker's new home in a Harlem brownstone to found the Frogs, a professional organization for artists. In doing so, they spearheaded an organiza-
tional move among artists endeavoring to raise the status of their work, as
well as firmly established themselves as prominent residents in uptown
Manhattan. The actors chose to call themselves "the Frogs" after the comedy written by Aristophanes, hoping that the reference to classical Greek
theater would help them in their quest. Although they named their group
after a play, they did not restrict membership to actors, or even artists.
Rather they invited noted black professionals to join as well, hoping to
earn their vocation similar professional status. By 1911, their roster included Booker T. Washington's personal secretary Emmett J. Scott, realtor
John E. Nail, and U.S. Customs official Charles Anderson. James Weldon
Johnson, a close friend of Anderson's, joined too, even though he had already left his stage career to study at Columbia University and to serve a
post as U.S. consul to Venezuela and later, Nicaragua.[1] Although established by the artists who had made their way on America's vaudeville
stages, the Frogs' membership seemed not so different from that of the
National Negro Business League.

Inspired by the Frogs and wary over changes in their West Fifty-third
Street community, other actors and musicians followed suit, forming the

Colored Vaudeville Benevolent Association (CVBA) in 1909 and the Clef Club in 1910. To some extent these organizations overlapped in goals and membership. Frog member and theater critic Lester Walton helped found the CVBA, and Frog member James Reese Europe, the orchestra conductor for Cole and Johnson's musical comedies, headed the Clef Club. Each group had a slightly different focus, but all continued the struggle begun years earlier to secure legitimacy for themselves and their art. The Frogs worked to enhance the status of actors among black professionals, while the CVBA sought both to elevate the status of vaudevillians and to provide benefits to members. The Clef Club, under the direction of Europe, responded to the different needs of musicians and functioned both as a labor organization, helping musicians negotiate contracts, and as a professional organization set on raising the status of black music. Their efforts coalesced around the social events they held uptown at the Manhattan Casino, and culminated with Europe's dream of demonstrating that black music was indeed symphonic—a dream he realized by organizing Clef Club musicians into a symphony-sized orchestra that played Carnegie Hall.[2]

The story of these organizations and of black artists' rise to a place of prominence in black middle-class life is also the story of the growth of black Harlem. Leading performers were among the first blacks to participate in the twentieth-century migration to Harlem, a trek that New York's black community had begun only a few years before the founding of the Frogs. Although the CVBA and Clef Club had both been founded on West Fifty-third Street, they moved their activities to Harlem shortly after inception. It was in large part due to black entertainers' great financial success in vaudeville and musical comedy that they were able to move uptown; J. Rosamond Johnson was one of the first African Americans to buy a home west of Lenox Avenue, and by 1908 George Walker, Bert Williams, Bob Cole, Lester Walton, and Ernest Hogan had all relocated to Harlem. By the time James Weldon Johnson returned from Venezuela, his brother and Bob Cole had moved, and Johnson recalled, "I felt less at home in the city than ever before . . . West 53rd Street was already beginning to lose its place as the Negro center, and the trek to Harlem was taking on significant proportions."[3]

The Marshall still held sway as a gathering place for African Americans downtown, but by then, Johnson said, the hotel "seemed to have deteriorated . . . there seemed to me to have been an all-round cheapening process going on." The Marshall's location near the theater district and the popu-

The Frogs, ca. 1908. Top row, left to right: Bob Cole, Lester Walton, Sam Corker, Bert Williams, James Reese Europe, Alex Rogers. Bottom row, left to right: Tom Brown, J. Rosamond Johnson, George Walker, Jesse Shipp, R. C. McPherson (Cecil Mack).
(Photographs and Prints Division, Schomburg Center for Research in Black Culture, The New York Public Library, Astor, Lenox and Tilden Foundations.)

larity of black musical comedy on Broadway had led to its becoming a favorite after-show spot for theatergoers, one that attracted increasing numbers of white patrons—a change that drew scrutiny from the city's vice agency. Believing that the "mixing of the races which when the individuals are of the ordinary class, always means danger," the city targeted the hotel as a center for prostitution. New cabaret laws required that the Marshall close at 1:00 a.m.—a death-knell for an after-theater venue, and Jim Marshall went out of business. When the hotel closed in 1913, its still-loyal clientele mourned its death with "one hundred disciples of good cheer," singing "more affectionately than melodiously 'Auld Lang Syne' . . . just as dawn was breaking," but by then, black bohemia had already relocated uptown.[4]

Black artists and professionals could buy in Harlem both because they had the money, and because a building boom had turned to bust. Practically all the houses in Harlem had been built between 1870 and 1910—a boom predicated on construction of new subway lines that anticipated the growth of an uptown residential neighborhood. Real estate investors had assumed that Harlem would develop into an upper- and middle-class white community—a community far removed from the vast numbers of immigrant arrivals from southern and eastern Europe. Thus, the buildings were spacious, and many had elevators and servants' quarters. But overspeculation had led to a glut in the market, and by 1904, realtors were left with an abundance of vacant buildings. The substantial increase in New York's black population between 1890 and 1914 meant that some section of the city was destined to become a black neighborhood because of the persistence of racial segregation; that it was this uptown locale was both a result of circumstance and the foresight of some moneyed blacks. Philip A. Payton, a black realtor, capitalized on the overspeculation, convincing Harlem landlords that he could fill the buildings with well-to-do African Americans. Payton knew that blacks were looking to move out of the midtown black neighborhood due to increased migration, overcrowding, substandard housing stock, and the riot of 1900 that had terrorized the black community. One friend of James Weldon Johnson never recovered from a beating he had received that night. By 1905 Payton's Afro-American Realty Company had become the most prominent black-owned real estate firm in New York, and his business success led some African Americans to name him the "father of colored Harlem."[5]

Payton's friends included prominent blacks like (future Frog) Charles Anderson and Fred Moore, editor of the *New York Age*—and Payton employed (future Frog) John E. Nail, the man who would become Harlem's most successful realtor after Payton's business failed. Yet Payton too had overestimated demand, and with a recession hitting in 1907, he went bankrupt. He had even asked Booker T. Washington to underwrite a loan in January 1908, and although Payton could not save his company, Washington's secretary (and future Frog) Emmett Scott supported him until the end. Nail and his colleague Henry C. Parker resigned their positions, set up their own firm, and soon took the lead in Harlem real estate. These men, and thus Harlem's early development as a black neighborhood, were well connected with performing artists. Nail's father, West Fifty-third Street saloon owner John B. Nail, had already made some money by taking advantage of Harlem's inflated real estate market, but he kept the connection to artists he had fostered at his downtown establishment. Before moving, he helped his loyal patrons set up a new social space downtown, even securing the venue, paying the first month's rent, and stocking it with supplies. As vaudevillian Tom Fletcher recalled, Nail encouraged the artists to form an organization, which became the CVBA.[6] Although clearly interested in bettering their own condition, Payton and the Nails saw themselves as race leaders as well, not unlike the artists who founded the Frogs. They envisioned their ventures in Harlem as building community—however much their real estate dealings took advantage of New York's segregated housing market and kept prices inflated. They rented houses to blacks, giving the houses names like the Langston (after John Mercer), the Douglass, the Dunbar, the Attucks, the Wheatley, and the Toussaint, hoping that pride in the housing stock might advance the race.

For black artists and black businessmen, the name Harlem connoted elegance and distinction. Originally developed as a white middle-class and elite community, its streets and avenues were broad, well-paved, clean, and tree-lined; its homes were spacious, replete with the best modern facilities. In short, it was an ideal place to live.[7] Black entertainers bought these homes as soon as they were available, greatly improving the living conditions they had endured in the crowded West Fifty-third Street neighborhood. At the same time, they must have hoped that their Harlem lifestyle would convey their success as skilled professionals much as their attention to dress and deportment signaled respectability. In effect, the Frogs, the CVBA, and Clef Club sustained the goals originally laid out by Williams and Walker, who had thrown open the doors to their flat on West Fifty-third and worked to mentor aspiring artists and build a viable profession for African Americans. What changed with the move to Harlem was that the leading performers directly linked their efforts with those of black professionals, who had become equally interested in the way that cultural production and participation might help race advancement.

Harlem was still racially mixed in 1910, but by then, the influx had earned the area its designation as a black neighborhood. Before World War I, Harlem's black population was 49,555, while the entire black population of Manhattan was 60,534, and by wartime, the neighborhood had earned the reputation of housing the largest concentrated black community in the country. By this time, practically every black institution was located in

Harlem, including the three oldest churches—Bethel AME, AME Zion, and St. Philip's Protestant Episcopal, along with the offices of the *New York Age,* the YMCA, the National Urban League, the NAACP, the AME Home and Foreign Missionary Society, and various fraternal orders. Most blacks moving to Harlem even before the Great Migration had originally moved to the city from somewhere else, usually from the South; only an estimated 14,309 black Manhattanites had been born in New York. Sometimes called the "advance guard" of the Great Migration, prewar migrants laid the foundations for twentieth-century northern black communities in Chicago and Philadelphia as well as in New York.[8] Harlem would experience a flowering of black culture in the 1920s—a flowering that came with its own class and generational tensions—but these tensions had begun to emerge among prewar migrants in Harlem's burgeoning social world.

To sustain their organizations, the Frogs, the CVBA, and the Clef Club held fundraising parties at the Manhattan Casino, a large dance hall located on West 155th Street and Eighth Avenue. These soirées became central to black middle-class life. One of several large so-called dance palaces that became popular in the years before the war, the Manhattan Casino held well over two thousand patrons and included a saloon, dance hall, and picnic grounds, all available for rent.[9] The Frogs inaugurated the fundraising parties, sponsoring annual formal balls that they called "Frolics of the Frogs" from 1908 through 1914. These late-night affairs began at 10:30 and continued through the night; overflowing crowds packed the hall, often leaving entertainers barely enough room to perform. With performances by "tightwire walkers, gymnasts, aerialists, bareback riders, clowns and equilibrists," along with "jesters, fakers, tribal chiefs, executioners, dancing girls, elephants, camels, and horses," one attendee described the Frolic of 1914 as more like a circus. With few exceptions, social dancing followed the show. Critic Lucien H. White wrote a poem published in the *New York Age* that encapsulates the festive spirit of the events. One stanza announced, "Froggies came dressed in their best, the late style costumes stood the test," and another described the party atmosphere, "The frogs and froggies danced till morn / and occasionally sipped the mellow corn."[10]

The CVBA joined the tradition begun by the Frogs and held their first fundraising picnic and dance at the Manhattan Casino on August 12, 1909. "The party started in the afternoon with games and outdoor sports," recalled vaudevillian Tom Fletcher. "In the evening there was a Grand Minstrel, the many vaudeville acts with a grand Prize Cake Walk and the finale. Dancing followed until the wee hours of the morning. That first party fattened the treasury of the CVBA and the organization adopted the practice of giving annual picnics and dances in the spring and winter." At another CVBA event in February of 1910, "dancing was the feature of the evening" and "all the members were in full dress." While there were performances, one reviewer complained that "a much better and smoother vaudeville entertainment should have been provided by professional performers." Still, he reported that "judging from the many evidences of good cheer and hilarity, those in attendance were doing their best to 'corner up' all the joviality and merriment extant in New York for the occasion."[11]

Unlike turn-of-the-century vaudeville, these events catered to an exclusively middle-class population. Admission charges ranged from fifty cents to one or two dollars, and some box seats for Clef Club performances cost as much as five dollars—or nearly half a month's rent for many working-class New Yorkers. Even one dollar was out of the range of what most workers could pay. At the Manhattan Casino, patrons would then have to spend more money for drinks and food. Accordingly, these benefit performances became major social events for the middle class, attracting black professionals—even W. E. B. Du Bois. Sometimes whites came to the events, but there is no direct evidence that they ever approached a majority of the audience, that they joined the organizations themselves, or that they stayed for the early morning dances.[12] The white middle classes would have been less likely to travel uptown to the Manhattan Casino because they had their choice of entertainment downtown. Instead, the uptown venue more often served as a dance hall for Manhattan's white working classes, whose union halls and fraternal orders would rent out the facilities for group events.[13] But because racial segregation kept them out of most downtown cabarets, middle-class African Americans made the club-sponsored events at the Manhattan Casino central to Harlem society.

The parties were not without critics. Sylvester Russell called the Frogs an "exclusive colored actors' society," and complained, "Nobody knows what the Frogs stand for . . . they have as yet no house or home . . . all we hear is news of no importance . . . the most important fiction in order is its exclusiveness." The organizers, he wrote, "haul in class politicians to swell the anthem" and have produced "a club supported by public summer cotillion dances or midnight sprees where mixed crowds of sporting people assemble to drink and carouse." Although not entirely opposed to the organization, Russell questioned whether they were for "the sake of social advancement or charity or for both." Russell had long championed an actor's fund that would provide social services for actors in need, and had seen these very same actors turn away from his earlier fundraising efforts.[14] With the addition of politicians and businessmen on its board of directors, the Frogs seemed to Russell more concerned with self-promotion than with helping fellow struggling actors. Frog leaders, however, did not see such goals as intrinsically separate. The uptown Frolics provided much needed leisure activities for black Americans excluded from downtown venues, and the Frogs entertained black middle-class audiences with black music and dance, thus raising the status of their art as well as their own standing as black professionals.

Although he enjoyed events held at the Manhattan Casino, Lester Walton, along with his fellow Frogs, also labored to facilitate the growth of black theater in Harlem, both to provide affordable amusement to local residents and to generate a production that would renew Broadway's interest in black stage shows. Bert Williams and J. Rosamond Johnson joined with Walton to campaign for a theater that would present affordable vaudeville performances and seat 1,200 to 1,400 people. They set up the Johnson Amusement Company to promote building a site at 138th Street between Fifth and Lenox and sold stock in the company at ten dollars a share, but since they wanted this theater to be owned solely by African Americans, they did not sell stock to whites. Enthusiastic about a black-owned theater in their community, black Harlemites wrote to the *New York Age* suggesting several names, including the "Menelik," "The Nubian," "The Progress," and "The Harlem." The Amusement Corporation, however, followed the trend of realtors and settled on the name Walker-Hogan-Cole Theater to commemorate the three stars who had died; Walker and Cole in 1911, and Hogan in 1909. Unfortunately, African Americans did not have the capital to build the theater and the company abandoned its venture in 1912. Walton blamed blacks for not getting the Walker-Hogan-Cole Theater off the ground, but building such a theater was an enormous undertaking, especially since two white-owned theaters in Harlem, the Lafayette and the Lincoln, already presented vaudeville at popular prices.[15] Harlem had become a black residential neighborhood, with black real estate agents managing nearly half of the property, but ownership stayed almost entirely in white hands. The largest black property owner in Harlem was St. Philips Episcopal Church, hardly an institution that would fund vaudeville.

When the Walker-Hogan-Cole Theater project died, Walton and Harlem's new black residents successfully desegregated the larger of Harlem's two established theaters, the Lafayette, which seated 1,500 patrons. "Managers should know that it is 'suicide' to draw the color line in colored neighborhoods," wrote Walton. While New York's black population had, on different occasions, individually challenged segregated seating for well over a decade, they had not desegregated an entire theater until their collective refusal to attend the Lafayette forced white management to allow African Americans to sit anywhere inside. A big victory for Harlem's new black community, this achievement earned front-page coverage in the *New York Age,* and, in turn, the Lafayette's management posted a full-page advertisement announcing its new policy. Walton feared that whites would show antipathy toward black patrons who sat in the orchestra, but noted that most white patrons, the majority of whom were local shopkeepers, posed little threat. While no black-owned theater emerged in pre-war Harlem, Walton heralded the moment when whites and blacks sat together in orchestra seating, and made sure to note that blacks "outclassed whites in dress."[16]

The Lafayette became central to Harlem's social and cultural life. Walton hoped that the Lafayette would not only provide entertainment for neighborhood residents, but also nourish the talent that would bring black shows back to Broadway. *Bandana Land* (1909) had been the last successful black show on Broadway, and with the deaths of Hogan, Walker, and Cole, the three major black companies had disbanded—leaving James Weldon Johnson to name the 1910s a "term of exile" of black acts from the Great White Way. In Harlem, Lester Walton's devotion to the Lafayette helped it thrive, and in October 1913, the theater hosted J. Leubrie Hill's *Darktown Follies,* a show that drew large crowds in part because the desegregated Lafayette kept its prices the same throughout the show's run—"matinees five and ten cents; evenings, ten, fifteen and twenty-five cents."[17] In 1911, Hill, who was originally from Memphis and who had performed in all the premier black vaudeville and comedic musicals, formed his own company and toured the show *My Friend from Kentucky*. The renamed *Darktown Follies*

excited Harlem audiences immensely, and even attracted Broadway producers to the theater. The Lafayette also featured performances by Will
Marion Cook and Abbie Mitchell, among others, and hosted a series of
well-attended dance contests for Harlem residents.[18]

Still, the crowds that frolicked with the Frogs at the Manhattan Casino
did not mingle freely with Lafayette patrons. Performers like Will Marion
Cook, Abbie Mitchell, and *Darktown Follies* dancer Ethel Williams played
and supported both venues, but ticket prices at each inevitably meant
that audiences differed. The introduction of the "country store" best exemplifies the class politics shaping the Lafayette. A venture that Lester
Walton introduced when he took over the Lafayette in 1914 after hearing
that other managers had already found the idea to be quite popular, the
country store was essentially a raffle where audience members were "given
an opportunity to win one of the many useful articles put up by the theater." On one typical Saturday "one man left the Lafayette Theatre with a
brass bed, while other men and women were seen carrying a ham, a set of
dishes, an umbrella, a bottle of wine, a bed quilt, a chicken, or some useful
article." This event proved so popular with Harlemites that the theater
eventually added an additional "country store" on Tuesday evenings. For
the cost of admission to a night of entertainment, working-class African Americans could also hope to return home with needed supplies.
By contrast, middle-class and elite blacks who typically spent fifty cents
on admission, plus extra money on food and drink at the Manhattan
Casino, would have been unlikely to want to be seen carrying home a
Sunday ham from their Saturday night out. Frolic attendees received gifts
as well, but the Frogs "distributed with profligate liberality to the ladies
present . . . souvenirs of handsome and expensive cut class, sliverware, articles of brass, English porcelain, valuable field glasses and rare water
colors."[19]

Although class differences were important to Harlem's social world, racial segregation guaranteed that the classes would engage one another,
and it was the overlapping worlds of the Manhattan Casino and the Lafayette Theater that gave birth to the craze for modern dances that swept
through prewar America. The dances from the *Darktown Follies* and the
musical breakthroughs fostered by Clef Club musicians together raised
the respectability of black music and dance in ways that soon had Americans flocking to cabaret dance floors. James Reese Europe blazed the path

COMING FROM THE LAFAYETTE THEATRE SATURDAY EVENING

"The Country Store" at the Lafayette Theater, *New York Age,* February 5, 1914.
(General Research and Reference Division, Schomburg Center for Research in Black Culture,
The New York Public Library, Astor, Lenox and Tilden Foundations.)

to the dance craze by arranging one hundred musicians into a symphony-sized concert orchestra for the Clef Club's first "Musical Melange and Dancefest" at the Manhattan Casino. The event so thoroughly pleased Lester Walton that he correctly predicted: "The time is not far distant when this organization will be afforded an opportunity to appear at Carnegie Hall or some large theater and deliver the message to our Caucasian brothers that the race is making advanced strides in the musical world."[20]

Arriving at Carnegie Hall (1912–1913)

A decade after Will Marion Cook first urged his mother and teenage bride to embrace his compositions, his "real Negro melodies" made their way to Carnegie Hall with the help of James Reese Europe and his Clef Club Orchestra. At first Cook criticized the effort, and "raved all over town about Jim not knowing anything about conducting and what right did he have going to Carnegie Hall with his inexperience."[21] Perhaps Cook was jealous that Europe seemed to be earning the recognition that he had long struggled for, but his fears echoed those of other black critics who worried that if whites did not accept the legitimacy of an African American orchestra, ·

their resulting derision would be a serious setback for African American musicians. Fortunately, the event was a tremendous success. When the applause thundered for "Swing Along," Cook "began to weep tears of joy and when he tried to speak he couldn't say a word. All he could do was just bow."[22] His victory was complete. Under his direction, 150 black voices filled Carnegie Hall with "Darktown Is Out Tonight," and at a later concert, Abbie Mitchell sang some of his songs there to the same grand acceptance. Surely James Reese Europe was thrilled as well. The concert prompted the *Crisis* to name him Man of the Month, and a white critic proclaimed that Europe's composing and conducting were "legitimizing the music of the negro."[23]

Artists' skills made the Carnegie concerts triumphant, but it was their professional networking that had gained the support from black and white progressives necessary to open the symphony hall's doors. The Clef Club's desire to raise the status of black music meshed well with a progressive impulse of uplift through music education: Europe's musicians arrived at Carnegie Hall by performing at a fundraiser for the Colored Music School Settlement, a music school for African American children in Harlem. David Mannes, a white reform-minded musician who had been deeply moved by his relationship with his first music teacher, the black concert violinist Charles Douglas, had long wanted to provide music education for African Americans. Mannes joined with black and white progressives to found the school, and while more than 75 percent of the board of directors was white, it included black men like Harry T. Burleigh and W. E. B. Du Bois. African Americans, however, sought to increase black participation on the board to at least 50 percent, and directed the school itself; David Irwin Martin headed the school for the first two years, after which J. Rosamond Johnson took over.[24]

The Music School Settlement refused to draw a color line at the Carnegie Hall concerts, so class became the determining factor, with well-dressed whites sitting next to well-dressed blacks. Lester Walton commended patrons, announcing that the "whites present represented the best element of their race" as did the "colored people in attendance." As he reported, "Some of the leading white citizens sat in evening dress in seats next to some of our highly respectable colored citizens, who were also in evening clothes."[25] Walton's exultations reflect the pride that blacks felt as African American bohemians moved into Harlem brownstones and played at the premier symphony hall in the nation.

Walton admitted that he spent most of his time "watching the white auditors" because he was anxious to know what they thought of the music. The concerts included spirituals, ragtime numbers, black classical compositions, and dance music. The St. Philips Church boys' choir sang compositions by Samuel Coleridge Taylor; Harry T. Burleigh performed both spirituals and popular tunes; Cook conducted a chorus singing his "real Negro melodies"; J. Rosamond Johnson played piano solos; and the Clef Club Orchestra played songs like "Swing Along." Walton worried about whites' response to the music, explaining, "Many white composers and writers do their best to disparage syncopated music, commonly known as ragtime, and do their utmost to show wherein this brand of music does not even merit passing consideration." At Carnegie Hall, however, he "noticed that not until the Clef Club had played 'Panama' did the audience evince more than ordinary interest. White men and women then looked at each other and smiled, while one lady seated in a prominent box began to beat time industriously with her right hand which was covered with many costly gems." He concluded, "Syncopation is truly a native product—a style of music of which the negro is originator, but which is generally popular with all Americans," and he exulted that Will Marion Cook's "Swing Along" alone was worth the price of admission. "The artistic way in which it was rendered bore out the statement often made that classical music is not the only kind that requires preparation and intelligent interpretation."[26]

Without a doubt, the Clef Club's dual success at Carnegie Hall and uptown at the Manhattan Casino earned them a central place among black professionals—a status demonstrated by their honored position at New York State's Emancipation Celebration. Du Bois served on the board of governors of this event held at the Armory at Sixty-second and Columbus Avenue from October 22–31, 1913. New York's event, the most elaborate of several celebrations held nationwide, planned exhibits to illustrate black progress and to speak to contemporary conditions—exhibits similar to those that Ida Wells and Frederick Douglass had wanted to display ten years earlier at the Chicago World's Fair. More than a decade of work came together at this event, and Du Bois premiered his own theatrical production, eventually titled *The Star of Ethiopia,* a drama celebrating black achievement from ancient Africa through the then-contemporary freedom struggle. Advertised as "The Historical Pageant of the Negro Race" and described as a "great scenic production . . . with 350 actors in full costume, orchestra and chorus, and a Regiment of boy Scouts," Du Bois's pageant characterized the excitement and hope surrounding the celebration.[27] Popular performers were not exempt from the tribute, but rather granted a prominent role. Will Marion Cook, James Reese Europe, along with J. Rosamond Johnson, James Weldon Johnson, and Bert Williams—the "Apostle of Laughter"—were all honored as among the "100 distinguished freedmen" and awarded certificates and gold medals.[28]

Like the music that filled Carnegie Hall, the music at the Emancipation Celebration included a diversity of forms. Europe directed a forty-member

Clef Club band for the final concert and costume ball, advertised as a "unique concert of Negro music." David Mannes and David Martin led a concert of the Music School Settlement, and Will Marion Cook, whose music was described in the program as "distinctly Negro and delightful," conducted musicians from the Washington Conservatory of Music. But New York's black community embraced more than the performed music at the Emancipation Celebration; they also reveled in the chance to dance to the music of Clef Club bands as African Americans had been doing at the Manhattan Casino for three years. The 150 Clef Club members

The Clef Club Orchestra, ca. 1913.

(Photographs and Prints Division, Schomburg Center for Research in Black Culture, The New York Public Library, Astor, Lenox and Tilden Foundations.)

provided dance music every afternoon and evening of the ten-day-long event.[29] Clef Club performances at the Manhattan Casino and Carnegie Hall had raised the respectability of black dance and black music so much that Harlem's leadership embraced these leisure pursuits, which had formerly been deemed disreputable.

The Carnegie concerts contributed to a surge in demand for black dance bands, and James Reese Europe used this enthusiastic demand to win rights for black musicians. Barred from the American Federation of Musicians' local union, African Americans would rarely be hired to entertain audiences. Instead hotel managers hired them at low wages for menial work like washing dishes or sweeping floors, but once there, the musicians had to perform for guests for tips.[30] Europe stipulated that Clef Club bands would only work for a fixed salary, would only entertain, and required that they would be compensated for travel, room, and board. The *Crisis* fully credited Europe for changing musicians' working conditions, explaining, "One would have to know how the Negro entertainers in cafes, hotels, at banquets, etc. were regarded before the organization of the Clef Club, and how they have been regarded since. Before they were prey to scheming head waiters and booking agents, now they are performers whose salaries and hours are fixed by contract."[31]

In return for fair contracts, Europe promised professionalism from his musicians. Not unlike Williams and Walker, who had written a rule book on public behavior for company members, Europe distributed a list of rules for Clef Club members. He established a dress code stipulating "tuxedos for engagements booked in advance and dark suits, white shirts, and bow ties for pick-up dates"—and as Tom Fletcher remembered, "no one was sent on a job if not dressed correctly."[32] In addition, Europe required some amount of maneuvering around racist stereotypes, since the increased demand for African American musicians did not eliminate the indignities suffered. Clef Club bands memorized all their music to reassure white audiences that blacks could not read music, thereby affirming that blacks were naturally musical rather than intellectual and creative. "I'd get all the latest Broadway music from the publisher," recalled pianist Eubie Blake, "and we'd learn the tunes and rehearse 'em until we had 'em all down pat." Disgusted with this practice, Blake lambasted "all the high-tone, big-time folks" who would say "isn't it wonderful how these untrained, primitive musicians can pick up all the latest songs instantly without being able to read music?"[33]

In Blake's view, Europe went overboard in tolerating abuse and endured humiliating situations that he and other Clef Club musicians could not. One such incident occurred after playing an all-evening private concert for the Wanamakers, when Europe asked their butler to see about getting dinner for the band. The waiter brought a "big china thing they use for soup," recalled Blake. "As soon as I tasted this stuff, I had to spit it out. And I see everybody else is doin' the same thing. This stuff, I'm still sure, is the water they washed the dishes in—soap, everything." Blake explained that the African American butler "thinks he ain't' like other Negroes" and was mad because he didn't "like no colored people to complain." Europe, though, was "eatin' the stuff just like it's soup," and Blake realized then that "Jim Europe didn't get where he is with the white folks by complainin'. At home or in the White House, it was all the same to him."[34] Europe's swallowing of abuse reveals the gritty reality that black musicians faced daily as they played the society party circuit—as well as how much Europe was willing to sacrifice to make his art public.

Suffering indignities paid off; Europe's music and his Clef Club bands were central to the Frolics and picnics held at the Manhattan Casino and to the rise of social dancing—an emerging popular entertainment in the 1910s. Americans were going out more and wanted to socialize in their leisure time. No longer content to only observe the show, they sought to fraternize with performers at after-hour clubs, and to try out the new dance steps themselves on the floors of a growing number of dance halls, palaces, and cabarets. The demand was so great after the Carnegie concerts that "the Clef Club had every amusement place outside of the legitimate theaters sewed up."[35] Given Europe's intimate link to the Clef Club, Lester Walton's claim that the Marshall Hotel actually introduced this style of entertainment rang true. "One hears much talk nowadays, even in 'Squeedunk,' about the cabaret," explained Walton in 1913, "but this form of entertainment was introduced at the Hotel Marshall many years before it came to New York as an imported product under the French *nom de plume*."[36] Europe himself surmised: "In the last few years a new type of Negro musician has appeared . . . due to the widespread popularity of the so-called modern dances, and the consequent demand for dance music of which the distinguishing characteristic is an eccentric tempo . . . such music usually takes the form of a highly syncopated melody, which in the early period of its development was known as 'rag-time' music. Since the dance is born of music it is quite apparent that the modern dance is a creature of the syncopated melody."[37] Black and white audiences embraced ragtime dance. Like the melodies and rhythms of the music, these "modern dances" seemed to mirror the temper of the times.

The popularity of dance music at the Emancipation Celebration, at Carnegie Hall, or in the quickly multiplying cabarets did not thrill everyone. In his New Year's message of 1914, Reverend A. Clayton Powell, pastor of the Abyssinian Baptist Church, echoed Du Bois's late-nineteenth-century fears that popular amusements threatened racial progress. Powell worried that "the Negro race is dancing itself to death," and he singled out the Emancipation Celebration for special criticism saying, "The race could not even celebrate its fifty years of progress without advertising 'Dancing every afternoon.'"[38] Several white publications also vehemently criticized the inclusion of Broadway tunes and dance music at Carnegie Hall. One *Musical America* reporter enjoyed the spirituals arranged and conducted by Harry T. Burleigh like "Deep River" and "Dig My Grave," but disliked Burleigh's inclusion of the popular "Why Adam Sinned," explaining, "It is impossible to applaud in Carnegie Hall his imitations of the vulgar dance music of Broadway originated by the tone poets of Tin Pan Alley." This reporter encouraged Europe "to give attention to a movement or two of a Haydn symphony and ignore the "tango and waltzes" that he "took obvious pleasure in conducting."[39] But Europe, like Cook before him, had little interest in playing the works of European composers. Both men remained committed to demonstrating that their music should be as highly regarded as any European opera.

Instead of playing European compositions, Clef Club members joined with the Frogs, combining their talents for a tour of black music and dance in August 1913. This much-hyped event marked the first time that Bert Williams performed with a black company since signing with the all-white Ziegfeld Follies in 1910. Aida Walker and S. H. Dudley, along with the Clef Club's Will Vodery and his Exclusive Society Orchestra, joined Williams on stage. The black press reminded its readers that this band was the same that caused "society folk to dance the tango and turkey trot with unwonted enthusiasm."[40] Whites and blacks turned out in droves to see this show. In Richmond, whites joined African Americans in the black section when the white section became overcrowded, and in Baltimore black patrons launched a boycott of the segregated theater, most likely hoping that their numbers would be large enough to change the theater's seating policy.[41] As much as black middle-class leaders like Du Bois sought to sort out "wholesome" from "hurtful" amusements, they, along with many whites, publicly acknowledged some popular music and dance as respectable by 1913. And clearly, public denunciations of modern commercial culture aside, both black and white middle-class folks found ways to shape the new urban leisure culture so that they, too, could dance.

Dancing Cheek-to-Cheek

The popularity of black dance styles predated the modern dance craze; it grew up alongside vaudeville and musical comedy. Williams and Walker had become well-known for their cakewalk routines with their early vaudeville act, and their company even made the dance a national fad in London when they toured there with *In Dahomey* in 1903. By then, hundreds of Americans, black and white, had become cakewalk enthusiasts. The cakewalk craze had more to do with the way George Walker danced with his partner and wife, Aida Overton, than with his comic routines with Williams, however, and it was Aida, and other black women like Dora Dean, who raised the bar of respectability on black dance. Done with a partner, the cakewalk included high stepping and exaggerated movements; the dance was a strut developed by enslaved Africans who mixed European dance styles like the waltz with their own dance steps to perform for (and subversively mock) slaveowners. Eager to learn the steps, and blind to the irony that the dance evolved out of satire, white women invited Aida Walker to teach them in the privacy of their homes. The press announced in 1903, "Product of Slavery Days Now the Craze of Fashion" among New York's Gilded Age elite—Astors' list of the top four hundred of society folk. One journalist marveled that Walker, "a well-known colored actress, has taken the '400' by storm by her graceful dancing . . . under her graceful leadership society has taken up the cakewalk until it is a perfect rage. Night after night the women of the younger society set glide and swing to the rhythmic strains of syncopated music."[42]

Aida Walker credited her generation with refining the dance and adding grace to its style. "The present cakewalk has been developed by the younger generation," she explained. "It has less of the old-time dignity and stiffness and more of grace and suppleness. It is devoid of the extravagant features of the earlier period." Part of this refinement had to do with eliminating some of the sexual overtones of the dance; as Walker instructed, "good form no longer permits a woman to place her foot on her partner's knee to have her shoe tied. The flourishing of handkerchiefs and that kind of coquetry is no longer popular with those who have developed the modern cakewalk."[43] Before James Reese Europe brought black music to Carnegie Hall, thus "legitimizing" it, Aida Walker had made the cakewalk respectable enough to inspire the Vanderbilts to seek dance instruction—news that in turn motivated Williams and Walker to publicly challenge them to a cakewalk competition. Predictably, the Vanderbilts did not respond.[44] As much as whites yearned to learn black dance styles, they did not wish to share their dance floors with African Americans. When whites like the Vanderbilts went out in public to dance, they did so in segregated spaces.

The segregated nature of public dance outlived the popularity of the cakewalk and became more evident with the prewar craze for so-called modern dances. As mentioned earlier, Aida Walker had earned attention for her cakewalk in *In Dahomey* (1902) and praise for her "Salome" with *Bandana Land* (1908), but her 1912 performance of "Salome" as a solo classical dance received criticism. One white critic called Walker the "best 'Salome' 'Tommy' dancer who ever hit Broadway on a warm day," referring to the Texas Tommy, an acrobatic partnered black dance (similar to the 1940s lindy hop) done in cabarets.[45] This critic categorized Walker's classical dance as social dance, as "low" culture, and made clear he thought black dance belonged in the dance hall rather than on the concert stage. By 1912, too, the dance craze was already under way. Americans, black and white, eagerly flocked to the city's dance halls and cabarets, more interested in trying out the steps themselves than watching black dancers perform.

In the early 1910s, one of the most popular black dancers, Ethel Williams, worked the vaudeville and cabaret circuits, and like Walker before her, discovered that whites sought her out for dance instruction, but did not want to share their dance floor with black people. Williams had begun her career in 1897 as a "pick"—a talented black child performer—hired to accompany headliners like Sophie Tucker and Eva Tanguay.[46] J. Leubrie Hill discovered Williams and hired her to dance with Johnny Peters in the *Darktown Follies*, a show that built itself around the new interest in dancing and whose success depended more on the expertise of the dancers than on a plot. She and Peters danced at Lafayette and Clef Club events uptown, as well as performed at Bustanoby's, a Broadway cabaret; they danced the

Aida Overton Walker and George Walker, 1905.
(Photographs and Prints Division, Schomburg Center for Research in Black Culture,
The New York Public Library, Astor, Lenox and Tilden Foundations.)

tango, the one-step, the waltz, the maxixe and the Texas Tommy, among others. Lauded as the strongest dancing act in vaudeville, Williams and Peters once exhausted themselves so much at a Clef Club bash that when they had finished, it was "impossible for them to respond to calls for more."[47] Ethel Williams recalled that in the *Darktown Follies*, "we had some wonderful dancers" who did "the Texas Tommy, and a fine cakewalk for the finale, but the most fun was the circle dance at the end of the second act. Everybody did a sort of sliding walk in rhythm with their hands on the hips of the person in front of them."[48] This dance, like the cakewalk, drew on aspects of the ring shout—a dance style derived from West African religious ritual—and makes clear the African and African American origins of the new dances sweeping the nation.[49]

Although the *Darktown Follies* was popular with Harlem audiences and attracted Broadway producers, it never made it to a Broadway stage—nor did Williams or Peters. Their dances, however, did. Florence Ziegfeld made the trek uptown and fell in love with the dance moves, particularly with the one known as "balling the jack," in which the dancer swivels her hips in a twisting motion. "I'd ball the jack on the end of the line every way you could think of," recalled Williams, "and when the curtain came down, I'd put my hand out from behind the curtain and ball the jack with my fingers." Black pianist and songwriter James P. Johnson wrote a song that included lyrics instructing dancers how to do the dance:

> First you put your two knees close up tight
> Then you sway 'em to the left, then you sway 'em to the right
> Step around the floor kind of nice and light
> Then you twis' around and twis' around with all your might
> Stretch your lovin' arms straight out in space
> Then you do the Eagle Rock with style and grace
> Swing your foot way 'round then bring it back
> Now that's what I call 'Ballin' the Jack.[50]

The Eagle Rock Baptist Church in Kansas City reputedly gave that dance move its name; the gesture of raising one's arms in space evolving from black religious devotion.[51] When Ziegfeld saw the *Darktown Follies*, he was so enamored with the dance movements that he brought Ethel Williams downtown to teach it to his dancers. "I went down to the New York theater and showed the cast how to dance it," she recalled. "They were having trouble." As one white critic told it, "The trouble is you have a might hard time getting white performers who can 'ball the jack' and do the 'Eagle Rock' as effectively as the colored performers."[52] Ziegfeld erased black authorship, never crediting Williams or Hill in the program. In addition, as Williams explained, "None of us was hired for the show and at that time I was supposed to be the best woman dancer in the whole country."[53]

White promoters frequently capitalized from black culture without giving credit or compensation to the innovators of the styles that drove American entertainment. Such "theft" of black culture helped launch its biggest white promoters—Irene and Vernon Castle, a couple who would become known for dancing to the tunes of James Reese Europe. After having seen Ethel Williams dance, Irene, who had long dreamed of a stage career, called her at home and asked that she teach her some of the steps.[54] No direct evidence exists showing whether Williams took her up on her offer, but Irene surely copied the steps she had seen Williams perform. The middle-class white woman from New Rochelle and her husband, Vernon, a British-born performer, brought these dances to Paris in 1912 where he was booked for a comedy engagement. His act failed, and the Castles struggled to make ends meet. Had they not traveled with Walter Ash, an African American employee whose skill at shooting craps kept them solvent, they might have been forced to leave Paris before "being discovered." With Ash supporting them, they developed the café act destined to bring the Castles fame on both sides of the Atlantic. Although they had never danced together professionally, the Castles drew on the modern dances from their New York social life. The turkey trot and grizzly bear thrilled Parisians, and soon the Castles were in demand in New York. They returned in late 1912 and worked in musical comedies, vaudeville, and most profitably, as exhibition dancers in the booming cabaret business. A second tour of Paris the following spring further increased their marketability in New York.[55]

Cabaret culture contributed to the Castles' rising fame. The standard New York cabaret act of performers emerging "spontaneously" from the audience to demonstrate their dances thrilled patrons and blurred the lines between audience and performer. Once on the dance floor, the paid exhibition dancers then invited audience members to join them. Racial segregation prohibited Ethel Williams and Johnny Peters from likewise emerging from the audience to perform. Turn-of-the-century black vaudevillians had successfully manipulated the politics of segregated theatrical seating by playing to two distinct audiences, but black dancers could not similarly negotiate the space of the cabaret. The lure of cabaret life was intimacy with performers, and the Castles' success lay, in part, in their ability to demonstrate that "the café was the place to become friendly with entertainers." Al Jolson, a Jewish immigrant blackface performer who made his career in the cabaret, used the runway to "get confidential with the audience by running up and down on this platform, stopping for a chat with people, and by kidding the audience and the performers in general."[56] While Jolson and other white performers found success performing in cabarets, no black entertainer, whether or not in blackface makeup, could regularly enter such a world where entertainment rested on that amount of physical and social intimacy. Some "well-dressed" whites may have felt somewhat relaxed about sitting next to "well-dressed" blacks in the orchestra at a Carnegie Hall fundraiser, but mixed-race dance audiences were not permitted; middle-class whites needed the guarantee of segregated public space to try out black dance styles.

Although segregated cabarets kept black dancers from rising to mainstream fame, black musicians were essential to both the Castles' celebrity and the white craze for modern dances. While the cabaret required segregated audiences, an all-male, all–African American band could be safely set apart from the audience while white dancers attempted the steps demonstrated by the Castles. Thus, James Reese Europe partnered with the Castles, and Clef Club musicians gave the dance craze its score. The performances began with the Castles' exhibition dance and followed with a dance contest where they "judged eager white couples on their ability to dance to the tune dictated by a black orchestra leader."[57]

The Castles further encouraged white participation in the dance craze by promoting themselves as having "refined" the popular dances from their original "primitive" forms. In 1914, the *New York Times* reported that the turkey trot of 1912 had "smacked strongly of the Dahomey-Bowery-Barbary Coast form of revelry, but since then it has been trimmed, expurgated, and spruced up until now it is quite a different thing." More than any other couple, the Castles are credited with transforming the turkey trot into what became known as the one-step. The Castles' version "was shorn of much of the arm pumping and body shaking of the original."

They "moderated the dips that revealed too much of the woman's leg . . . and placed women in a sexually suggestive position." The Castles wrote a book of instruction that told dancers: "Do not wriggle the shoulders, do not shake the hips . . . drop the turkey trot, the grizzly bear . . . these dances are ugly, ungraceful and out of fashion."[58] When they opened their dance studio, the Castle House, in 1914, they renamed their turkey trot the "Castle Walk." Years before, Aida Walker had already "refined" the cakewalk while instructing white women on a more graceful, less sexual dance style, and she had performed "Salome" as classical dance as part of the move by black artists to raise the respectability of black music and dance in public venues. Yet, along with "legitimacy," "refinement" had come to have racially charged meanings. While white Americans had sought privately to learn the dance steps that Aida Walker and Ethel Williams had mastered, they required the Castles to bring them out in public to dance.

Although descended from early vaudeville, the modern dance craze differed from its predecessor in that it rested on white admiration for black style rather than on derogation of black images. In the late nineteenth century, black vaudevillians had become stars by capitalizing on white racist desire to laugh at black caricatures on stage. Whites laughed at, pitied, and feared the black images fed to them by the amusement business. In this way, white audiences distanced themselves from black stereotyped imagery and reinforced their own sense of status as civilized—even as African American artists tried to show how they were not that which they portrayed. Ironically, through their skillful use of stage and sound, black artists succeeded in making black style and black art products of desire rather than of derision or repulsion. Twentieth-century whites still sought escape, a reprieve from the staid, rigid Victorian sensibilities that suppressed pleasure and abandonment. Indeed, "'Coon' songs peaked in the 1910s just as whites began to admit their deeper interest in the new impulses as something capable of being integrated into their own culture," and it was the cabaret that "relaxed boundaries between the sexes, between audiences and performers, between ethnic groups and Protestants, between black *culture* and whites."[59] By the 1910s, black performers had raised the bar on black music and dance so much that modern whites were no longer content to laugh at (performed) black ineptitude; rather, whites sought ownership over this new product of black style. Whereas late-nineteenth-century whites understood their civilized status through distance from blackness, by the 1910s, whites understood their status as modern through their ability to buy the blackness that the new culture of consumption produced. For the most part, however, whites did this without interacting with black artists or even acknowledging African Americans' contributions.

Since black music was essential to the dance craze, James Reese Europe did find ways to make music, earn money, and advance racial interests within the new cabaret culture—a culture that kept African American artists segregated but gave black music a central role. For Europe, opportunity lay with his association with the Castles, and he resigned from most of his responsibilities with the Clef Club in 1914, forming a new orchestra, the Tempo Club, devoted solely to providing music for the dancing duo. He maintained an organizing role with the Clef Club, but Will Vodery and Will Marion Cook took on larger roles conducting Clef Club bands. Europe's enormous success with the Castles and with organizing Clef Club musicians helped him "break the color line" in the local musician's union. Tensions in the all-white union had surfaced when the Castles insisted that Europe's Tempo Club band play for them at Hammerstein's Broadway vaudeville theater in January of 1914. The union feared that black orchestras would dominate theaters as they did the cabaret business. When white union members vociferously objected to blacks playing in the pit orchestra, the Castles refused to appear. Willie Hammerstein negotiated the dispute by bringing Europe's band on stage to perform, leaving the orchestra pit empty. At subsequent performances, the band occupied the pit. That March, the musician's union invited black musicians to join; Europe himself joined in the fall. Still, there remained vast inequities in pay; the battle for equal treatment was hardly over.[60]

Europe's success in marketing black music and his work with the Castles resulted in some of the more revealing and peculiar events of the dance craze. With the craze in full swing, Irene and Vernon Castle starred uptown at the Manhattan Casino in May and October of 1914, thus demonstrating their interpretations of black dance to Harlem's black audiences. The *Age* announced on its front page, "Tempo Club Gives Class Dansant before Big Throng" and by April 2, black and white patrons had reserved all the boxes and loges for the May event. J. Rosamond Johnson,

S. H. Dudley, and Abbie Mitchell all took part in the demonstration, and Will Marion Cook, W. E. B. Du Bois, Aida Walker, and the white music publisher Joseph Stern were among those who made up the "large and brilliant" audience. The boxes at the Manhattan Casino that night "were occupied by representative members of both races." In October, "not only did the Castles do their most attractive and interesting dances," reported the *Age*, "but at the end of their performance Mr. Castle advanced to the front of the stage and in a felicitous manner, with words appreciative of the services rendered by Mr. Europe and his orchestra, presented a bronze statue of himself and Mrs. Castle, showing them in characteristic tango pose." Europe and his band had not been told that this gift would be offered, and "the presentation took the boys by surprise." When the crowd urged Europe to speak, "the best the talented composer and conductor could do was to call on the orchestra to help him out by playing the 'Castle Walk,' a Europe song composed for and dedicated to the Castles." Over his lifetime Europe had swallowed so much of his anger while playing for white society that it is difficult to discern just how he felt receiving a bronze of the white dancers. The Castles were blind to the irony of the event and the presentation. After their performance, they personally supervised and judged a dance contest of nearly one hundred black couples and awarded "two massive silver loving cups as trophies to . . . the best exponents of the one-step and of the hesitation waltz."[61]

The Lafayette Theater hosted dance contests as well, but differences between the prizes at these contests, which were geared more to Harlem's working-class audiences, and those awarded by the Castles at the Manhattan Casino mirrored the differences in goods won at the Lafayette's "country store" and gifts given by the Frogs at their Frolics. Although the contests at both venues resembled those held in cabarets across the country, Lester Walton made sure to provide monetary prizes to winners at the Lafayette. He explained: The "management decided to give money to the winners instead of medals, believing that at this time that gold would be more acceptable."[62] Notably, Walton made his announcement only weeks after the Castles had given Europe the statue of themselves and had awarded black dance contestants silver cups at the Manhattan Casino. The monetary prizes were not insignificant for working-class New Yorkers; first place received ten dollars, second earned seven dollars and fifty cents, and third collected five dollars. Not unlike Harlem patrons who went to shows at the Lafayette hoping to return home with needed supplies, black dancers envisioned their night out as competition—if not exactly work—since winnings could well pay a month's rent or more.

Both white and black middle-class people distanced themselves from Victorian gentility in large part by participating in new leisure pursuits that carefully loosened and refigured racial and gender boundaries. Hungry for middle-class status, black patrons appreciated the new legitimacy awarded James Reese Europe and African American music through his affiliation with the Castles. Black artists had made black style a desirable consumer product, and the Castles became its best advertisement. But although this new desire for black entertainment meant earnings for working-class African Americans and enabled some middle-class blacks to cross the color line—at least temporarily—it allowed middle-class whites to appropriate black music and dance and call it their own without acknowledging the African Americans who created them. Thus the Castles, and whites generally, became arbiters of modernity as they appropriated black style—a dynamic well epitomized by the gift of white bodies bronzed in a tango pose.

As Ziegfeld and the Castles did to African American dance steps, Irving Berlin, a Russian Jewish immigrant, had already done to ragtime. In 1911, Berlin's "Alexander's Ragtime Band" was a big hit. While resembling more of a march than the syncopated rhythms of Scott Joplin or Will Marion Cook, the tune capitalized on the popularity of black music, dance, and cabaret trends. The song became so well-known so quickly that the Clef Club Orchestra was to play it at one of their Musical Melanges.[63] Three years later, with *Watch Your Step,* a Broadway show with a Berlin-authored score, white appropriation of black expressive culture was complete. The Castles starred in the show, which featured an orchestra made up of white musicians. It is unclear whether Europe was ever approached to do the music for the show, and one account has him resigning a few days before opening night. Based on Europe's work in white society, with the Castles, and earlier in black musical comedy, it is difficult to imagine him refusing the contract or resigning from this show without good reason. *Watch Your Step* became the most successful Broadway show that season, running for 171 performances—an especially remarkable feat since the 1914–1915 season had the lowest attendance American theater had experienced up to that time.

White management and white audiences seemingly preferred seeing whites perform music and dance credited to white artists. The Great White Way had finally headlined black expressive culture, but ironically, without employing any African Americans. Notably, the Castles brought the fox-trot, the new dance step that they had carefully worked out with James Reese Europe, to Broadway in this show and performed it without black musicians. The fox-trot's origins actually lay with W. C. Handy's song "Memphis Blues." Europe "would sit at the piano and play slowly the 'Memphis Blues,'" recalled Handy, and "he did this so often that the Castles became intrigued by its rhythm, and Jim asked why they didn't originate a slow dance adaptable to it." As Handy told it, "the Castles liked the idea and a new dance was introduced by them which in a magazine article they called the 'Bunny Hug,'" but quickly changed to the "Fox Trot." While whites raved about the new dance in *Watch Your Step,* Vernon Castle explained that the fox-trot was not new, "but had been danced by negroes, to his personal knowledge, for fifteen years."[64] This comment reveals that the Castles did acknowledge where they got their inspiration, but at the same time, they acquired black style for personal gain, barely crediting black innovators. The book they authored, *Modern Dancing,* included four chapters on dress alone, whereas music garnered only a three-page chapter—with no mention of Europe. In her autobiography, Irene barely mentioned Europe, noting only that he provided the music for their new dances and had been "one of the first to take jazz out of the saloon and make it respectable."[65] The Castles' talent and spectacle cannot be denied, but neither can their debt to black artists.

While Europe did not provide the music for Broadway's *Watch Your Step,* he and his Tempo Club Orchestra continued to perform with the Castles at private parties throughout the 1914–1915 season to a still-growing market—one that earned the Castles, at least, $5,000 a week. Europe explained in the *New York Tribune* that he supplied "a majority of the orchestras which play in the various cafes of the city and also at the private dances" and that African Americans were "peculiarly fitted for the modern dances . . . rhythm is something that is born in the negro, and the modern dances require rhythm above all else." As Europe maintained, "Both the tango and the fox-trot are really Negro dances, as is the one step. The one step is the national dance of the Negro, the Negro always walking in his dances."[66] Still, before World War I white audiences preferred to see how white performers incorporated such rhythm into their own dancing and singing—a choice that left African Americans generally offstage.

"Colorphobia" Hits the Stage

Although black arts played such a central role in the making of a modern American sensibility, black artists could not find their way back to Broadway, leaving Lester Walton to lament in 1913 that several stage acts would have made the big circuits had they emerged before "colorphobia hit the stage."[67] Black musical comedy might have spurred the dance craze, but whites no longer needed black performers once they decided that they could dance. The "term of exile" from Broadway had begun. Certainly, the deaths of some of its leading stars—deaths that broke up the major partnerships of Williams and Walker, and Cole and Johnson—dealt a blow to black musical comedy. But many other talented company members, like J. Leubrie Hill, who seemingly should have been able to capitalize on the earlier successes, could not attract Broadway's interest. "There is no colored star in a white theater except Mr. Bert Williams in vaudeville," wrote a *Freeman* critic in 1914, "and now the white man is saying that he is not a Negro." The *Darktown Follies* and similar shows did not make it out of Harlem nor off the black circuit, because whites were more interested in learning to sing and dance themselves. "White men and women are browning up, blacking up and turning up, and our colored men are training them to do the colored people's work," added the *Freeman* critic, "therefore there is nothing for our acts to do . . . big-time white women . . . have offered . . . much money" to black singers to "teach them how to do a coon song." One black performer refused to participate in white plagiarism of black art, saying, "I never teach a white woman something to make about six hundred dollars per week, when for the same thing, the manager would not give me fifty dollars," and he implored *Freeman* readers, "Let us look at all these things which are killing us every day."[68] Will Marion Cook had similarly protested the racism of Harry Von Tilzer, a music publisher who had published Cook's songs. With Cook's popularity, many other African American composers called on Tilzer, a trend that provoked his company's manager, Max Winslow, to complain to Cook, "Entirely too many spades come into the office." Cook, in turn, implored black performers to seek firms where their presence was "not only welcomed but eagerly sought." Moreover, after *Clorindy,* Cook never again published with Witmark and Sons, because "they robbed him terribly," and he sought legal redress as late as 1941 for songs he claimed Irving Berlin and others had stolen from him.[69]

Performers not only confronted new racial boundaries on the dance floor and the racism of music publishers; they also could not circumvent the segregated seating at Broadway theaters. The early stars made their way in the popular-priced houses of vaudeville with tickets ranging from five to twenty-five cents a show. The move to higher-priced houses presented African Americans with a particular dilemma. Most working-class blacks could not afford the dollar houses, and middle-class blacks preferred to frolic with the Frogs uptown than to pay higher prices in segregated theaters downtown. The Frogs had once considered trying to secure a downtown theater for one of their Frolics, but decided to stay at the Manhattan Casino, "thereby enabling hundreds to witness the performance who would find it impossible to secure admission in any of the local theaters."[70] Even Williams and Walker's *Bandana Land* had gotten off to a slow start in 1908 because, as a *Freeman* critic explained, the "high prices were unpopular" and "white people simply will not tolerate the black brother in their midst on the lower floor of these $1.50 houses, even if the colored people were able or inclined to separate themselves from that amount to see a show."[71]

Additionally, by the 1910s, black stage artists faced "the stranglehold the movies are getting on the public." The film industry further robbed black Americans of the possibilities for self-portrayal. When D. W. Griffith's racist classic *Birth of a Nation* was released in 1915, Walton joined the many editors who regularly denounced the film, reporting on protests around the country and lamenting that relatively little could be done about its distribution and popularity. But his film criticism had begun at least two years earlier, when he started to respond to images included in film shorts interspersed between live acts at vaudeville and variety theaters. He condemned one film that pictured flood victims in Memphis as comical, and denounced another of "a Negro woman . . . who was subjected to vigorous disinfecting by health officials" who "squirted a fluid down her throat in large doses." He lambasted films that producers marketed as "all colored" but which showed the "lazy, indolent type of Negro, who proceed to 'ball the Jack,' drink gin, shoot dice and steal watermelons."[72]

Not only was the abundance of racist imagery problematic, but the inexpensive admission fees for moving pictures also drew audiences away from full-length musical comedy. Between 1900 and 1908, the number of nickelodeons (storefront theaters where patrons paid a nickel to see a moving picture) rose from fifty to over five hundred. Cheaper than the average vaudeville show, these theaters attracted growing numbers of working-class patrons. "Cole & Johnson saw the handwriting on the wall and closed *The Red Moon* with its pretty name," explained Walton, "as the movies were, even then, making great inroads on popular-priced houses. And to-day the movies are now closing the $2 houses throughout the country, New York included." Moreover, not unlike the cabaret, the nickelodeons invariably ended up being white-only spaces, since as storefronts they were too small to house segregated audiences. Although white and black entrepreneurs attempted to set up all-black small moving picture theaters, none succeeded; one manager speculated that, in part, this was probably due to blacks wanting to see black actors.[73]

Vaudeville and variety theaters interspersed short films between live acts, so black audiences were subject to the film reels like the ones criticized by Lester Walton. But in many predominantly black theaters, black musicians hired to accompany the silent flicks often found ways to mediate the racist imagery for African Americans, not unlike the ways that black vaudevillians had earlier addressed black audiences in the balcony. As the soundtrack for predominantly white performances, some African American bands subverted racist imagery with what they chose to play—choices that often angered theater owners and critics. "During a death scene . . . you are likely to hear the orchestra jazzing away on 'Clap Hands, Here Comes Charlie,'" reported black columnist Dave Peyton in the *Defender,* complaining, "There is entirely too much 'hokum' played in our Race picture houses. It only appeals to a certain riff-raff element who loudly clap hands when the orchestra stops, misleading the leader to believe that his efforts are winning the approval of the entire audience."[74] Perhaps disgruntlement with this type of boisterous communication with audiences led Chicago's black-owned Pekin Theater to "discontinue the use of the moving pictures and talking machines which have been the attraction all summer."[75] Although perhaps similar in some ways to the culture fostered by early vaudevillians, this sort of audience participation was no longer what critics like Walton wanted; his goal was to raise the status of black performance and to attract black shows (and black audiences) to downtown theaters. Thus, Walton and other managers stressed decorum in audience behavior, much like Sylvester Russell had disparaged artists for their communication with "gods of the gallery."[76]

Walton's determination to attract Broadway's attention led him to blame the quality of actors as well as black audiences, and reflecting the tendency present in the uplift politics, he particularly singled out southerners. "Quite a large crop of colored acts have come from the South recently," wrote Walton, "and while many of them are very entertaining, there is every indication that they could be more so with more up-to-date songs." Further, he explained, "Many colored performers from the South, while they are good singers and dancers, often they find themselves at a disadvantage by reason of the material they bring East." Even more blatantly, on another occasion he announced that "colorphobia" was most severe downtown at Forty-second and Seventh, where "poor broken down actors with southern tendencies abound in numbers." A *Crisis* letter writer echoed Walton's concerns, reporting that "every town of any consequence, in the South, has its colored picture or playhouse, but I am sorry to say that the major portion of the young women and men entering this profession are ignorant, and aside from a natural talent for singing and dancing are all unqualified to appear before intelligent audiences."[77] While this criticism resembled comments reported for over a decade as to the demeanor of stage people, he and others noticeably began to identify uncouth, unintelligent behavior specifically with southerners.

Along with the continued stranglehold of Jim Crow, changes in the entertainment industry, in the generational shift of black communities, and in regional and class politics contributed to the "term of exile" of black artists from Broadway. The new black middle class was not content to view well-dressed African Americans onstage or in the balcony. Instead they desired a status equal to the white middle class: they wanted to sit in the orchestra side-by-side with well-dressed whites at Carnegie Hall. A group that established their own art forms, their own organizations, and their own burgeoning residential community in Harlem—complete with the Frolics at the Manhattan Casino—wanted to share equally with whites in the culture they had helped to create. They sought more alliances with the white middle class, and segregation in New York's theaters began to have as much to do with class position as it did with race.

Still, Walton and his colleagues held fast to their earlier formula of producing black-themed musical comedy that appealed to both black and white audiences, albeit for different reasons. They wanted to raise the respectability and acceptance of black art on their own terms; they stayed true to their desire to produce music and dance that emerged from black America, and they did not as a rule shift their method to performing European classics to prove their worth. Seeking to bring back the heady days of *In Dahomey,* they premiered in October 1915 *Darkydom,* a show that Walton hoped would spark a "Negro renaissance."[78] Combining the talents of black musical comedy's heyday, Will Marion Cook wrote the score, Jesse Shipp did the staging, and Walton himself directed the show. James Reese Europe helped with the music and conducting, S. H. Dudley with the casting, and Abbie Mitchell performed. Even the "new" stars, Flournoy Miller and Aubrey Lyles, two Fisk students, had earlier made their names as authors of Ernest Hogan's *Oysterman.* Of the stars still living, only Bert Williams and the Johnson brothers were absent from *Darkydom*'s roster. Williams had committed to Flo Ziegfeld's Follies, James Weldon had left stage life, and J. Rosamond was busy with the Colored Music School Settlement. It was up to "Miller & Lyles," reported the *Age,* "to perform for the stage and for their race . . . to them has fallen the lot to pick up where Williams & Walker left off, thereby making the colored musical show a commodity greatly to be desired instead of a drug on the market, and it is believed that they will take advantage of this golden opportunity and make good."[79]

The style of *Darkydom* replicated that of the earlier productions by following one plot throughout the show and relaying the story through dialogue, song, and dance. Miller and Lyles played two vagabonds caught stealing a ride on the private train of the railroad company president. When the engineer pulls the train over in order to remove the offenders, a wreck with an approaching train traveling on the same track is avoided. The president wants to give the pair a five-hundred-dollar reward, but because they fear that he will have them arrested, they flee into the local town of Mound Bayou, Mississippi. The play primarily takes place in this all-black town with the railroad president's valet searching for the stowaways, and two local tramps trying to scam the money for themselves.[80]

Darkydom's setting also continued the tradition of the earlier shows. Hardly of interest to white audiences, Mound Bayou would have been well-known to black audiences as the Mississippi town founded by former slave Isaiah T. Montgomery in 1887. Mound Bayou was one of a few all-black towns, and it testified to the resilience of black Americans' post-bellum search and struggle for a homeland after Reconstruction's failures. The town had so impressed W. C. Handy that he brought a band there from Memphis at his own expense for the grand opening of their oil mill.[81] *Darkydom*'s libretto, although no longer extant, probably contained references specific to Mound Bayou and directed at African American audiences, much in the same way that Williams and Walker's shows commented on Africa. Harlem's opening night audience responded well to the story; as one critic reported, there was "nothing startling about the music," but the story line was well received.

On opening night a "long line of automobiles" filled the streets, reminding one reporter "of similar scenes enacted nightly in front of the big downtown theaters." Harlem's new residents eagerly supported the show, just as black performers and critics had hoped. As local admirers adorned the stage with "many large and beautiful floral pieces," it seemed that the much-desired "renaissance" had arrived.[82] But the formula that had much success in white America in 1903 did not bear fruit in 1915. White managers and song publishers, including Irving Berlin, music publisher Joseph F. Stern, and *Bandana Land* financier F. Ray Comstock, ventured uptown for the show's opener, but only John Cort, a white independent theater owner, liked the show enough to book it for a small circuit of theaters.[83] While Walton had conceived of this show the same year that Irving Berlin had planned *Watch Your Step*, *Darkydom* did not hit the stage until the year after Berlin's show, and by then Broadway was even less interested in black musical comedy.

Despite the turnout on opening night and interest in the plot, *Darkydom* failed to thrive in the black community as well. In 1915 many black critics could not get beyond the show's name to consider the script. *Birth of a Nation* had opened that year, adding momentum to black stereotypes; consequently any black production referencing potentially stereotypical language or imagery was considered even more harmful to racial progress. The Baltimore *Afro-American Ledger* criticized *Darkydom*, along with the *Darktown Follies* and another black musical revue, *Broadway Rastus*, for their chosen names. "It is perfectly true that these shows do not belie their names; they abound in catchy songs, dances whose degree of suggestiveness depends on the character of the audience, and scenes in which the simple country Negro finds himself at a disadvantage when matching wits with his city brother."[84] Even the *Freeman* chimed in, "If the management consults the wishes of the masses of the colored patrons of the show, they will select a title that will convey the idea that it is a genuine Negro entertainment without using a term that is banned by polite society."[85] Unlike a decade earlier, "darky" was no longer an acceptable stage term. Walton, however, defended the choice of language as a business decision to insure bookings in white-owned theaters, explaining to the Baltimore critic, "When the colored theatrical public is big enough to support colored shows and the patronage of white theatregoers is not needed, when cities of large colored population, Baltimore in particular, can furnish large theatres under colored management, conditions, then, will be such that the friendly consideration of white managers will not be necessary. But today a colored attraction can get only three weeks consecutive booking in colored houses—the Lafayette Theatre, New York; the Standard Theatre, Philadelphia, and the Howard Theatre, Washington."[86]

While Walton defended the show's naming, he still expressed serious concern in the press about the persistence of certain remnants from the minstrel stage as well as ambivalence about the continued use of blackface makeup. Moreover, he had already begun a campaign to require capitalization of the word "Negro," and had declared that the days that black acts had to include blackface or an act of theft must end, asking, "How much good are they doing for blacks with exaggerated character?"[87] But even though he raised concerns about stereotyped imagery, he continued to praise the work of Bert Williams who performed during these years in the Ziegfeld Follies in blackface; more significantly, in *Darkydom*, Miller and Lyles both performed in blackface makeup, as they would later do in *Shuffle Along* in 1921. Nor did Walton find problematic the title of a song he wrote for *Darkydom*—"Mammy." "No disparagement is meant" by the song's title, wrote Walton, "even if some confuse the word with the obnoxious term 'nigger,' a term many of our people unfortunately use in conversation with one another."[88] Although clearly ambivalent about terminology as he strove to attract white managers and audiences, Walton held fast to his goal of bringing black art back downtown with *Darkydom*.

Walton had staged this show at an impossible time, however. Not only had *Darkydom* opened during the same year as *Birth of a Nation*, but six months before opening night, too, the sinking of the *Lusitania* had intensified America's war preparedness, shifting the country's attention away from musical farce. The war-inspired migration lured more than half a million black southerners north, forever changing cities like New York and Chicago. Harlem's population and geographic area expanded; black audiences grew exponentially. The influx led to increased tensions with white urban communities—over jobs, housing, and community space that erupted into a series of race riots, notably in East St. Louis (1917) and Chicago (1919)—hardly conditions under which Broadway would embrace black song and dance. Black New Yorkers were also less interested in hokum: Harlem's leaders, for example, launched a silent protest parade after the East St. Louis riot to raise awareness of racial violence. The race riots, along with other postwar political and labor unrest, kept America preoccupied through the summer of 1919 and alert to the fear of communism in the wake of the Russian Revolution. But by 1921, with a successful government suppression of the strike wave and "Red Scare," as well as an economic boom fueled in large part by the auto industry, America was ready for the Jazz Age. Postwar confidence and prosperity inspired a more eager, more adventurous white consumption of black style. Although black artists had inspired a bohemian white market for black arts in the past, wartime experiences and the 1920s economic boom helped make that market a mass market. Now whites from a variety of backgrounds danced to the music of black artists to make their claim as modern Americans.

Black Moderns

While *Darkydom* did not take off that year, it arguably made it to Broadway in 1921 reformulated as *Shuffle Along*, a show that starred Miller and Lyles in blackface as the same duo they had played in their vaudeville act and in *Darkydom*—Sam Peck and Steve Jenkins. Eubie Blake and Noble Sissle provided *Shuffle Along*'s music. (James Reese Europe had died in 1918 from a knife wound suffered during a fight with a band member.) Although most of the leading stars from the earlier generation had died by 1921, *Shuffle Along* rested on their work and legacy. John Cort, the white promoter who had earlier liked *Darkydom*, brought *Shuffle Along* to his Broadway theater on May 23, 1921, and it ran for over five hundred performances, grossing close to eight million dollars before closing in 1923.[89]

Shuffle Along's Broadway audiences were 90 percent white, but the production was received enthusiastically by black Americans as well. James Weldon Johnson credited this show with breaking the color line in New York City's theaters, even though two-thirds of the orchestra seating had still been reserved for whites. One critic noted that on opening night "colored patrons were noticed as far front as the fifth row."[90] W. E. B. Du Bois heartily endorsed the performance, and Langston Hughes remembered it as a "honey of a show . . . to see *Shuffle Along* was the main reason I wanted to go to Columbia." Hughes continued, "When I saw it, I was thrilled and delighted. From then on I was in the gallery of the Cort Theatre every time I got a chance."[91] Notably, Hughes sat in the gallery—maybe because of the high price of orchestra tickets or because he wanted to sit with other black patrons in the balcony.

That both Du Bois and Hughes reveled in *Shuffle Along* demonstrates just how much turn-of-the-century performers had accomplished. Although not fond of vaudeville, Du Bois had by this point left his Victorian sensibility behind, and he applauded the production whose stars performed in blackface and whose popularity lay in the singing and dancing of chorus girls. Hughes, nineteen years old when he saw *Shuffle Along*, may have imagined possibilities similar to those envisioned by Paul Laurence Dunbar who, at practically the same age, had ventured to the Chicago World's Fair. Still, their experiences were remarkably different. Born in 1902, and unburdened by the dilemma faced by Dunbar and Cook, Langston Hughes came of age enamored by their successes. Black art and black style—although not black artists—had become foundational to America's popular culture and, arguably, to white conceptions of American modernity. While in the last years of the nineteenth century Dunbar had struggled for cultural representation against perverse images of blackness on the midway, in 1921 Hughes enjoyed a successful black-produced Broadway show—the culmination of a generation's cultural work.

Although *Shuffle Along* was an updated and slightly altered combination of *Darkydom* and the *Darktown Follies*, it was geared more toward marketing black culture than toward asserting black perspectives. Clef Club member Eubie Blake composed the music for *Shuffle Along*, and in some ways, the differences between his songs and those of Will Marion Cook highlight the generational shift, as well as the influence of the burgeoning white market for black culture. Many artists, including Blake and Duke Ellington, sought advice from Cook, whom they embraced as the found-

Still from *Shuffle Along*, 1921. Flourney Miller and Aubrey Lyles are in the center;
the chorus includes Allegretti Anderson, Wilsa Caldwell, Goldie Cisco,
Adelaid Hall, Evelyn Irving, and Margaret Weaver.

(Helen Armstead-Johnson Theater Photograph Collection, Photographs and Prints Division,
Schomburg Center for Research in Black Culture, The New York Public Library,
Astor, Lenox and Tilden Foundations.)

ing father of syncopated music. Blake actually called Cook "Pop," while
Ellington called him "Dad." Once in 1906, Cook introduced Blake to music publishers and tried to sell them Blake's first rag. When the publisher
asked for changes in the music, Cook "flared up and said, 'What right have
you, to question my protégé? How long have you been a Negro?'" Blake's
song, however, went unpublished until 1919; by then, Blake had changed
the more nationalist name that Cook had chosen for his song, "Sounds of
Africa," to the more marketable "Charleston Rag."[92]

American modernity rested, in part, on a new equation of continued racial segregation and the popularity of black expressive culture—thus testifying to the success of black performing artists who brought black musical
comedy to Broadway, black music to Carnegie Hall, and black dance to society ballrooms. By carefully negotiating the market for black images and
singing so-called coon songs, Williams and Walker and their cohort sold
America on the beauty and value of black music—something W. E. B. Du
Bois had yearned to do with the "sorrow songs." Wary of popular amuse-

ments, Du Bois did not then understand how much the artists' project paralleled his own—how well aware they were of the "double consciousness" he had so eloquently named in *The Souls of Black Folk*. For over a decade, black artists had carefully orchestrated their productions in an attempt both to stay true to an expressive black authenticity and to open doors to further performances in a white-dominated performance world.

The cultural acceptance of the 1920s, however, did not translate into the kind of racial advancement that African Americans had hoped for. Instead Jim Crow whites found ways to embrace black culture without acknowledging—and while continuing to destroy—black lives. White America's understanding of modernity rested, in part, on the co-opting of black style—but in the process, this style was tainted by Jim Crow (and gender) politics. As white moderns imagined themselves "playing in the dark," they distinguished themselves from their more Victorian parents; they cast black Americans as their id and rushed to the dance floor—something they needed black music and dance to do, but refused to do with black dancers in their midst. Thus even though black moderns had created the very sound and style underlying modernity, they were still dehumanized as "primitive" and "other"—albeit in a "kinder, gentler" way than their minstrel predecessors had been.

Even so, as black artists created, performed, and struggled at the dawn of the twentieth century, they gave meaning and definition to black modernity. Their lives demonstrate how a double consciousness was lived daily. They critiqued the black middle class even while they were some of its most visible representatives. They celebrated Africa and their connections to the continent, even though they mocked emigration and loudly proclaimed themselves American. And they created comedy built on racist ideas while critiquing racism. In many ways, turn-of-the-century black performers were beyond "modernity": they well understood the racist underpinnings of a modern culture they had helped create, and were hard at work exposing its foundations.

Hokum Redux

As BOHEMIAN VISIONARIES, Williams, Walker, and their cohort of artists saw America's fixation on being entertained as an opening into
a Jim Crow public culture that excluded, segregated, and mocked them.
These muckraking performers played stereotypes as a way of showing the
falseness of the images, imagining that whites as well as blacks would see
their performances as exposés of American racism. Black vaudevillians ex-
ploited the ubiquity of the minstrel mask and used humor to combat the
rhetoric of violence just when mass entertainment businesses were taking
off and just when Americans began devoting more time and energy to
play.[1] For this generation of eccentrics and intellectuals, the art of entertainment promoted social change along with laughter; it elevated the race
along with black music and dance; it soothed souls hungry for black song;
and it provided jobs, skills, and professional opportunities during hard
times for African Americans.

At the beginning of the twentieth century, too, black popular artists
sold white Americans on the idea that black style was the very essence of
cool. Fascinated by technology, nightlife, urbanity, and most of all themselves, white moderns turkey-trotted their way into a new era. White cabaret crowds congratulated themselves on their mastery of black dance
styles—a dramatically different moment than when white midway patrons
twenty years earlier had reinforced their sense of themselves as civilized by
collecting cotton-ball souvenirs from plantation exhibits and trembling
before depictions of "Darkest Africa."

During a period marked by a passionate self-obsession and replete with new spaces for self-presentation, black entertainers marketed black arts through hokum—putting on the minstrel mask just enough to be seen and heard. Certain they could demonstrate the complexity of black life through their staging of race but not yet fully aware of how painful the interplay between artistic expression and market distribution would quickly become, black performers enacted fictive types onstage to debunk racial mythologies offstage. Black artists negotiated consumer culture through hokum, trusting that once whites heard the tunes, they would not only move to the music, but also embrace its creators as equals. Hokum became a kind of weapon—a dissemblance, a disguise of authenticity, a marketing of fictions—a technique nurtured by the modern era's heightened focus on self-presentation and a necessary survival strategy for black Americans negotiating Jim Crow.

The cakewalk, Williams and Walker's "Two Real Coons," and W. C. Handy's musicians' strike all involved hokum, but wearing "the mask that grins and lies" has a much longer history. Its antecedents existed at least from the beginnings of the Atlantic slave trade; as the lyrics of one song explain, "Got one mind for white folks to see / 'Nother for what I know is me / He don't know, he don't know my mind." Black writers like Zora Neale Hurston, Richard Wright, and Ralph Ellison have commented similarly on this kind of manipulation of audience, but perhaps Alberta Roberts's 1970s comment is most on point for black vaudevillians: "The biggest difference between us and white folks," she said, "is that we know when we are playing."[2]

With hokum, turn-of-the-century black performers broke the color line on Broadway and in the musician's union, but they could not break the color line defining America's social and political landscape or the one deeply embedded in white America's psyche. White Americans embraced black culture, but they did so to elevate their own status rather than to accept African Americans as equal citizens. White audiences coveted black music and black dance—in effect, black style. But with the mechanics of reproduction still in the hands of white-owned businesses, black artists could not substantially control the marketing of their wares. At every turn black artists and critics tried to shape black theater in ways that would earn black Americans equal status, but they did not count on the depths of white determination to buy and own black culture.

White commitment to controlling black art and representation was particularly fierce in part because white peoples' interpretation of the "other" was essential to their own sense of themselves as civilized in the nineteenth century and modern in the twentieth. Social Darwinist displays of the world's cultures maintained Anglo-Saxon dominance; even in the Chicago World's Fair the midway's geographical distance from the White City assured whites of how far away they had come from a "savage" and "primitive" past. With Jim Crow firmly in place at home and American imperial expansion rampant abroad, white Americans, confident of their global hegemony and secure in their segregated spaces, emulated black cultural styles as they loosened Victorian constraints in celebration of a twentieth-century hopefulness and exuberance. White Americans embraced the Castles for their interpretation of black dance, and congratulated themselves for their own modernity—a sensibility they enjoyed with their Jim Crow café society, their (constrained) public sexuality, and their ability to maintain "civility" even while "losing" themselves in rhythms of black music.

The commodification of black music and dance that accelerated with the prewar fox-trot thus resulted in a level of commodification of black style, of black culture, and in a sense, of black identity. By the time of the Jazz Age and Harlem Renaissance of the 1920s, "all the Negro artist had to do," asserted historian Nathan Huggins, "was to be true to himself, and he would be honored and sustained . . . how grand it was to be valued not for what one might become—the benevolent view of uplift—but for what was thought to be one's essential self, one's Negro-ness." But the more that whites sought to incorporate black style, the more interested and invested they were in what depictions of "Negro-ness" they would buy. Since white audiences desired black imagery that "freed" them from their nineteenth-century social conventions, they sought black cultural products that countered their Victorian notions of civility, met their expectations of black primitivism, and fulfilled their desires for an essential "Negro-ness." This market and desire presented black artists with a more complex white audience, one that demanded a fictive authenticity it could embrace. "Even if Harlem blacks had wanted it," assessed Huggins, "there was little chance they would have been left alone to shape and define their own identity."[3] In some ways, then, success trapped African American artists. Their hokum had hooked white audiences, so much so that white moderns could not fully exist without the rhythms of black music or the movements of black dance. Thus, African Americans had to grapple with two interdependent identities to be both "modern" and black. This predicament highlights another aspect of Du Boisian double consciousness: "Modern" identity itself was hybrid—an unequal mixing of black and white culture that rested on the segregation and continued oppression of black people.

White America's consumer culture did not simply rob black artists of the material rewards for their artistic production; it also denied black Americans the cultural rewards of self-presentation. Mass markets and mass production limited the ability of black artists like James Reese Europe and Ethel Williams to sell their own wares, while helping white imitators like Irene and Vernon Castle to take center stage. Bert Williams's success led him to his job with the white Ziegfeld Follies, but his onstage act with this company affirmed white assumptions; white chorus girls "balled the jack" and danced the Eagle Rock that they had learned from Ethel Williams while Bert Williams, in blackface, portrayed a buffoonish character that met white expectations. There is a reason that the story of Thomas "Daddy" Rice stealing his minstrel act from a sole black man, "jumping Jim Crow," has survived throughout the years.[4] The apocryphal story—minstrelsy's foundation myth—serves as an allegory for America's popular culture. Over the years, white artists like Irving Berlin and Elvis Presley have profited from their interpretations of black song, while the grossly unequal relations of production have kept black artists from accessing their share of the market.

This familiar selling of black culture and style was the historic backdrop against which generations of black artists worked as they sought to claim ownership of their art and culture. The younger generation of Harlem Renaissance artists rebelled against the acute attention to audience reception. Exhausted with white desires for the "primitive" and the black middle-class search for "uplifting" imagery that would advance the race, several black artists who came of age in the 1920s decried the practice of making art that had propaganda or profit as its overriding goal. In his 1926 manifesto "The Negro Artist and the Racial Mountain," Langston Hughes declared: "If white people are pleased we are glad. If they are not, it doesn't matter. We know we are beautiful and ugly too. The tom-tom cries and the tom-tom laughs. If colored people are pleased we are glad. If they are not, their displeasure doesn't matter either . . . We build our temples for tomorrow, strong as we know how, and we stand on top of the mountain, free within ourselves." Even more loudly rejecting consumer culture, artists associated with the 1960s Black Arts Movement embraced black power politics and saw their artistic work as likewise supporting black peoples' desire for self-determination and nationhood. They gave up the "futile practice of speaking to whites" and instead understood the "Black Aesthetic" as "a means of helping black people out of the polluted mainstream of Americanism."[5] For this generation of black artists, art was revolutionary; Black Arts Movement artists hoped to mobilize mass black populations with their expressive culture. Their cultural production was not for white markets—soul was not for sale.

Perhaps late-twentieth-century rap and hip-hop artists—with their mix of play, profit, and politics—more closely resembled turn-of-the-century vaudevillians in their intent and hopes. Coming of age in the post–Civil Rights era and in the postindustrial landscape of America's cities, many young rappers—not unlike the young actors and musicians who had come of age with the rise of Jim Crow—sought to make money, create art, and critique racism. Rap and hip-hop artists often mixed their art with humor, consumerism, and politics, and like their vaudeville predecessors, they took hold of the "double-edged sword" of "mass-mediated culture" to make their expressive cultures and political messages public.[6] Commercial distribution of their music meant as well that white suburban audiences often thrilled to rap music and performance for a "romance" with "ghetto" life, not unlike white orchestra patrons who desired depictions of the "primitive" at the beginning of the twentieth century. While during this period more than a few black rappers and producers benefited significantly from commercial distribution of their wares (far more than their ragtime predecessors), they continued to grapple with a market for racist stereotypes—a demand that could quickly drown out the combination of art and social commentary that had inspired much of the genre.

The late-twentieth-century mechanics of production made the commodification of art a virtual overnight phenomenon, but the commodification of popular culture happened quickly even in the days of Williams and Walker. While the comedy duo led their company in Broadway productions and tried to set up their own publishing house, thousands of spin-off "coon song" singers and writers joined white publishers to reproduce racist imagery as fast as it could be sold; the black publishing house Gotham-Attucks went out of business in the period of a few years. Will Marion Cook's and Billy Kersands's renditions of black song—and the mix of politics, art, and commerce that interested turn-of-the-century black performers—disappeared under the onslaught of white consumption of "coon songs," plantation minstrelsy, and Aunt Jemima products.

The Williams and Walker generation succeeded in selling America on black song and dance, but their expressive culture was never just a song, a dance, or a joke. Rather, these black performers had created an aesthetic sense and public style—one that revolved around black music and dance, but whose influence cannot be easily understood by reading the lyrics to "Who Dat Say Chicken in Dis Crowd?" or tapping a foot to "Darktown Is Out Tonight." The moment the joke, song lyric, or syncopated rhythm left its black creator, producers turned it into a static consumer product to be bartered over, bought, and sold, hardly representative of the intent of the artists or the moment of authenticity that inspired their work. Certainly, Bert Williams cannot be understood by looking at his work in the white Ziegfeld Follies. A lone photograph of a blackfaced Williams, or even one of the few moving images of his solo film performances, erases the politics and hokum in his art. Without gallery laughter and applause, without his banter with George Walker, and without the support of a large black cast, Williams's art has no perceptible hokum, no bright moment, no instant that makes clear that Williams and Walker—and their black audiences—knew when and how they were playing.

In the business of fantasy, dreams, and imagination, and coming of age with the rise of Jim Crow, turn-of-the-century black performers envisioned a better place. With a mix of African-descended and American-lived culture, their creative moment was a hybrid one—a bricolage—of European classics, American minstrelsy, *The Wonderful Wizard of Oz*, and the "souls of black folk." As a totality, the creative work of turn-of-the-century black performers—their vaudevillian mix of comedy and politics—was popular culture. These artists expressed the despair, desires, hopes, and dreams of their generation. At the heart of their art was an authentic mix of black music, dance, and humor—and an authentically black approach to the marketing of black culture. Rather than a capitulation to racism, hokum was their modus operandi. These black artists played with language, melodies, and self-presentation; they composed black song and choreographed black dance; they entertained themselves as well as their black audiences; they provoked laughter in the face of tragedy; and they derived pleasure from their attempt to loosen the stranglehold of Jim Crow on their lives and cultural expression. Hardly intended to be direct representations, their expressive cultures were enactments of their feelings, thoughts, and imaginations. These black artists used hokum for more than just fooling white folks; they deftly employed it to reimagine their world.

NOTES ◆ INDEX

Notes

Abbreviations

BRTC   Billy Rose Theater Collection, The New York Public Library
KAC   Keith/Albee Collection, Special Collections, University of Iowa, Iowa City
SC   Schomburg Center for Research in Black Culture, The New York Public Library

Introduction

1. Among the books that address some of these artists are Reid Badger, *A Life in Ragtime: A Biography of James Reese Europe* (New York: Oxford University Press, 1995); Susan Curtis, *The First Black Actors on the Great White Way* (Columbia: University of Missouri Press, 1998); Ann Douglas, *Terrible Honesty: Mongrel Manhattan in the 1920s* (New York: Farrar, Straus, and Giroux, 1995); Nathan Irvin Huggins, *Harlem Renaissance* (New York: Oxford University Press, 1971); David Krasner, *A Beautiful Pageant: African American Theater, Drama and Performance in the Harlem Renaissance, 1910–1927* (New York: Palgrave MacMillan, 2002); David Krasner, *Resistance, Parody, and Double Consciousness in African American Theatre, 1895–1910* (New York: St. Martin's Press, 1997); Lawrence Levine, *Black Culture and Black Consciousness: Afro-American Thought from Slavery to Freedom* (New York: Oxford University Press, 1977); David Levering Lewis, *When Harlem Was in Vogue* (New York: Oxford University Press, 1979); Thomas L. Riis, *Just before Jazz: Black Musical Theater in New York, 1890–1915* (Washington, D.C.: Smithsonian Institution Press, 1989); Mel Watkins, *On the Real Side: Laughing, Lying, and Signifying* (New York: Simon and Schuster, 1994); Shane White and Graham White, *Stylin' African American Expressive Culture from Its Beginnings to the Zoot Suit* (Ithaca, N.Y.: Cornell University Press, 1998); and Allen Woll, *Black Musical Theatre: From Coontown to Dreamgirls* (Baton Rouge: Louisiana State University Press, 1989).

2. Leon L. Litwack and Steven Hahn have recently explored the ways that south-

ern African Americans of this generation responded to the particularities of the rise of Jim Crow. See Hahn, *A Nation under Our Feet: Black Political Struggles in the Rural South from Slavery to the Great Migration* (Cambridge, Mass.: Belknap Press of Harvard University Press, 2003); and Litwack, *Trouble in Mind: Black Southerners in the Age of Jim Crow* (New York: Knopf, 1998).

3. Selected significant books on minstrelsy and stereotype include W. T. Lhamon, *Raising Cain: Blackface Performance from Jim Crow to Hip Hop* (Cambridge, Mass.: Harvard University Press, 1998); W. T. Lhamon, *Jump Jim Crow: Lost Plays, Lyrics, and Street Prose of the First Atlantic Popular Culture* (Cambridge, Mass.: Harvard University Press, 2003); Eric Lott, *Love and Theft: Blackface Minstrelsy and the American Working Class* (New York: Oxford University Press, 1993); M. M. Manring, *Slave in a Box: The Strange Career of Aunt Jemima* (Charlottesville: University of Virginia Press, 1998); Robert Toll, *Blacking Up: The Minstrel Show in Nineteenth-Century America* (New York: Oxford University Press, 1974); and Alexander Saxton, *The Rise and Fall of the White Republic: Class Politics and Mass Culture in Nineteenth-Century America* (London: Verso, 1990).

4. W. C. Fields was Williams's colleague and reportedly close friend during his years with the Ziegfeld Follies. See Ann Charters, *Nobody: The Story of Bert Williams* (New York: Macmillan, 1970), 11; quotation is from Mabel Rowland, ed., *Bert Williams, Son of Laughter: A Symposium of Tribute to the Man and His Work* ([1923?]; repr., New York: Negro Universities Press, 1969), 94.

5. Gail Bederman, *Manliness and Civilization: A Cultural History of Gender and Race in the United States, 1880–1917* (Chicago: University of Chicago Press, 1995); Lewis Erenberg, *Steppin' Out: New York Nightlife and the Transformation of American Culture, 1890–1930* (Chicago: University of Chicago Press, 1981); John Kasson, *Amusing the Millions: Coney Island at the Turn of the Century* (New York: Hill and Wang, 1978); David Nasaw, *Going Out: The Rise and Fall of Public Amusements* (New York: Basic Books, 1993); Kathy Peiss, *Cheap Amusements: Working Women and Leisure in Turn of the Century New York* (Philadelphia: Temple University Press, 1986).

6. Willard B. Gatewood Jr., ed., *Slave and Freeman: The Autobiography of George L. Knox* (Lexington: University of Kentucky Press, 1979), 26–32. Knox relocated the press to larger quarters and made this claim in 1893.

7. Linda O. McMurry, *To Keep the Waters Troubled: The Life of Ida B. Wells* (New York: Oxford University Press, 1998), 192–197.

8. Kevin Gaines, *Uplifting the Race: Black Leadership, Politics and Culture in the Twentieth Century* (Chapel Hill: University of North Carolina Press, 1996); Deborah Gray White, *Too Heavy a Load: Black Women in Defense of Themselves, 1894–1994* (New York: Norton, 1999); Evelyn Brooks Higginbotham, *Righteous Discontent: The Women's Movement in the Black Baptist Church, 1880–1920* (Cambridge, Mass.: Harvard University Press, 1993); Victoria W. Wolcott, *Remaking Respectability: African American Women in Interwar Detroit* (Chapel Hill: University of North Carolina Press, 2001).

9. Erenberg, *Steppin' Out;* Susan A. Glenn, *Female Spectacle: The Theatrical Roots of Modern Feminism* (Cambridge, Mass.: Harvard University Press, 2000); Kasson, *Amus-*

ing the Millions; Nasaw, *Going Out;* Christine Stansell, *American Moderns: Bohemian New York and the Creation of a New Century* (New York: Metropolitan Books, 2000).

1. Minstrel Men and the World's Fair

1. W. C. Handy, *Father of the Blues: An Autobiography by W. C. Handy,* ed. Arna Bontemps (New York: Da Capo Press, 1941), 24–26.

2. Ibid.

3. *Toledo Blade,* January 29, 1906, Williams and Walker clipping file, BRTC.

4. Virginia Cunningham, *Paul Laurence Dunbar and His Song* (New York: Dodd, Mead, 1947), 92–94; Eugene Levy, *James Weldon Johnson: Black Leader, Black Voice* (Chicago: University of Chicago Press, 1973), 37; Christopher Robert Reed, *All the World Is Here: The Black Presence at the White City* (Indianapolis: Indiana University Press, 2000), 8–9, 58, 76.

5. Levy, *James Weldon Johnson,* 40, n. 36; Reed, *All the World Is Here,* 101–104.

6. Robert Rydell, *All the World's a Fair* (Chicago: University of Chicago Press, 1984), 40, 42–43; James Weldon Johnson, *The Bulletin of Atlanta University,* quoted in Christopher Robert Reed, "The Black Presence at 'White City': African and African American Participation at the World's Columbian Exposition, Chicago, May 1, 1893–October 31, 1893," Paul V. Galvin Library, Digital History Collection, http://columbus.gl.iit.edu/reed2.html (accessed May 13, 2005); James Gilbert, *Perfect Cities: Chicago's Utopias of 1893* (Chicago: University of Chicago Press, 1991), 121; John Kasson, *Amusing the Millions: Coney Island at the Turn of the Century* (New York: Hill and Wang, 1978); David Nasaw, *Going Out: The Rise and Fall of Public Amusements* (New York: Basic Books, 1993), 3.

7. Rydell, *All the World's a Fair,* 46.

8. Reid Badger, *The Great American Fair: The World's Columbian Exposition and American Culture* (Chicago: Nelson Hall, 1979), 107–109; Nasaw, *Going Out,* 66–72.

9. Kasson, *Amusing the Millions,* 23–28.

10. George A. Dorsey, "Man and His Works," *Youth's Companion,* World's Fair, 1893, as quoted in Lee D. Baker, *From Savage to Negro: Anthropology and the Construction of Race, 1896–1954* (Berkeley: University of California Press, 1998), 253. n. 18; Rydell, *All the World's a Fair,* 5–8.

11. Rydell, *All the World's a Fair,* 47–48; Badger, *The Great American Fair,* 80–81.

12. As quoted in the American Social History Project (ASHP) film *Savage Acts* (New York: American Social History Project, 1995); Nasaw, *Going Out,* 78; Gail Bederman, *Manliness and Civilization: A Cultural History of Gender and Race in the United States, 1880–1917* (Chicago: University of Chicago Press, 1995), 35; Rydell, *All the World's a Fair,* 47–49, 62, 65.

13. Nasaw, *Going Out,* 74–79, 91–94; Rydell, *All the World's a Fair,* 68–69; Lester Walton, "The 'African Dodger,' a Menace to the Race," *New York Age,* February 1, 1917.

14. Mitch Kachun, *Festivals of Freedom: Memory and Meaning in African American Emancipation Celebrations, 1808–1915* (Boston: University of Massachusetts Press, 2003).

15. Reed, *All the World Is Here*, 117; *Cleveland Gazette*, March 25, 1893, and *Huntsville Gazette*, May 6, 1893, as quoted in August Meier and Elliott Rudwick, "Black Man in the 'White City': Negroes and the Columbian Exposition, 1893," *Phylon* 26 (1965): 354.

16. M. M. Manring, *Slave in a Box: The Strange Career of Aunt Jemima* (Charlottesville: University of Virginia Press, 1998), 74–75.

17. W. T. Lhamon, *Raising Cain: Blackface Performance from Jim Crow to Hip Hop* (Cambridge, Mass.: Harvard University Press, 1998), 180–195; W. T. Lhamon, *Jump Jim Crow: Lost Plays, Lyrics, and Street Prose of the First Atlantic Popular Culture* (Cambridge, Mass.: Harvard University Press, 2003), 1–19; Eric Lott, *Love and Theft: Blackface Minstrelsy and the American Working Class* (New York: Oxford University Press, 1993), 8–9, 15–18, 22–24 (quotation of song lyric "Eb'ry time I weel about," from first song sheet edition in the early 1830s, is on p. 23); Robert Toll, *Blacking Up: The Minstrel Show in Nineteenth Century America* (New York: Oxford University Press, 1970), 28; and Marshall Stearns and Jean Stearns, *Jazz Dance: The Story of American Vernacular Dance* (New York: Da Capo Press, 1994), 39–40. Shane White discusses black performers in New York before the rise of T. D. Rice and American minstrelsy in *Stories of Freedom in Black New York* (Cambridge, Mass.: Harvard University Press, 2002).

18. Toll, *Blacking Up*, 54–57; Lott, *Love and Theft*, 5–6; Alexander Saxton, *The Rise and Fall of the White Republic* (London: Verso, 1990); Manring, *Slave in a Box*, 67.

19. Henry Sampson, *Blacks in Blackface: A Sourcebook on Early Black Musical Shows* (Metuchen, N.J.: Scarecrow Press, 1980), 171, 388–391; Toll, *Blacking Up*, 200, 256; Manring, *Slave in a Box*, 69; Tom Fletcher, *One Hundred Years of the Negro in Show Business* (New York: Burdge & Co., 1954), 62; Handy, *Father of the Blues*, 17.

20. Manring, *Slave in a Box*, 69–70.

21. Toll, *Blacking Up*, 201–209, 262–263; Fletcher, *One Hundred Years of the Negro in Show Business*, 94; Thomas L. Riis, *Just before Jazz: Black Musical Theater in New York, 1890–1915* (Washington, D.C.: Smithsonian Institution Press, 1989), 23–24.

22. Unidentified clippings, *Black America* clipping file, BRTC.

23. Rydell, *All the World's a Fair*, 87, 119, 146–147; on "acting naturally" and the quotation by Salisbury about "attempting affectation," see unidentified clippings from *Black America* clipping file, BRTC; for Salisbury's description of the participants, see *Boston Transcript*, July 1895, clipping file, BRTC. For Dundy's training of participants, see Nasaw, *Going Out*, 77–78; for the myth of Aunt Jemima, see Manring, *Slave in a Box*, 76–78.

24. Rydell, *All the World's a Fair*, 67; *St. Louis Republic*, Saturday, August 6, 1904, as reproduced in Phillips Verner Bradford and Harvey Blume, *Ota Benga: The Pygmy in the Zoo* (New York: St. Martin's, 1992), 252.

25. Emmett J. Scott, "The Louisiana Purchase Exposition," *Voice of the Negro*, as quoted by Baker, *From Savage to Negro*, 64; quotation from *Frank Leslie's Popular*

Monthly is in Baker, *From Savage to Negro,* 58; *Harper's Weekly,* August 19, 1893 edition as cited in Rydell, *All the World's a Fair,* 55.

26. George Walker, "The Real 'Coon' on the American Stage," *Theater Magazine,* August 1906, Williams and Walker clipping file, BRTC.

27. Frederick Douglass, "Haiti and the Haitian People: An Address Delivered in Chicago, Illinois, on 2 January 1893," *The Frederick Douglass Papers: Series One, Volume Five, 1818–1895,* eds. John W. Blassinghame, C. Peter Ripley, Lawrence N. Powell, Fiona E. Spiers, and Clarence L. Mohr (New Haven, Conn.: Yale University Press, 1979), 509–510.

28. *Topeka Call,* May 7, 1893, and *Indianapolis Freeman,* April 15, 1893, as quoted in Meier and Rudwick, "Black Man in the 'White City,'" 360.

29. Marva Griffin Carter, "The Life and Music of Will Marion Cook," Ph.D. diss., University of Illinois, Urbana-Champaign, 1988, 32–33; Cunningham, *Paul Laurence Dunbar and His Song,* 99–109; for quotation by Cook, see Will Marion Cook, Autobiographical Notes, Mercer Cook Papers, Moorland-Spingarn Research Center, Howard University; for Dunbar's comment, see Ida B. Wells, *Crusade for Justice: The Autobiography of Ida B. Wells,* ed. Alfreda M. Duster (Chicago: University of Chicago Press, 1970), 117–118.

30. Carter, "The Life and Music of Will Marion Cook," 12; William S. McFeeley, *Frederick Douglass* (New York: Norton, 1991), 370–371; Cunningham, *Paul Laurence Dunbar and His Song,* 95–99.

31. For all quotations in the paragraph, see *Indianapolis Freeman,* April 15, 1893, as quoted in Meier and Rudwick, "Black Man in the 'White City,'" 356.

32. Meier and Rudwick, "Black Man in the 'White City,'" 357; Rydell, *All the World's a Fair,* 52; Robert Rydell, ed., *The Reason Why the Colored American Is Not in the World's Columbian Exposition* (1893; repr., Urbana: University of Illinois, 1999), xiii, 8.

33. *Cleveland Gazette,* July 15, 22, 1893; *Topeka Call,* July 15, 1893, Wells as quoted in Meier and Rudwick, "Black Man in the 'White City,'" 359–360; drawing is reproduced in Rydell, *All the World's a Fair,* 54; for the minstrel show, see Toll, *Blacking Up,* 263.

34. *Indianapolis Freeman,* April 15, 1893 and *Chicago Inter Ocean,* August 22, 1893, as quoted in Meier and Rudwick, "Black Man in the 'White City,'" 359.

35. Wells, *Crusade for Justice,* 116, 119; Mary Church Terrell, *A Colored Woman in a White World* (New York: Simon and Schuster Reprint, 1996), 110–111.

36. Reed, *All the World Is Here,* 52. Kachun, *Festivals of Freedom,* 55.

37. Edwin Redkey, *Black Exodus: Black Nationalist and Back-to-Africa Movements, 1890–1910* (New Haven, Conn.: Yale University Press, 1969), 182–183.

38. Cunningham, *Paul Laurence Dunbar and His Song,* 104; Dunbar, "Colored Soldiers," as published in Lida Keck Wiggins, ed., *The Life and Works of Paul Laurence Dunbar* (New York: Kraus Reprint, 1975), 171.

39. *Topeka Call,* September 9, 1893; *Cleveland Gazette,* September 16, 1893, as quoted in Meier and Rudwick, "Black Man in the 'White City,'" 361.

40. Wells, *Crusade for Justice,* 118–119; Paul Laurence Dunbar, "Frederick

Douglass," in Wiggins, *Life and Works of Paul Laurence Dunbar,* 139; Meier and Rudwick, "Black Man in the 'White City,'" 360–361; *Cleveland Gazette,* August 26, 1893, as quoted in Carter, "The Life of Will Marion Cook," 31.

41. Quoted in Thomas Riis, "Bob Cole: His Life and His Legacy to Black Musical Theater," *Black Perspective in Music* 13 (Fall 1985): 137; *Indianapolis Freeman,* September 20, 1890, printed in Henry T. Sampson, *Blacks in Blackface: A Sourcebook on Early Black Musical Shows* (Metuchen, N.J.: Scarecrow Press, 1980), 7; Mel Watkins, *On the Real Side* (New York: Simon and Schuster, 1994), 143.

42. Nasaw, *Going Out;* Robert W. Snyder, *Voice of the City: Vaudeville and Popular Culture in New York* (New York: Oxford University Press, 1989).

43. "Classic music" as quoted in Susan Curtis, *Dancing to a Black Man's Tune* (Columbia: University of Missouri Press, 1994), 49–50; for the *Chicago Inter Ocean* quotation, see James Gilbert, *Perfect Cities* (Chicago: University of Chicago Press, 1991), 128–129.

44. Isidore Witmark and Isaac Goldberg, *The Story of the House of Witmark: From Ragtime to Swingtime* (New York: Da Capo Press, 1976), 122, 169; all quotations are in Edward Berlin, *King of Ragtime: Scott Joplin and His Era* (New York: Oxford University Press, 1994), 11, 21; for a discussion of Joplin at the fair, see Curtis, *Dancing to a Black Man's Tune,* 46–47.

45. Handy, *Father of the Blues,* 35–36, 149.

46. Alain Locke, *The Negro and His Music* (1936; repr., New York: Da Capo Press, 1969), 59.

47. Handy, *Father of the Blues,* 62.

2. Vaudeville Stages and Black Bohemia

1. Although some of these accounts conflict in their details, they all attest to the violence perpetrated and that artists were targeted. See James Weldon Johnson, *Black Manhattan* (1930; repr., New York: Atheneum Press, 1969), 127; James Weldon Johnson, *Along This Way* (New York: MacMillan, 1933), 157–158; Roi Ottley and William Weatherby, eds., *The Negro in New York* (New York: New York Public Library, 1967), 167; undated clipping, *New York Telegraph,* with the headline "All Coon Photos Alike to Boy Jeffs," Williams and Walker clipping file, BRTC.

2. *New York Journal* as printed in Henry T. Sampson, *The Ghost Walks: A Chronological History of Blacks in Show Business, 1865–1910* (Metuchen, N.J.: Scarecrow Press, 1988), 221–222; the *New York Dramatic Mirror* reported on August 25, 1900, that Walker and Hogan had a "hot time in the Old town"; for Dunbar's claims of being drugged and robbed the night of the riot, see *New York Times,* August 20, 1900; for other accounts of the riot, see Citizen's Protective League, *Story of the Riot* (New York: Arno Reprint, 1969); Gilbert Osofsky, *Harlem: The Making of a Ghetto* (New York: Oxford University Press, 1969), 46–52; and Jervis Anderson, *This Was Harlem, 1900–1950* (New York: Farrar Straus Giroux, 1981), 43–45.

3. When an African American man, Arthur Harris, discovered Robert Thorpe, a white plainclothes New York City policeman, accosting his wife, he went to her rescue. Thorpe hit him with his club and Harris retaliated with an ultimately fatal penknife wound to the abdomen. After Thorpe's funeral on August 15, 1900, a white mob gathered, and a fight broke out between an African American, Spencer Walters, and a white man, Thomas J. Healy. Before long, a group of whites attacked Walters and marauding whites, including several members of the New York Police Department, mobbed the city. Ottley and Weatherby, *Negro in New York,* 166.

4. Allen Woll, *Black Musical Theatre: From "Coontown" to "Dreamgirls"* (Baton Rouge: Louisiana State University Press, 1989), 7; Mel Watkins, *On the Real Side* (New York: Simon and Schuster, 1994), 150; Henry Sampson, *Blacks in Blackface: A Sourcebook on Early Black Musical* Shows (Metuchen, N.J.: Scarecrow Press, 1980), 8.

5. Robert W. Snyder, *Voice of the City: Vaudeville and Popular Culture in New York* (New York: Oxford University Press, 1989), 26–32; David Nasaw, *Going Out: The Rise and Fall of Public Amusements* (New York: Basic Books, 1993), 20–27.

6. Managers' Report Books, 1902–1914, KAC.

7. David Nasaw, *Going Out,* chapter 5.

8. Watkins, *On the Real Side,* 143–144; Ann Charters, *Nobody: The Story of Bert Williams* (New York: MacMillan, 1974); quotation is from Marshall Stearns and Jean Stearns, *Jazz Dance: The Story of American Vernacular Dance* (New York: Da Capo Press, 1994), 197.

9. Will Marion Cook, "Clorindy, the Origin of the Cakewalk," *Theatre Arts,* September 1947, as reprinted in Eileen Southern, *Readings in Black American Music* (New York: Norton, 1971), 223.

10. *New York Morning Telegraph,* quoted in the *New York Age,* July 6, 1911, emphasis mine; Manager's Report Books, May 28, 1906, October 19, 1903, December 8, 1902, December 22, 1902, and September 19, 1904, KAC.

11. Sampson, *Blacks in Blackface,* 381–383; Manager's Report Books, New York, October 13, 1902, September 28, 1905, Pittsburgh, October 9, 1905, New York, July 17, 1905, Boston, July 24, 1905, and Cleveland, October 16, 1905, KAC.

12. For the burlap sack story, see Mabel Rowland, ed., *Bert Williams, Son of Laughter: A Symposium of Tribute to the Man and His Work* (1923; repr., New York: Negro Universities Press, 1969), 158; the Hogan story is in Tom Fletcher, *One Hundred Years of the Negro in Show Business* (New York: Burdge & Co., 1954), 141; and the Elk pin anecdote can be found in *Indianapolis Freeman,* November 14, 1903. For more stories of violence endured, see W. C. Handy, *Father of the Blues: An Autobiography by W. C. Handy,* ed. Arna Bontemps (New York: Da Capo Press, 1941), 43–46, and Robert Toll, *Blacking Up: The Minstrel Show in the Nineteenth Century America* (New York: Oxford University Press, 1970), 220–222.

13. *Indianapolis Freeman,* March 14, 1908. This story was earlier published in the *Toledo Courier,* December 20, 1907, but without the drink invitation.

14. *Indianapolis Freeman,* July 25, 1903.

15. Aida Overton Walker, *Colored American Magazine* 9 (October 1905): 571–575.

16. *Indianapolis Freeman,* January 13 and 27, 1906; Anderson, *This Was Harlem,* 18.

17. George Walker, "The Real 'Coon' on the American Stage," *Theater Magazine,* August 1906, Williams and Walker clipping file, BRTC.

18. Snyder, *Voice of the City,* 59. In the 1880s and 1890s, the offices of prominent white vaudeville theater proprietors John Koster and Albert Bial were at Twenty-third Street; B. F. Keith's offices were at Twenty-sixth and Broadway in a white residential neighborhood known as Madison Square.

19. *Indianapolis Freeman,* July 27, 1907.

20. James Weldon Johnson, *Along This Way* (New York: MacMillan, 1933), 171, 175.

21. Johnson, *Along This Way,* 171, 195; *Indianapolis Freeman,* December 8, 1906. The Marshall was the scene of a Thanksgiving party whose participants included Ernest Hogan, Will Marion Cook, and a secretary to Booker T. Washington.

22. *Indianapolis Freeman,* November 26, 1904.

23. Reid Badger, *A Life in Ragtime* (New York: Oxford University Press, 1995), 27.

24. James Weldon Johnson, *Autobiography of an Ex-Colored Man* (1912; repr., New York: Penguin, 1990); Paul Laurence Dunbar, *Sport of the Gods* (New York: Arno Reprint, 1969); *New York Age,* July 9, 1908.

25. *New York Age,* July 9, 1908; Ottley and Weatherby, *Negro in New York,* 157.

26. Lewis Erenberg, *Steppin' Out: New York Nightlife and the Transformation of American Culture, 1890–1930* (Chicago: University of Chicago Press, 1981), 22–23; Ottley and Weatherby, *Negro in New York,* 145. Ottley also notes that there was a back room with a piano and tables used by both performers and patrons. It is unclear where he acquired this description, because one very much like it appears in Johnson's fictional *Autobiography of an Ex-Colored Man,* which Johnson first published anonymously in 1912. Johnson was probably describing the same establishment; see *Indianapolis Freeman,* January 13, 1906, and January 27, 1906. For Harrison Stewart on Walker, see *New York Age,* July 9, 1908.

27. Anderson, *This Was Harlem,* 15, 26–29; Willard B. Gatewood, *Aristocrats of Color: The Black Elite, 1880–1920* (Bloomington: Indiana University Press, 1990), 105, 192–197.

28. *New York Age,* March 26, 1908.

29. John Hope Franklin and Alfred A. Moss Jr., *From Slavery to Freedom: A History of African Americans,* 7th ed. (New York: Knopf, 1994), 310; Robin D. G. Kelley and Earl Lewis, *A History of African Americans* (New York: Oxford University Press, 2000), 345, 355; Joe William Trotter, *The African-American Experience* (Boston: Houghton Mifflin, 2001), 379.

30. Marvin Griffin Carter, "The Life and Music of Will Marion Cook," Ph.D. diss., University of Illinois, 1988, 1–21.

31. *Indianapolis Freeman,* June 22, 1907.

32. Eric Ledell Smith, *Bert Williams: A Biography of the Pioneer Black Comedian* (Jefferson, N.C.: McFarland, 1992), 1–4. Accounts differ as to whether Williams actually attended Stanford as well as to why he left. He told one reporter that he left to begin working when his father "suddenly lost his money." Unidentified clipping, Williams and Walker clipping file, Robinson Locke Collection, folder 2593, BRTC.

33. For Dunbar, see *The Collected Poetry of Paul Laurence Dunbar,* ed. and with an introduction by Joanne M. Braxton (Charlottesville: University Press of Virginia, 1993), x–xi; for Overton see Susan A. Glenn, *Female Spectacle: The Theatrical Roots of Modern Feminism* (Cambridge, Mass.: Harvard University Press, 2000); for Mitchell, see autobiographical notes, Mercer Cook Papers, Moorland-Spingarn Research Center, Howard University.

34. *New York Age,* August 10, 1911; Thomas L. Riis, *Just before Jazz: Black Musical Theater in New York, 1890–1915* (Washington, D.C.: Smithsonian Institution Press, 1989), 26; Johnson, *Along This Way,* 12.

35. *Indianapolis Freeman,* May 7, 1904, June 9, 1900.

36. Ibid., July 25, 1903.

37. Ibid., March 24, 1900, July 11, 1903, October 19, 1907.

38. Unidentified clipping dated April 29, 1903, Robinson Locke Collection, folder 2461, BRTC; postcards, Helen-Armstead Johnson Collection, SC; *New York Age,* August 24, 1905; Sampson, *Blacks in Blackface,* 397–401.

39. Fletcher, *One Hundred Years of the Negro in Show Business,* 316–319; Handy, *Father of the Blues,* 24–26, 116–117.

40. Paul Laurence Dunbar, *Sport of the Gods,* 87, 94.

41. Snyder, *Voice of the City,* 107–109; *Indianapolis Freeman,* November 30, 1907.

42. *New Republic,* 1922, as quoted in Snyder, *Voice of the City,* 104–105,

43. Both quotations are from ibid., 104–105, 127.

44. *New York Times,* April 20, 1910, quoted by Woll, *Black Musical Theatre,* 51.

45. "The Shoofly Regiment" at the Globe Theater, Boston, August 27, 1907, unidentified clipping, clipping file, Harvard Theater Collection, Houghton Library, Harvard University; unidentified clipping, *Mr. Lode of Koal,* Williams and Walker clipping file, BRTC.

46. *New York Telegraph,* February 27, 1906, Williams and Walker clipping file, BRTC. For a similar description, see *New York Age,* April 30, 1908. Snyder reports on different responses from different parts of the house with cheap versus expensive seats, but makes no note of Jim Crow seating, though some of his evidence comes from a 1903 show by a black act "The Watermelon Trust." See Snyder, *Voice of the City,* 107.

47. Managers' Report Books, Providence, September 28, 1902, Boston, June 23, 1903, Philadelphia, November 18, 1907, KAC.

48. Unidentified clipping, Helen-Armstead Johnson Collection, SC; *Brooklyn Eagle* review reprinted in *New York Age,* April 30, 1908.

49. The story line recorded here regarding *Bandana Land* appears in many different reviews. See, for example, *Variety,* February 22, 1908, Williams and Walker clipping file, BRTC; *Indianapolis Freeman,* February 13, 1909; and *New York Dramatic News,* February 15, 1908.

50. Several unidentified clippings, Williams and Walker clipping file, Robinson Locke Collection, folder 2593, BRTC; for the comments by black critics, see *Indianapolis Freeman,* February 13, 1909, and February 15, 1908.

51. Bert Williams Jokebooks, Manuscripts Division, SC.

52. Ibid.

53. Aida Overton Walker, undated clipping from the *Chicago Herald*, Williams and Walker clipping file, BRTC; Johnson, *Autobiography of an Ex-Colored Man*, 14–15; *Indianapolis Freeman*, December 27, 1902.

54. Lyrics to "Swing Along," published in Marva Griffin Carter, "Life and Music of Will Marion Cook," Ph.D. diss., University of Illinois, Urbana-Champaign, 1988. Sheet music is available in *African American Sheet Music, 1850–1920*, Sheet Music Collection, John Hay Library, Brown University.

55. *Indianapolis Freeman*, October 26, 1901; *New York Age*, January 5, 1911; Report Book, March 9, 1914, Cleveland, KAC.

56. *Chicago Daily News*, November 9, 1909, Williams and Walker clipping file, Robinson Locke Collection, folder 2593, BRTC.

57. Unidentified article by Eric P. Waters, clippings, writings about Will Marion Cook, Mercer Cook Papers, Moorland-Spingarn Research Center, Howard University.

58. *Indianapolis Freeman*, December 21, 1901. The Williams and Walker Company also received a huge homecoming and send-off when they toured London; see *Indianapolis Freeman*, May 9, 1903, July 4, 1903 and July 11, 1903.

59. For performances in Utah, see *Indianapolis Freeman*, May 31, 1902; for performances in Oregon, see *Indianapolis Freeman*, May 3, 1902, and *Chicago Daily News*, November 9, 1909; for the "empty seats" quotation, consult Williams and Walker clipping file, BRTC.

60. Paul Laurence Dunbar, *Sport of the Gods*, 101, 104–105, 177; Dudley as quoted in Sampson, *The Ghost Walks*, 383–384. Cole and Johnson were at the debut of Williams and Walker's *In Dahomey* in Stamford, Conn.; see *Indianapolis Freeman*, September 27, 1902, and August 22, 1903.

61. *The Telegraph*, September 20, 1901, reprinted in Henry Sampson, *The Ghost Walks*, 237; *New York Age*, April 2, 1908; for the quotation about Black Patti's Troubadours performance see *Indianapolis Freeman*, January 30, 1904. The *Indianapolis Freeman* article made no specific mention that the audience for Black Patti's Troubadours was black, but it seemed to be assumed.

62. *Indianapolis Freeman*, November 25, 1899; unidentified clipping, November 19, 1899, George Walker clipping files, Harvard Theater Collection, Houghton Library, Harvard University; Mary Church Terrell, *A Colored Women in a White World* (1940; repr., New York: Simon and Schuster, 1996), 247–248; *Indianapolis Freeman*, September 17, 1904.

63. Report book, Philadelphia, September 21, 1903, KAC; unidentified clipping, *Mr. Lode of Koal*, Williams and Walker clipping file, BRTC.

64. *New York Age*, January 5, 1911.

65. Unidentified clipping, Williams and Walker clipping file, BRTC; *New York Age*, November 2, 1911.

66. *New York Age*, January 25, 1912.

67. Woll, *Black Musical Theatre*, 72.

68. *Indianapolis Freeman*, January 4, 1902; *New York Age*, February 13, 1908; Robin

D. G. Kelley, *Race Rebels: Culture, Politics, and the Black Working Class* (New York: Free Press, 1994), Chapter 3.

69. *Indianapolis Freeman,* June 16, 1900. While Hogan won only $2,250 of the $586,000 he had sued for, this case does show that use of stereotype did not translate into acceptance of a Jim Crow state; *New York Age,* July 6, 1911; Walton quoted in *New York Age,* November 23, 1911.

70. Evelyn Brooks Higginbotham, *Righteous Discontent: The Women's Movement in the Black Baptist Church, 1880–1920* (Cambridge, Mass.: Harvard University Press, 1993), 8–10; Farah Jasmine Griffin, *"Who Set You Flowin'?": The African American Migration Narrative* (New York: Oxford University Press, 1995), 9; Robin D. G. Kelley explains that similarly in the Jim Crow South, segregation law ironically facilitated the development of barbershops, bars, churches, and even alleyways as "black" space; see Kelley, "'We Are Not What We Seem': Rethinking Black Working-Class Opposition in the Jim Crow South," *Journal of American History* 80 (June 1993): 79. For scholarship documenting this era as one of black activism and struggle, see Charles Payne and Adam Green, eds., *Time Longer than Rope: A Century of African American Activism, 1850–1950* (New York: New York University Press, 2003).

71. Higginbotham, *Righteous Discontent,* 8–10; Elsa Barkley Brown, "Negotiating and Transforming the Public Sphere: African-American Political Life in the Transition from Slavery to Freedom," in Black Public Sphere Collective, *The Black Public Sphere: A Public Culture Book* (Chicago: University of Chicago Press, 1995), 114–115.

72. Elsa Barkley Brown describes a decline in the authority of the church in the late nineteenth and early twentieth centuries—the same period during which rose the secular world of commercial amusement—in her "Negotiating and Transforming the Public Sphere," 134.

73. *New York Age,* March 12, 1908, emphasis mine; *Indianapolis Freeman,* April 20, 1901; Veronica Adams, "The Dramatic Stage as an Upbuilder of the Races," *Chicago Inter Ocean,* January 17, 1909, Bert Williams clipping file, SC; Ida B. Wells, *Crusade for Justice: The Autobiography of Ida B. Wells,* ed. Alfreda M. Duster (Chicago: University of Chicago Press, 1970), 289–295.

74. Aida Overton Walker quoted in the *New York Age,* June 11, 1908; the George Walker quote is in Veronica Adams, "The Dramatic Stage as an Upbuilder of the Races," *Chicago Inter Ocean,* January 17, 1909, Bert Williams clipping file, SC; *New York Age,* October 26, 1911.

75. *Indianapolis Freeman,* October 10, 1903; *Chicago Record,* October 2, 1907, Ernest Hogan clippings, Robinson Locke Collection, folder 717, BRTC.

76. James Weldon Johnson, *Along This Way,* 218–221.

77. Booker T. Washington praises Bert Williams in *American* 70 (September 1910), 600–604, included in *Booker T. Washington Papers,* ed. Louis R. Harlan (Urbana: University of Illinois Press, [1972–1989]), 388–391; the "encouraging letters" quotation is from unidentified clipping, February 8, 1906, Williams and Walker clipping file, BRTC; on Washington's clerk attending the Marshall, see *Indianapolis Freeman,* December 8, 1906, and February 15, 1908; see also David Levering Lewis, *W. E. B. Du Bois: Biography of a Race* (New York: Henry Holt, 1993), 431.

78. *Indianapolis Freeman,* February 8, 1908.

79. W. E. B. Du Bois, *The Souls of Black Folk* (New York: Vintage Books/Library of America, 1990), 8; Paul Laurence Dunbar, *Life and Works of Paul Laurence Dunbar* (New York: Kraus Reprint, 1975), 186.

3. The "Coon Craze" and the Search for Authenticity

1. "Who Dat Say Chicken in Dis Crowd?" sheet music in *African American Sheet Music, 1850–1920,* Sheet Music Collection, John Hay Library, Brown University; lyrics are published as well in Marva Griffin Carter, "Life and Music of Will Marion Cook," Ph.D. diss., University of Illinois, Urbana-Champaign, 1988.

2. Carter, "Life and Music of Will Marion Cook," 360; Will Marion Cook, "Clorindy, the Origin of the Cakewalk," *Theatre Arts,* September 1947, as reprinted in Eileen Southern, *Readings in Black American Music* (New York: Norton, 1971); Mitchell is quoted in Mercer Cook, "From *Clorindy* to the Red Moon," miscellaneous clippings, Theater Papers, Helen Armstead Johnson Collection, Manuscript Division, SC.

3. Cook wrote that Grandpa Lewis had been born free, was a wagon-maker and blacksmith by trade, and was "highly respected." At the same time, he mentions that his grandfather was "a former slaveholder, a hard and, at times, brutal man" and details the severity of the beatings he was to receive in Tennessee. Unless noted otherwise, Cook's descriptions of his early years in this chapter can be found in Will Marion Cook, "The Young Will Marion," as published in Carter, "Life and Music of Will Marion Cook," 386–421.

4. Will Marion Cook, Autobiographical Notes, Mercer Cook Papers, Moorland-Spingarn Research Center, Howard University.

5. Willard Gatewood, *Aristocrats of Color: The Black Elite, 1880–1920* (Chicago: University of Chicago Press, 1989), 6, 21–22.

6. Anne Key Simpson, *Hard Trials: Life and Music of Harry T. Burleigh* (Metuchen, N.J.: Scarecrow Press, 1990), 13–14; Cook, "Clorindy, the Origin of the Cakewalk," 61; for the anecdote on violin smashing, see Carter, "Life and Music of Will Marion Cook," 175–176.

7. The quotation is from a student's reminiscence, "Dvořák as I Knew Him," *Etude,* November 1919, as documented in Emanuel Rubin, "Dvořák at the National Conservatory," in John C. Tibbets, ed., *Dvořák in America* (Portland: Amadeus Press, 1993), 71.

8. Walton included this statement in a 1908 article about Cook, but since Dvořák left America in 1895 and died in 1904, it is possible he misinterpreted a statement Dvořák had made about Burleigh. *New York Age,* May 7, 1908.

9. Will Marion Cook, "Clorindy, the Origin of the Cakewalk"; for the quotation see Cunningham, *Paul Laurence Dunbar and His Song* (New York: Biblo and Tannen, 1969), 167.

10. Simpson, *Hard Trials,* 17–19; Cook, "Clorindy, the Origin of the Cakewalk."

11. *New York Age,* May 7, 1908; Witmark as quoted in Cook, "Clorindy, the Origin of the Cakewalk," 229.

12. Ibid. Unfortunately, there is no extant copy of *Clorindy*'s libretto; although Allen Woll says it is in the Music Collection, Library of Congress, it could not be found. See Woll, *Black Musical Theatre: From Coontown to Dreamgirls* (Baton Rouge: Louisiana State University Press, 1989).

13. Cook, "Clorindy, the Origin of the Cakewalk"; *New York Age*, May 5, 1908; James Weldon Johnson, *Along This Way* (New York: MacMillan, 1933), 173.

14. *New York Dramatic Mirror*, October 29, 1898, as quoted by Carter, "Life and Music of Will Marion Cook," 51–52. Sylvester Russell frequently criticized use of the term opera for Cook's work, though he did use "comic opera" at times. See *Indianapolis Freeman*, February 5, 1902, February 15, 1902, November 8, 1902, December 6, 1902; Joplin as quoted in *New York Age*, April 3, 1913. See also Susan Curtis, *Dancing to a Black Man's Tune* (Columbia: University of Missouri Press, 1994), 47.

15. Thomas L. Riis, *Just before Jazz: Black Musical Theater in New York, 1890–1915* (Washington, D.C.: Smithsonian Institution Press, 1989), 42, 67, 78.

16. *Negro Music Journal* (March 1903): 138; *Musical Courier* 40 (May 23, 1900): 20, and *Musical Observer* 11 (September 1914): 15, as quoted by Edward A. Berlin, *Ragtime: A Musical and Cultural History* (Berkeley: University of California Press, 1980), 42; Willie "the Lion" Smith, *Music on My Mind: The Memoirs of an American Pianist* (New York: De Capo Press, 1975), 25–26.

17. Since Joplin did not move to New York until 1908, he did not participate in the "coon" song craze of New York's performing world. He would, however, work with Lester Walton and others in vaudeville organizations of the 1910s, and like them, felt strangled by the relegation of ragtime to variety stages and barroom accompaniment. He struggled unsuccessfully until his death in 1917 to produce *Treemonisha*, an opera of syncopated music that he hoped would raise ragtime's status. See Curtis, *Dancing to a Black Man's Tune*.

18. Tricia Rose, *Black Noise: Rap Music and Black Culture in Contemporary America* (Hanover, N.H.: Wesleyan University Press, 1994), 17.

19. Alain Locke described him as a white man; Eubie Blake refers to him as black; and Tom Fletcher said he was white. Leah Kathleen Cothern excluded him from her study because of this conflicting evidence. See Cothern, "The Coon Song: A Study of American Music, Entertainment, and Racism," master's thesis, University of Oregon, 1990, 34. Thomas Riis names him a ragtime pianist with no reference to race in *Just before Jazz*. Williams H. Talmadge provides the most credible evidence by locating one census report that listed Harney's family as white in 1880. See Talmadge, "Ben Harney: The Middlesborough Years, 1890–1893," *American Music* (Summer 1995): 169.

20. Ernest Hogan, "All Coons Look Alike to Me," sheet music, *African American Sheet Music, 1850–1920*, Sheet Music Collection, John Hay Library, Brown University.

21. Cothern notes an increase in the use of the word "coon" in popular songs, citing the white comedy team of Edward Harrigan and Tony Hart from 1875 to 1880, but she argues that what could be called the "coon" craze was made by white and black songsters and mostly white publishing houses and lasted from 1887 through 1912. She identifies most characters in "coon" songs as male buffoons and dandies,

with the fewer number of females most often typed as a gal rather than a mammy. The most common "props" were chickens, guns, and razors, although the most common themes were love, marriage, and courting. See Cothern, "Coon Song," 23–26, 58–60, 77–78.

22. For "coon" as a linguistic coup, see James Dormon, "Shaping the Popular Image of Post-Reconstruction American Blacks: The 'Coon Song' Phenomenon of the Gilded Age," *American Quarterly* 40 (December 1988): 452–454; for use of word coon, see David Roediger, *Wages of Whiteness: Race and the Making of the American Working Class* (London: Verso, 1991), 98, 100; Cothern, "Coon Song," 12–15.

23. Tom Fletcher, *One Hundred Years of the Negro in Show Business* (1954; repr., New York: De Capo Press, 1984), 138.

24. There were also instances where African Americans used the term coon in situations unrelated to the popular song craze. For example, emigrationist Bishop Henry McNeal Turner attacked his black opponents as "northern coons" and "miserable black coons who are everlastingly trying to berate Liberia." But for the most part the term appeared in the black press in reference to the song and vaudeville craze. Turner's comments appeared in his own publications *Voice of Missions* and *Voice of the People* in 1893 and 1903 as cited by Edwin Redkey, *Black Exodus: Black Nationalist and Back-to-Africa Movements, 1890–1910* (New Haven, Conn.: Yale University Press, 1969), 178, 270.

25. Russell quoted in *Indianapolis Freeman,* July 19, 1902; *Indianapolis Freeman,* October 20, 1900, February 1, 1901, March 2, 1901, December 28, 1901, February 16, 1901, July 11, 1903, September 19, 1903, October 19, 1907; and *New York Age,* April 9, 1908.

26. *Indianapolis Freeman,* April 5, 1902. More examples of the language can be found in the paper on April 12 and April 26, 1902.

27. *Indianapolis Freeman,* July 4, 1903, December 27, 1902.

28. Lester Walton, "The Future of the Negro on the Stage," *Colored American Magazine* 6, no. 6 (May 1903): 439–442.

29. *New York Age,* March 5, 1908; Walton called *Hottest Coon in Dixie* "one of the most enjoyable 'coon' shows which has been seen here in a long time," *New York Age,* April 9, 1908. On the Pekin Theater see Carter, "Life and Music of Will Marion Cook," 97–101; for the fictional quotation see Paul Laurence Dunbar, *Sport of the Gods* (1902; repr., New York: Arno Press, 1969), 123.

30. Samuel A. Floyd Jr., *The Power of Black Music* (New York: Oxford University Press, 1995), 70; Berlin, *Ragtime: A Musical and Cultural History,* 28–29; *Indianapolis Freeman,* May 13, 1905.

31. Eileen Southern, *The Music of Black Americans: A History,* 2d ed. (New York: W. W. Norton, 1983), 314–315.

32. Readers were told to send forty cents to E. C. Knox and Company, and a later advertisement on May 18, 1901, encourages professionals to send twelve cents for a copy of "the latest and best coon song." *Indianapolis Freeman,* March 4, 1901.

33. Ann Charters, ed., *The Ragtime Songbook* (New York: Oak Publications, 1965), 33.

34. *Indianapolis Freeman,* December 14, 1901, review of Sons of Ham, as published in Henry T. Sampson, *The Ghost Walks: A Chronological History of Blacks in Show Business, 1865–1910* (Metuchen, N.J.: Scarecrow Press, 1988), 241.

35. Cothern, "Coon Song," 86–88, 100; Riis, *Just before Jazz,* 52.

36. Riis, *Just before Jazz,* 239–241.

37. "Who Dat Say Chicken in Dis Crowd?" lyrics as printed in Carter, "Life and Music of Will Marion Cook."

38. Cothern, "Coon Song," 23–26, 58–60, 77–78.

39. Sheet Music for "Darktown Is Out Tonight," "Who Dat Say Chicken in Dis Crowd?" and "Swing Along" are in *African American Sheet Music, 1850–1920,* Sheet Music Collection, John Hay Library, Brown University; "Swing Along" also appears in Thomas L. Riis, ed., *The Music and Scripts of "In Dahomey"* (Madison, Wis.: A-R Editions, 1996), 156.

40. Tera Hunter, *To Joy My Freedom: Southern Black Women's Lives and Labors after the Civil War* (Cambridge, Mass.: Harvard University Press, 1997).

41. *New York Age,* May 7, 1908. "The Young Will Marion" in Carter, "Life and Music of Will Marion Cook."

42. Music reprinted in Carter, "Life and Music of Will Marion Cook."

43. *Indianapolis Freeman,* October 25, 1902, and December 30, 1899.

44. Unidentified clipping, November 8, 1905, Robinson Locke Collection, BRTC; unidentified clipping, *In Dahomey* folder, BRTC; *Toledo Times,* September 21, 1907, Ernest Hogan clippings, Robinson Locke Collection, BRTC.

45. *Minneapolis Journal,* April 30, 191?, a very tattered clip from the Williams and Walker clipping file, Robinson Locke Collection, folder 2593, BRTC.

46. *Indianapolis Freeman,* August 24, 1901; Charters, *Ragtime Songbook,* 33.

47. Simpson, *Hard Trials,* 27; *Negro Music Journal,* September 1902, October 1902, January 1903, and March 1903.

48. *Negro Music Journal,* January 1903 and March 1903.

49. Ibid., May 1903.

50. Ibid.

51. Carter, "Life and Music of Will Marion Cook," 97–101.

52. *Indianapolis Freeman,* May 13, 1905, December 31, 1904.

53. Burleigh, *Musical America* (March 1924) as published in Simpson, *Hard Trials,* 292, 295; Tricia Rose, *Black Noise,* 24, 83. Amiri Baraka concludes that ragtime was not "Negro music," but was rather the debris of "vanished emotional references": see Baraka (published as Leroi Jones), *Blues People: Negro Music in White America* (New York: William Morrow, 1963), 221. Ronald Radano points out that even African American folksongs as performed by Jubilee singers had been "built upon white assumptions of black natural musical gifts," and as such, created a "kind of produced authenticity that was intimately connected to the institutional matrices of modernization," see Radano, "Soul Texts and the Blackness of Folk," *Modernism/Modernity* 2, no. 1 (1995): 71–95, 84; see also Stuart Hall, "What Is This 'Black' in Black Popular Culture?" in *Black Popular Culture,* ed. Gina Dent (Seattle: Bay Press, 1992), 24.

54. George Walker, "The Negro on the American Stage," *Colored American Magazine* 11, no 4 (October 1906): 248.

55. *Indianapolis Freeman,* May 31, 1902; Lester Walton, "The Future of the Negro on the Stage," *Colored American Magazine* 6, no. 6 (May 1903): 439–442.

56. *New York Age,* February 20, 1908, April 2, 1908; in the February 20, 1909, edition, *Indianapolis Freeman* critics also commented on *Bandana Land*'s "naturel" depiction of "Negro life."

57. *New York Age,* February 6, 1908. M. M. Manring cites Cyril V. Briggs's post–World War I comments in the *Crusader* as among the earliest critiques of Aunt Jemima in his *Slave in a Box: The Strange Career of Aunt Jemima* (Charlottesville: University of Virginia Press, 1998), 151–152.

58. *New York Age,* February 20, 1908.

59. Riis, *Music and Scripts of "In Dahomey,"* xlix–l; Kathy Peiss, *The Making of America's Beauty Culture* (New York: Henry Holt, 1998), 203–210.

60. *New York Age,* February 20, 1908.

61. Ibid.

62. Ibid. A common misperception is that the straightening of hair always has to do with black desire to appear white. As Robin D. G. Kelley has argued, working-class African American men in the 1940s "conked" their hair to protest the "dominant, stereotyped image of the Southern migrant or the black bourgeoisie" rather than to imitate whites. Likewise, Shane White and Graham White show how important the styling of hair was in African American culture and point out that straightening was frequently the first step in styling. See Kelley, *Race Rebels: Culture, Politics, and the Black Working Class* (New York: Free Press, 1994), 167–168; as well as White and White, *Stylin': African American Expressive Culture from Its Beginnings to the Zoot Suit* (Ithaca, N.Y.: Cornell University Press, 1998), 42–62.

63. *New York Age,* February 20, 1908.

64. Leah Kathleen Cothern speculates that similar to Dunbar, who used dialect for character development, African American lyricists used dialect "to stand aside from the caricature by consciously satirizing it, as if to subtly say, 'I know the difference between him and me.'" She notes that twice as many black songwriters used this technique. Cothern, "Coon Song," 78.

65. The Hughes quotation is from "Our Wonderful Society," *Opportunity* (August 1927): 226–227, quoted in Willard B. Gatewood, *Aristocrats of Color: The Black Elite, 1880–1920* (Bloomington: Indiana University Press, 1990), 27, 143, 338.

66. *The Globe,* February 24, 1908, "Theater before 1925" clipping file, SC.

67. Will Marion Cook, Autobiographical Notes, Mercer Cook Papers, Moorland-Spingarn Research Center, Howard University.

68. *Indianapolis Freeman,* January 4, 1908; Walton in *New York Age,* March 19, 1908; Will Marion Cook letter to his son, Mercer, April 29, 1931, Mercer Cook Papers; Paul Laurence Dunbar, *Sport of the Gods,* 203.

69. Letter to friend, reprinted in Cunningham, *Paul Laurence Dunbar and His Song,* 182, 190. Also see Gatewood, *Aristocrats of Color,* 60–62.

70. Lida Keck Wiggins, *The Life and Works of Paul Laurence Dunbar* (Naperville, Ill.: Nichols & Company, ca. 1907), 109, 117–118; James Weldon Johnson, *Along This Way*, 160–161.

71. Eugene Levy, *James Weldon Johnson: Black Leader, Black Voice* (Chicago: University of Chicago Press, 1973), 87.

72. *Indianapolis Freeman*, April 2, 1904, May 6, 1905, and June 22, 1907.

73. *Negro Music Journal*, March 1903; *Indianapolis Freeman*, January 2, 1909.

74. Cook was founder of Gotham when it merged with Attucks; see *Indianapolis Freeman*, March 25, 1905. Wayne D. Shirley names the man as Ferdinand E. Mierisch and describes "song sharks" as scam artists who agreed to publish an artist's song for a fee, but then would produce a limited run that would gather dust in a warehouse rather than reach consumers. See Shirley, "The House of Melody: a List of Publications of the Gotham-Attucks Music Company at the Library of Congress," *Black Perspective in Music* 15 (Spring 1987): 79–112; *New York Age*, March 19, 1908.

75. W. C. Handy, *Father of the Blues: An Autobiography by W. C. Handy*, ed. Arna Bontemps (New York: Da Capo Press, 1941), 108.

76. Tom Fletcher, *One Hundred Years of the Negro in Show Business* (New York: Burdge & Co., 1954), 139–143. Nathan Huggins interprets the same information to say that Hogan had "misgivings," but qualified this by saying, "If not misgivings, at least he had been made sensitive enough by the criticism of other black performers that he felt moved to justify himself." See Huggins, *Harlem Renaissance* (New York: Oxford University Press, 1971), 277. Brooke Baldwin argues that too many authors have apologized for Hogan's song and that Hogan "repeatedly expressed regret for writing this song later in life" in her article "The Cakewalk: A Study in Stereotype and Reality," *Journal of Social History* 15 (Winter 1981): 212, although she does not cite sources for this statement. Lester Walton wrote that Hogan had lamented his work as well, but again, he published his comments two years after Hogan's death—see *New York Age*, March 30, 1911.

77. Handy explained that the song's lyrics used "the same down-home medium that conveyed the laughable woe of lamp-blacked lovers in hundreds of frothy songs," but that the mood of the song and plight of the protagonist were "much too real to provoke much laughter." Handy, *Father of the Blues*, 120, 143–144.

78. Lawrence Levine, *Black Culture and Black Consciousness: Afro-American Folk Thought from Slavery to Freedom* (New York: Oxford University Press, 1977), 166–168. The Trotter quotation is on p. 167.

4. "No Place Like Home"

1. Will Marion Cook with additional lyrics by Paul Laurence Dunbar, *Jes Lak White Fo'ks*, libretto, Music Division, Library of Congress, Washington, D.C., 1900. All quotations from *Jes Lak White Fo'ks* are taken from this source.

2. *Freeman* editor George Knox lamented in 1897 that the future of Africa was

dismal and explained that "Africa is slipping away piece meal into the clutches of the land grabbing countries." *Indianapolis Freeman,* July 17, 1897, as quoted by Sylvia Jacobs, *The African Nexus: Black American Perspectives on the European Partitioning of Africa, 1880–1920* (Westport, Conn.: Greenwood, 1981), 45.

3. William R. Scott, *The Sons of Sheba's Race: African Americans and the Italo-Ethiopian War, 1935–1941* (Indianapolis: Indiana University Press, 1993), 13; Robert G. Weisbord, *Ebony Kinship: Africa, Africans, and the Afro-American* (Westport, Conn.: Greenwood, 1973), 6; Wilson J. Moses, *The Golden Age of Black Nationalism,* 1850–1925 (New York: Oxford University Press, 1978), 23, 24, 200; Wilson Moses, *The Wings of Ethiopia: Studies in African American Life and Letters* (Ames: Iowa State University Press, 1990), 101; Wilson J. Moses, *Afrotopia: The Roots of African American Popular History* (New York: Cambridge University Press, 1998), 50–58; Sidney Lemell and Robin D. G. Kelley, *Imagining Home: Class, Culture, and Nationalism in the African Diaspora* (New York: Verso, 1994), 3.

4. Scott notes that the New Orleans *Black Republican* also had the phrase in its masthead, and gives a succinct overview of the history of the Ethiopian tradition— see Scott, *Sons of Sheba's Race,* 20; Colin Palmer, *Passageways: An Interpretive History of Black America* (New York: Harcourt Brace, 1998), 89–90; and Virginia Cunningham, *Paul Laurence Dunbar and His Song* (New York: Dodd, Mead and Co., 1947) 73, 88–89.

5. *Clorindy* opened on July 5, 1898, and *Jes Lak White Fo'ks* on June 26, 1900. Irving Jones had performed in Sam T. Jack's *Creole Show* in 1893. See James Weldon Johnson, *Black Manhattan* (1930; repr., New York: Atheneum Press, 1969), 95; Bernard Peterson, *A Century of Musicals in Black and White: An Encyclopedia of Musical Stage Works by, about, or Involving African Americans* (Westport, Conn.: Greenwood, 1993).

6. Cunningham, *Paul Laurence Dunbar and His Song,* 161; Walter L. Williams, *Black Americans and the Evangelization of Africa, 1877–1900* (Madison: University of Wisconsin Press, 1982); Moses, *Golden Age of Black Nationalism,* 61–73 (the Crummell quotation is on p. 73).

7. W. E. B. Du Bois, "Conservation of the Races," in Wilson J. Moses, ed., *Classical Black Nationalism* (New York: New York University Press, 1996), 237.

8. Cook and Dunbar, *Jes Lak White Fo'ks* libretto; *Washington Bee,* February 9, 1889, as quoted by Willard B. Gatewood, *Aristocrats of Color: The Black Elite, 1880–1920* (Bloomington: Indiana University Press, 1990), 211.

9. Gatewood, *Aristocrats of Color,* 211–212, 223–224; Jervis Anderson, *This Was Harlem, 1900–1950* (New York: Farrar Straus Giroux, 1981), 26–29; Tera Hunter, *To Joy My Freedom: Southern Black Women's Lives and Labors after the Civil War* (Cambridge, Mass.: Harvard University Press, 1997), 148–149.

10. Gatewood, *Aristocrats of Color,* 69, 172, 344; on Turner, see Edwin Redkey, *Black Exodus: Black Nationalist and Back-to-Africa Movements, 1890–1910* (New Haven, Conn.: Yale University Press, 1969), 45; on Crummell, see Moses, *Golden Age of Black Nationalism,* 62.

11. Cook and Dunbar, *Jes Lak White Fo'ks* libretto.

12. As quoted in Gatewood, *Aristocrats of Color,* 22.

13. Paul Laurence Dunbar, *New York Tribune*, August 23, 1897, Vassar Scrapbook, vol. 2, Special Collections, Vassar College Library; Jillian A. Sim, Hemmings's great-granddaughter, explores the possibility that she was related to Sally Hemmings. See her "Fading to White," *American Heritage* (February/March 1999).

14. Dunbar, *New York Tribune*, August 23, 1897, Vassar Scrapbook, vol. 2.

15. For the Fannie Williams quotation, see Gatewood, *Aristocrats of Color*, 175–177; for the company member "jabbering" French, see *New York Age*, February 20, 1908; on the prevalence of passing narratives in songs, see Leah Kathleen Cothern, "The Coon Song: A Study of American Music, Entertainment, and Racism," master's thesis, University of Oregon, 1990, 77–78; for Cole and Johnson passing as Spanish dignitaries, see *New York Telegraph*, August 7, 1910, Robinson Locke Collection, Cole and Johnson clipping file, BRTC; for the hiring of a black doorman, see Gatewood, *Aristocrats of Color*, 337–338.

16. *Indianapolis Freeman*, August 10, 1901, and November 9, 1901; Peterson, *Century of Musicals in Black and White*.

17. James Weldon Johnson recalled that Cook and Cole argued repeatedly at the Marshall Hotel over the role of African Americans in theater. See Johnson, *Along This Way* (New York: Viking, 1933), 173; Marva Griffin Carter, "The Life and Music of Will Marion Cook," Ph.D. diss., University of Illinois, Urbana-Champaign, 1988; Will Marion Cook, autobiographical notes, Mercer Cook Papers, Moorland-Spingarn Research Center, Howard University.

18. Cole and the Johnson Brothers signed with Joseph Stern and Company to begin their career publishing "coon" songs for white shows in 1899 with "Louisiana Lize," written for May Irwin. See Eugene Levy, *James Weldon Johnson: Black Leader, Black Voice* (Chicago: University of Chicago Press, 1973), 85–93.

19. Bert Williams, unpublished manuscript notes, Williams and Walker clipping file, BRTC. The "pigeon wing" dance is described in Marshall Stearns and Jean Stearns, *Jazz Dance: The Story of American Vernacular Dance* (New York: Da Capo Press, 1994), 28, 191.

20. Thomas L. Riis, ed., *The Music and Scripts of "In Dahomey"* (Madison, Wis.: A-R Editions, 1996), introduction; Thomas Riis, *Just before Jazz: Black Musical Theater in New York, 1890–1915* (Washington, D.C.: Smithsonian Institution Press, 1989), 90–111.

21. Tom Fletcher, *One Hundred Years of the Negro in Show Business* (New York: Burdge & Co., 1954), 237; George Walker, "The Real 'Coon' on the American Stage," *Theater Magazine*, August 1906, Williams and Walker clipping file, BRTC; *Indianapolis Freeman*, September 1, 1900; *New York Herald Tribune*, May 3, 1934, in Jesse Shipp clipping files, BRTC.

22. Shipp was breaking new ground because few popular shows of the period, black or white, followed one plot to its conclusion. By the turn of the century, artists had begun to merge the popular theater styles of comic opera, burlesque, minstrel, and variety shows into a new type of production—the musical comedy. See Levy, *James Weldon Johnson*, 85. Gerald Bordman states, "Precisely how many revues were

produced in this period is moot, since the line between the plotted revues and the slap-dash musical comedies of the era was often impossible to discern." Bordman, *American Musical Revues from the Passing Show to Sugar Babies* (New York: Oxford University Press, 1985), 27.

23. *Indianapolis Freeman,* October 25, 1902. This was the only direct reference to Turner in a review of *In Dahomey* that I found.

24. Moses, *Golden Age of Black Nationalism,* 201; Redkey, *Black Exodus,* 28, 45–46, quotation on p. 45; Robert Weisbord, *Ebony Kinship: Africa, Africans, and the Afro-American* (Westport, Conn.: Greenwood, 1973); 27; Walter Williams, *Black Americans and the Evangelization of Africa, 1877–1900* (Madison: University of Wisconsin Press, 1982), 48–52.

25. Weisbord, *Ebony Kinship,* 32; James Grossman, *Land of Hope: Chicago, Black Southerners, and the Great Migration* (Chicago: University of Chicago Press, 1989), 25; Redkey, *Black Exodus,* 177; Jacobs, *African Nexus,* 46–48. See also Kenneth C. Barnes, *A Journey of Hope: The Back to Africa Movement in Arkansas in the Late 1800s* (Chapel Hill: University of North Carolina Press, 2004); Steven Hahn, *A Nation under Our Feet: Black Political Struggles in the Rural South from Slavery to the Great Migration* (Cambridge, Mass.: Harvard University Press, 2003).

26. Redkey, *Black Exodus,* 33, 120 (Fortune quotation), 230.

27. Jacobs, *The Black Nexus,* reprint of *Indianapolis Freeman,* November 9, 1907.

28. W. C. Handy, *Father of the Blues: An Autobiography* (1941; repr., New York: Da Capo, 1969), 159–160.

29. Barnes, *Journey of Hope,* 139–140.

30. *Savannah Tribune,* March 21, 1896, as quoted by Weisbord, *Ebony Kinship,* 30–31.

31. Redkey, *Black Exodus,* 102–107, 174–175; Barnes, *Journey of Hope,* 101–104.

32. *Indianapolis Freeman,* June 22, 1907; Redkey, *Black Exodus,* 199, 286.

33. Unidentified clipping, Williams and Walker clipping file, BRTC; *Indianapolis Freeman,* June 22, 1907.

34. *New York Times,* December 12, 1892; Redkey says Lightfoot was "lynched" in his *Black Exodus,* 174–175; Barnes reports in *Journey of Hope,* 104, that "G. P. F." Lightfoot's body was "riddled with bullets, and hands hacked with knives and razors."

35. *Indianapolis Freeman,* October 25, 1902; synopsis of *In Dahomey* found on a program of the New York Theater of the week commencing March 9, 1903, clipping file, Theater Collection, Museum of the City of New York.

36. *New York Times,* February 19, 1903, *In Dahomey* clipping file, Harvard Theater Collection, Houghton Library, Harvard University.

37. Turner as quoted in Williams, *Black Americans and the Evangelization of Africa,* 107; see also Jacobs, *African Nexus,* 57–58.

38. Riis, *Music and Scripts of "In Dahomey."* All quotations from *In Dahomey* are taken from this source.

39. *Indianapolis Freeman,* April 20, 1901, December 26, 1903; unidentified clipping, October 3, 1907, Robinson Locke Collection, folder 717, BRTC.

40. This plot description is from *New York Globe*, November 26, 1907, Ernest Hogan clipping file, BRTC. No libretto survives from Hogan's show, and accounts vary as to where Hogan's character was setting sail for. All, however, mention a swindle rather than attempt at emigration. Redkey, *Black Exodus*, 236–238; Weisbord, *Ebony Kinship*, 31.

41. *New York Globe*, November 26, 1907, Ernest Hogan clipping file, Robert Locke Collection, folder 717, BRTC; Skinner, *African Americans and U.S. Policy toward Africa*, 282, 284.

42. Elliot Skinner, *African Americans and U.S. Policy toward Africa, 1850–1924* (Washington, D.C.: Howard University Press, 1992), 281–286. Also see Richard Pankhurst, "William H. Ellis—Guillaume Enriques Ellesio: The First Black American Ethiopianist?" *Ethiopia Observer* 15 (1972): 89–121.

43. Skinner, *African Americans and U.S. Policy toward Africa*, 283–284.

44. *New York Globe*, November 26, 1907; Skinner, *African Americans and U.S. Policy toward Africa*, 282, 284; quotation is from Pankhurst, "William H. Ellis," 91.

45. Thomas Riis, "Bob Cole: His Life and Legacy to Black Musical Theater," *Black Perspective in Music* 13 (Fall 1985): 141; Skinner, *African Americans and U.S. Policy toward Africa*, 245–275; Jacobs, *African Nexus*, 127–128.

46. "Evah Dahkey Is a King," in Riis, *Music and Scripts of "In Dahomey,"* 47–50.

47. Mabel Rowland, *Bert Williams, Son of Laughter: A Symposium of Tribute to the Man* (1923; repr. New York: Negro Universities Press, 1969).

48. *Abyssinia*, libretto, 1905, Music Division, Library of Congress, Washington, D.C. The copyright was 1905, but the show did not make it to the stage until 1906. All further quotations from the libretto are from this source. Both "Abyssinia" and "Ethiopia" seemed to be used with equal meaning in the literature of the period, and are still defined as interchangeable.

49. The *Cleveland Gazette* editor's quotation is from Skinner, *African Americans and U.S. Policy toward Africa*, 279; for the Knox quote, see Jacobs, *African Nexus*, 187, 194–195. The journalist's quote is from an interview with Harold Isaacs taken from his book *The New World of Negro Americans* (New York: John Day, 1963), 185; William Scott also points this out in his *Sons of Sheba's Race*, 21. See also Palmer, *Passageways*, 207.

50. Moses, *Afrotopia*, 61, 69–72; the Russell quotations and comments are from *Indianapolis Freeman*, September 27, 1902, October 25, 1902, February 29, 1908.

51. Klaw and Erlanger Collection, Wa-We, 1904–1905, George Walker folders, Schubert Archives, New York; Wayne D. Shirley, "The House of Melody: A List of Publications of the Gotham-Attucks Music Company at the Library of Congress," *Black Perspective in Music* 15 (Spring 1987): 83–86.

52. Robert P. Skinner, *Abyssinia of To-Day: An Account of the First Mission Sent by the American Government to the Court of the King of Kings, 1903–1904* (1906; repr., New York: Negro Universities Press, 1969), 131–133; Elliot Skinner commented, "What Skinner failed to report was the obvious incongruity of this statement, since Menelik was more 'negroid' in appearance than most Ethiopians." See Skinner, *African Americans*

and U.S. Policy toward Africa, 280. Harold G. Marcus reported on European attempts to redefine the race of Ethiopians in *The Life and Times of Menelik II: Ethiopia, 1844–1913* (Oxford, Eng.: Clarendon, 1975), 3.

53. Program for show at the Majestic Theater, Feb. 20, 1906, *Abyssinia* clipping file, BRTC (the translations are also printed in the libretto); Marcus, *Life and Times of Menelik II,* 185–190.

54. Skinner, *African Americans and U.S. Policy toward Africa,* 281–286.

55. While not appearing regularly in the black press, the term cracker was common vernacular at the time. In one instance in 1905, the *Indianapolis Freeman* quoted an Oxford-educated clergyman denouncing Booker T. Washington as "bowing hat in hand, to an unwashed cracker." As quoted in David Krasner, *Resistance, Parody, and Double Consciousness in African American Theatre, 1895–1910* (New York: St. Martin's, 1997), 103–104.

56. Nell Painter, *Exodusters: Black Migration to Kansas after Reconstruction* (New York: Knopf, 1977).

57. Mark Evan Swartz, *Oz before the Rainbow: L. Frank Baum's "The Wonderful Wizard of Oz" on Stage and Screen to 1939* (Baltimore: Johns Hopkins University Press, 2000), 71.

58. Sylvia Jacobs claims that the black middle-class community paid less attention to the politics of North Africa in part because of the heavy presence of Islam. No missionaries were sent to the region before 1920. See Jacobs, *African Nexus,* 183. Williams was known to have read the works of Muhammed, and perhaps he had a role in encouraging the inclusion of Islam in this production. See Green Book Album, 1913, Williams and Walker clipping file, BRTC.

59. Marcus, *Life and Times of King Menelik II,* 197; Chris Prouty, *Empress Taytu and Menelik II: Ethiopia, 1883–1910* (Trenton, N.J.: Red Sea Press, 1986), 14.

60. As quoted by Blanche Ferguson, "Black Skin, Black Mask: The Inconvenient Grace of Bert Williams," *American Visions* (June/July 1992): 16. The quote was retold by Mercer Cook, Will Marion and Abbie Mitchell's son, who became a noted African scholar and who remembered, "The name of Bert Williams was very much alive in our home during my childhood."

61. *Indianapolis Freeman,* February 29, 1908.

62. Ibid., February 29, 1908, March 3, 1906.

63. For the quotation by the first critic, see *Theatre Magazine,* April 1906, *Abyssinia* clipping file, BRTC; for the second critic's opinion, see one of several unidentified clippings, Williams and Walker clipping file, Robinson Locke Collection, BRTC.

64. *Theatre Magazine* 6, no. 62 (April 1906): xvi, *Abyssinia* clipping file; one of many unidentified clippings, Robinson Locke Collection, BRTC; *New York American,* February 23, 1906, Robinson Locke Collection, BRTC; unidentified New York clipping, Williams and Walker clipping file, Robinson Locke Collection, envelope 2461, BRTC.

65. *Theatre Magazine* 6, no. 62 (April 1906): xvi, *Abyssinia* clipping file; *New York American,* February 23, 1906; for "barbaric splendor," see unidentified clippings, Williams and Walker clipping file, envelope 2461, Robinson Locke Collection, BRTC.

66. W. E. B. Du Bois, "Conservation of the Races," in Wilson J. Moses, ed., *Classical Black Nationalism*, 228–240.

67. Ernest Hogan, "The Phrenologist Coon," *African American Sheet Music, 1850–1920*, Sheet Music Collection, John Hay Library, Brown University; on Williams's interest in reading, see Rowland, *Bert Williams, Son of Laughter*, 185; Bert Williams, "My Trip Abroad," datebook ca. 1903, San Francisco Performing Arts Library and Museum.

68. *Indianapolis Freeman*, January 13, 1906.

69. Ibid., May 13, 1905.

70. Ibid., January 13, 1906, May 13, 1905, and September 2, 1893, as quoted in Carter, "Life and Music of Will Marion Cook," 28–29.

5. Morals, Manners, and Stage Life

1. This song was written by Clarence A. Stout of Vincennes, Indiana, performed by W. C. Handy's Memphis Students, and made famous by Bert Williams. See W. C. Handy, *Father of the Blues: An Autobiography by W. C. Handy*, ed. Arna Bontemps (New York: Da Capo, 1941), 203; the sheet music for the song is in Historic American Sheet Music, Rare Books, Manuscripts and Special Collections, Duke University. This copy of sheet music was published in 1918 by Pace & Handy, Memphis, Tennessee. Handy did not identify the race of the author but did call the work a "Negro comic song."

2. Kevin Gaines, *Uplifting the Race: Black Leadership, Politics, and Culture in the Twentieth Century* (Chapel Hill: University of North Carolina Press, 1996), 3, 93, 217; Willard Gatewood, *Aristocrats of Color: The Black Elite, 1880–1920* (Chicago: University of Chicago Press, 1989), 182; Evelyn Brooks Higginbotham, *Righteous Discontent: The Women's Movement in the Black Baptist Church, 1880–1920* (Cambridge, Mass.: Harvard University Press, 1993), 198–199; James Grossman, *Land of Hope: Chicago, Black Southerners, and the Great Migration* (Chicago: University of Chicago Press, 1989), 145–154; Hazel Carby, "Policing the Black Woman's Body in an Urban Context," *Critical Inquiry* 18 (Summer 1992): 738–755; Tera Hunter, *To Joy My Freedom: Southern Black Women's Lives and Labors after the Civil War* (Cambridge, Mass.: Harvard University Press, 1997); Victoria Wolcott, *Remaking Respectability: African American Women in Interwar Detroit* (Chapel Hill: University of North Carolina Press, 2001).

3. W. E. B. Du Bois, "The Problem of Amusement," *Southern Workman* 26 (September 1897), as published in Herbert Aptheker, ed., *Writings by W. E. B. Du Bois in Periodicals* (New York: Kraus-Thomson Organization Limited, 1982), 31–39.

4. As quoted in Wolcott, *Remaking Respectability*, 53.

5. Du Bois, "Problem of Amusement."

6. Ibid., 31–39; *Atlanta University Publications*, no. 18, "Morals and Manners among Negro Americans," Eighteenth Conference for the Study of the Negro Problems, May 26, 1913 (New York: Arno Press, 1968), 92, 95 (reprint in the Moorland-Springarn Research Center, Howard University).

7. Du Bois, "Problem of Amusement," 38.

8. Ibid.

9. For the NACW quotation, see Deborah Gray White, *Too Heavy a Load: Black Women in Defense of Themselves, 1894–1994* (New York: Norton, 1999), 42–43; the "strong manhood" quotation is from Gaines, *Uplifting the Race,* 52, 135. See also Hunter, *To Joy My Freedom;* Higginbotham, *Righteous Discontent;* Carby, "Policing the Black Woman's Body in an Urban Context;" Wolcott, *Remaking Respectability,* 63.

10. *Indianapolis Freeman,* October 1, 1910, as published in Henry T. Sampson, *The Ghost Walks: A Chronological History of Blacks in Show Business, 1865–1910* (Metuchen, N.J.: Scarecrow Press, 1988), 531–532.

11. *Indianapolis Freeman,* October 29, 1904, July 21, 1900, and August 4, 1900; Gatewood, *Aristocrats of Color,* 183 (for pamphlet), and 192 (for Hope quotation).

12. *Indianapolis Freeman,* September 21, 1901.

13. Ibid., October 10, 1903.

14. As published in Eugene Levy, *James Weldon Johnson: Black Leader, Black Voice* (Chicago: University of Chicago Press, 1973), 71–72. Although I was struck by the similarity of the song titles, I could find no direct evidence that Stout might have been satirizing Johnson's song.

15. James Weldon Johnson, *Autobiography of an Ex-Colored Man* (New York: Avon, 1968). The book was first published anonymously by a small company in 1912, and was published under Johnson's name in 1927.

16. White, *Too Heavy a Load,* 70, 76–78.

17. Mary Church Terrell, *A Colored Women in a White World* (1940; repr., New York: Simon and Schuster, 1996), 109, 247.

18. *Indianapolis Freeman,* December 22, 1906. Pinckney Benton Stewart Pinchback had been a member of the New Orleans elite, and was elected lieutenant governor during Reconstruction. He moved to D.C. in 1893 and was known as "Governor" Pinchback for the rest of his life. See Gatewood, *Aristocrats of Color,* 42.

19. Paul Laurence Dunbar, *Sport of the Gods* (1902; repr., New York: Arno Press, 1969), 166–167.

20. Mercer Cook, "From Clorindy to the Red Moon," Helen-Armstead Johnson Collection, Manuscript Division, SC; Abbie Mitchell, "Autobiographical Notes" and "A Negro Invasion of Buckingham Palace in 1903" confirm her age—see Mercer Cook Papers, Moorland-Spingarn Research Center, Howard University.

21. See Paula Giddings, *When and Where I Enter: The Impact of Black Women on Race and Sex* (New York: Bantam, 1984), 137, whose information comes from W. E. B. Du Bois's *Gift of Black Folk.* Du Bois states that by 1910, 27 percent of women were still single at the age of fifteen, whereas "their grandmothers married at twelve and fifteen." For a discussion of black reform efforts to end "child marriage," and of sexuality, marriage, and reproduction generally, see Michele Mitchell, *Righteous Propagation: African Americans and the Politics of Racial Destiny after Reconstruction* (Chapel Hill: University of North Carolina Press, 2004), 76–107.

22. Henry T. Sampson claims that Mitchell had been in a Baltimore convent in his *Blacks in Blackface: A Sourcebook on Early Black Musical Shows* (Metuchen, N.J.: Scare-

crow Press, 1980), 404. He also notes that she studied voice with Harry T. Burleigh. See also Sampson, *Ghost Walks,* 516. Press clippings in the Cook papers also refer to Mitchell in a convent, but her own notes omit this fact. She did write, "The books say when writing about me that I made my debut at the age of 14 in *Clorindy.* As a matter of fact I was 12 years old." Abbie Mitchell, autobiographical notes, Mercer Cook Papers, Moorland-Spingarn Research Center, Howard University.

23. *Indianapolis Freeman,* July 21, 1900.

24. Ibid., June 28, 1902.

25. Ibid., April 23, 1904.

26. Sampson, *Ghost Walks,* 381. In one place he says that Dean and Johnson broke up in 1910; in another he reports 1914 as the date. See *San Fran Times Weekly* March 16, 1936, Dean and Johnson clipping file, SC. *Dance Magazine,* March 1943, recounts that Dean and Johnson traveled to Budapest and that Dora Dean had her life-size portrait done "by a European celebrated portrait painter." The portrait apparently hung in the Paris Exposition of 1902 before being shipped to Hammerstein's Victoria Theater for Dean and Johnson's 1903 engagement. They did 150 consecutive nights at Koster and Bial's and on August 30, 1897, were the first black act to headline a big time vaudeville bill at Tony Pastor's Fourteenth Street theater.

27. Susan A. Glenn, *Female Spectacle: The Theatrical Roots of Modern Feminism* (Cambridge, Mass.: Harvard University Press, 2000), 6–7.

28. Richard Newman, "'The Brightest Star': Aida Overton Walker in the Age of Ragtime and Cakewalk," in Jack Salzman, ed., *Prospects: An Annual of American Cultural Studies* (New York: Cambridge University Press, 1993), 477; Higginbotham, *Righteous Discontent,* 210.

29. *New York Age,* May 7, 1908, places Walker at the White Rose Mission fundraisers; see also White, *Too Heavy a Load,* 31; Higginbotham, *Righteous Discontent,* 199–201; Carby, "Policing the Black Woman's Body in an Urban Context."

30. Newman, "Brightest Star," 477.

31. Darlene Clark Hine, "Rape and the Inner Lives of Black Women in the Middle West: Preliminary Thoughts on the Culture of Dissemblance," *Signs* 14 (Summer 1989): 912–920; Higginbotham, *Righteous Discontent,* 193–194; Wolcott, *Remaking Respectability,* 23–25.

32. Glenn, *Female Spectacle,* 96–108.

33. Ibid., 114–115.

34. Ibid., 117.

35. Ibid., 115.

36. Hunter, *To Joy My Freedom,* 155–158, 174; Marshall Stearns and Jean Stearns, *Jazz Dance: The Story of American Vernacular Dance* (1968; repr., New York: Da Capo, 1994), 85–91; Nadine George-Graves, *The Royalty of Negro Vaudeville: The Whitman Sisters and the Negotiation of Race, Gender, and Class in African American Theater, 1900–1940* (New York: St. Martin's, 2000), 18–21; Sampson, *Ghost Walks,* 245, 464. Sampson lists their father's name as Albert instead of Albany, perhaps because one sister's name was Alberta.

37. See the "just for exercise" quotation in Hunter, *To Joy My Freedom,* 158; Stearns and Stearns, *Jazz Dance,* 85.

38. Elsa Barkley Brown and George Kimball, "Mapping the Terrain," *Journal of Urban History* (March 1995): 329–333.

39. The booklet was quoted at length in *New York Globe and Commercial,* October 27, 1905, Robinson Locke Collection, folder 2461, BRTC.

40. "Helpful Hints" leaflet, Detroit Urban League Papers, box 1, folder 9, Bentley Library, University of Michigan, Ann Arbor, reprinted in Elsa Barkley Brown and Thomas Holt, eds., *Major Problems in African American History* (New York: Houghton Mifflin, 2000), 132; Grossman, *Land of Hope,* 145–146.

41. *Indianapolis Freeman,* July 21, 1900.

42. *Detroit Times,* December 7, 1906, clipping files, p. 35, Robinson Locke Collection, BRTC.

43. *Indianapolis Freeman,* August 22, 1903.

44. Dunbar, *Sport of the Gods,* 117–118, 212–213.

45. *Indianapolis Freeman,* May 6, 1905.

46. Ibid., February 18, 1905.

47. Hunter, *To Joy My Freedom,* chapter 9.

48. Tom Fletcher, *One Hundred Years of the Negro in Show Business* (New York: Burdge & Co., 1954), 57.

49. *Indianapolis Freeman,* August 23, 1902.

50. Ibid., December 10, 1904.

51. Higginbotham, *Righteous Discontent,* 195.

52. Gatewood, *Aristocrats of Color,* 182–209.

53. *Indianapolis Freeman,* February 20, 1904.

54. Ibid., February 18, 1905.

55. Ibid., February 27, 1904.

56. Ibid., March 8, 1902, February 18, 1905.

57. Ibid., August 23, 1902.

58. Gatewood, *Aristocrats of Color,* 182–209.

59. Marva Griffin Carter, "Life and Music of Will Marion Cook," Ph.D. diss., University of Illinois, Urbana-Champaign, 1988, 361.

60. *Telegraph,* August 5, 1905, Abbie Mitchell clipping folder, envelope 1484, Robinson Locke Collection, BRTC.

61. Eleanor Alexander, *Lyrics of Sunshine and Shadow. The Tragic Courtship and Marriage of Paul Laurence Dunbar and Alice Ruth Moore: A History of Love and Violence among the African American Elite* (New York: New York University Press, 2001).

62. *Indianapolis Freeman,* March 7, 1908.

63. Most likely, Hogan too died of illnesses related to syphilis, but several accounts name pneumonia as the cause of his death.

64. Ann Charters, *Nobody: The Story of Bert Williams* (New York: MacMillan, 1974), 89; Glenn, *Female Spectacle,* 108–110.

65. Gatewood, *Aristocrats of Color,* 190–191.

66. Libretto, *Abyssinia*, scene 4, p. 6, Music Division, Library of Congress, Washington, D.C.

67. Special dispatch to *The Morning Telegraph*, 1906, Williams and Walker clipping file, Robinson Locke Collection, BRTC.

68. *New York Star*, February 27, 1909, Williams and Walker clipping file, Robinson Locke Collection, BRTC.

69. *Indianapolis Freeman*, January 1, 1910, December 27, 1902; see also S. Tutt Whitney, "The Negro on the Stage," *New York Age*, February 22, 1910.

70. Ibid., December 14, 1901; *Toledo Blade*, November 9, 1908, and other undated clips from the Williams and Walker and Cole and Johnson clipping files, BRTC.

71. *New York Mirror*, November 13, 1909, Williams and Walker clipping file, BRTC.

72. *Indianapolis Freeman*, December 28, 1901, September 27, 1902, and December 22, 1906.

73. James Weldon Johnson, *Black Manhattan* (1930; repr., New York: Atheneum Press, 1969), 171.

74. "Says Negro on the Stage Cannot Be Serious," *Indianapolis Freeman*, January 4, 1908.

75. *Indianapolis Freeman*, February 8, 1908.

76. Johnson, *Black Manhattan*, 171.

77. *Green Book* (July 1909), Robinson Locke Collection, BRTC. *Evening Sun*, May 5, 1909, Cole and Johnson clipping file, BRTC. Also see Susan Curtis, *The First Black Actors on the Great White Way* (Columbia: University of Missouri Press, 1998), 51.

78. *New York Age*, June 25, 1908.

79. Ibid., May 14, 1908.

80. *Indianapolis Freeman*, ca. October 1, 1910, as published in Sampson, *Ghost Walks*, 533–534.

81. Mabel Rowland, ed., *Bert Williams, Son of Laughter: A Symposium of Tribute to the Man and His Work* ([1923?]; repr., New York: Negro Universities Press, 1969), 3, 213. Emphasis in the original.

82. Bert Williams, *American Magazine*, 1918, Williams and Walker clipping file, BRTC.

83. *New York Globe and Commercial*, October 27, 1905, envelope 2461, Robinson Locke Collection, BRTC.

84. Bert Williams, *American Magazine* (1918), Williams and Walker clipping file, BRTC.

85. *Variety*, December 14, 1907, as published in Sampson, *Ghost Walks*, 421.

86. *Indianapolis Freeman*, November 1, 1902.

87. Ibid., December 6, 1902, December 27, 1902.

88. Wolcott, *Remaking Respectability*, 56; "Helpful Hints" leaflet, Detroit Urban League Papers, box 1, folder 9, Bentley Library, University of Michigan, reprinted in Elsa Barkley Brown and Thomas Holt, eds., *Major Problems in African American History* (New York: Houghton Mifflin, 2000), 132.

89. *Indianapolis Freeman*, October 24, 1903.

90. Ibid., March 7, 1908.

91. Ibid., November 1, 1902.

92. *New York Age,* February 6, 1908. Curtis argues similarly about Walton in her *First Black Actors,* 49.

93. Elsa Barkley Brown, "Negotiating and Transforming the Public Sphere," in Black Public Sphere Collective, eds., *The Black Public Sphere* (Chicago: University of Chicago Press, 1995), 122, 139.

94. Manager's report, B. F. Keith's Hippodrome, Cleveland, Ohio, March 9, 1914, KAC.

95. Washington's address is in *New York Age,* March 13, 1913 (emphasis mine); see also Gaines, *Uplifting the Race,* 3, 93; Higginbotham, *Righteous Discontent,* 193; and Wolcott, *Remaking Respectability,* 15–16.

6. Black Bohemia Moves to Harlem

1. *New York Age,* July 9, 1908, June 6, 1911; *Indianapolis Freeman,* February 5, 1910. For information on Johnson as consul, see James Weldon Johnson, *Along This Way* (1933; repr., New York: Da Capo Press, 1973), 227–293.

2. *New York Age,* June 10, 1909, December 5, 1912; Henry T. Sampson, *The Ghost Walks: A Chronological History of Blacks in Show Business, 1865–1910* (Metuchen, N.J.: Scarecrow Press, 1988), 474; Reid Badger, *A Life in Ragtime: A Biography of James Reese Europe* (New York: Oxford University Press, 1995), 260; Tom Fletcher, *One Hundred Years of the Negro in Show Business* (New York: Burdge & Co., 1954), 173–176; Susan Curtis, *The First Black Actors on the Great White Way* (Columbia: University of Missouri Press, 1998), 45, and her *Dancing to a Black Man's Tune* (Columbia: University of Missouri Press, 1994), 150–154.

3. Gilbert Osofsky, *Harlem: The Making of a Ghetto* (New York: Oxford University Press, 1969), 110–112; Johnson quoted in his *Along This Way,* 240, 252; Nathan Huggins, *Harlem Renaissance* (New York: Oxford University Press, 1971), 17.

4. James Weldon Johnson, *Along This Way,* 240, 252; for another mention of the Marshall's demise, see Fletcher, *One Hundred Years of the Negro in Show Business,* 251–252; "mixing of the races" quoted in George Chauncey, *Gay New York: Gender, Urban Culture, and the Making of the Gay Male World, 1890–1940* (New York: Basic Books, 1994), 139; for more on cabaret laws, see Lewis Erenberg, *Steppin' Out: New York Nightlife and the Transformation of American Culture, 1890–1930* (Chicago: University of Chicago Press, 1981), 74–77; for "disciples of good cheer" quotation, see *New York Age,* October 9, 1913.

5. Osofsky, *Harlem,* 46–52, 84, 88–104; Johnson, *Along This Way,* 157–158.

6. *New York Age,* February 2, 1911; Edward Berlin, *King of Ragtime: Scott Joplin and His Era* (New York: Oxford University Press, 1994), 189, 194, 199; Fletcher, *One Hundred Years of the Negro in Show Business,* 175.

7. Osofsky, *Harlem,* 110–112.

8. Jervis Anderson, *This Was Harlem, 1900–1950* (New York: Farrar Straus Giroux, 1981), 62; Osofsky, *Harlem,* 17.

9. One event was reportedly "overflowing" with 2,500 patrons. Another review reported that four thousand patrons filled the house. It is likely that "capacity" depended on how many rooms were rented for any one event. See Badger, *A Life in Ragtime*, 84, 101; Kathy Peiss, *Cheap Amusements: Working Women and Leisure in Turn of the Century New York* (Philadelphia: Temple University Press, 1986), 120. The Manhattan Casino was later renamed the Rockland Palace and also became known for the interracial drag balls it sponsored in the 1920s and 1930s. See Chauncey, *Gay New York*, 270, 294.

10. Ann Charters, *Nobody: The Story of Bert Williams* (New York: MacMillan, 1980), 94; *New York Age*, June 18, 1914, and for the poem, July 3, 1913.

11. Fletcher, *One Hundred Years of the Negro in Show Business*, 176; *New York Age*, February 3, 1910.

12. At one of the more popular events, only one hundred whites were in attendance in an estimated crowd of 2,500. Badger, *A Life in Ragtime*, 101–102.

13. Peiss, *Cheap Amusements*, 120–121.

14. *Indianapolis Freeman*, November 26, 1904, and August 10, 1907.

15. *New York Age*, November 30, 1911, December 7, 1911, December 26, 1912, and various articles through January 1913; the March 7, 1912, issue describes the decision to name the theater Walker-Hogan-Cole.

16. *New York Age*, January 9, 1913, and February 20, 1913.

17. James Weldon Johnson, *Black Manhattan* (1930; repr., New York: Atheneum Press, 1969); New *York Age*, July 23, 1914.

18. *New York Age*, March 6, 1913, October 29, 1914.

19. Ibid., February 5, 1914, June 18, 1914, and July 3, 1913.

20. *New York Age*, June 2, 1910, as quoted in Badger, *A Life in Ragtime*, 57.

21. Badger, *A Life in Ragtime*, 65.

22. Ibid., 66–68; Al Rose, *Eubie Blake* (New York: Schirmer Books, 1979), 43; as quoted in Fletcher, *One Hundred Years of the Negro in Show Business*, 260.

23. Marva Griffin Carter, "Life and Music of Will Marion Cook," Ph.D. diss., University of Illinois, Urbana-Champaign, 1988, 113–114; *New York Age*, April 25, 1912; Badger, *A Life in Ragtime*, 97.

24. Osofsky, *Harlem*, 35–67; "In Retrospect: Black-Music Concerts in Carnegie Hall, 1912–1915," *Black Perspective in Music* (Spring 1978); David Mannes, *Music Is My Faith* (New York: Norton, 1938), 213–220.

25. Walton's quotation is in *New York Age*, May 9, 1912, as published in "In Retrospect: Black-Music Concerts in Carnegie Hall, 1912–1915," 74–75; see also Badger, *A Life in Ragtime*, 67.

26. *New York Age* 1912; "In Retrospect: Black-Music Concerts in Carnegie Hall, 1912–1915."

27. Freda L. Scott, "*The Star of Ethiopia*: A Contribution toward the Development of Black Drama and Theater in the Harlem Renaissance," in Amritjit Singh, William S. Shiver, and Stanley Brodwin, eds., *The Harlem Renaissance: Revaluations* (New York: Garland, 1989), 257–269; Joshua Berrett, "The Golden Anniversary of the Emancipation Proclamation," *Black Perspective in Music* 16, no. 1 (Spring 1988): 75–79.

28. "A Memento of the Emancipation Proclamation Exposition of the State of New York," October 22–31, 1913, SC.

29. Ibid.

30. Fletcher, *One Hundred Years of the Negro in Show Business,* 264.

31. *Crisis* 2 (June 1912): 66–67, as quoted in Badger, *A Life in Ragtime,* 266 (n. 73).

32. Fletcher, *One Hundred Years of the Negro in Show Business,* 261; Badger, *A Life in Ragtime,* 59.

33. As quoted in Badger, *A Life in Ragtime,* 135; and Rose, *Eubie Blake,* 59.

34. As quoted in Badger, *A Life in Ragtime,* 135–136; and Rose, *Eubie Blake,* 58–59.

35. Fletcher, *One Hundred Years of the Negro in Show Business,* 261; as quoted in Badger, *A Life in Ragtime,* 69.

36. *New York Age,* October 9, 1913.

37. Ibid., September 30, 1915.

38. Ibid., January 8, 1914.

39. *Musical America,* March 21, 1914, as reprinted in "In Retrospect: Black-Music Concerts in Carnegie Hall, 1912–1915," 81–82.

40. *New York Age,* August 7, 1913; Badger, *A Life in Ragtime,* 85.

41. Charters, *Nobody,* 125–126.

42. Undated, unidentified clipping and unidentified clipping dated March 29, 1903, Robinson Locke Collection, envelope 2461, BRTC; Marshall Stearns and Jean Stearns, *Jazz Dance: The Story of American Vernacular Dance* (1968; repr., New York: Da Capo Press, 1994), 22, 123.

43. Undated, unidentified clipping and unidentified clipping dated March 29, 1903, Robinson Lock Collection, envelope 2461, BRTC.

44. Fletcher, *One Hundred Years of the Negro in Show Business;* Johnson, *Black Manhattan,* 105.

45. The white critic is quoted in Susan A. Glenn, *Female Spectacle: The Theatrical Roots of Modern Feminism* (Cambridge, Mass,: Harvard University Press, 2000), 117–118; see also Stearns and Stearns, *Jazz Dance,* 96, 108, 109, 125, 128–129, 323.

46. Stearns and Stearns, *Jazz Dance,* 80–82, 128. "Pick" was short for "pickaninny" (a stereotyped image). Neither term was used regularly in the black press, although black child actors were frequent on the Keith circuit and Keith managers used both terms in their reports. See Managers' Reports, 1902–1914, KAC.

47. *New York Age,* May 15, 1913; Badger, *A Life in Ragtime,* 84.

48. As quoted in Stearns and Stearns, *Jazz Dance,* 125.

49. For more on the ring shout, see Sterling Stuckey, *Slave Culture: Nationalist Theory and the Foundations of Black America* (New York: Oxford University Press, 1987), Chapter 1.

50. Stearns and Stearns, *Jazz Dance,* 26–27.

51. Ibid., 98–99.

52. Williams is quoted in Stearns and Stearns, *Jazz Dance,* 130; for the quotation by the white critic, see *New York Age,* July 23, 1914.

53. Stearns and Stearns, *Jazz Dance,* 130.

54. Ibid., 128.

55. Badger, *A Life in Ragtime;* Susan Cook, "Passionless Dancing and Passionate Reform: Respectability, Modernism, and the Social Dancing of Irene and Vernon Castle," in William Washabaugh, ed., *The Passion of Music and Dance: Body, Gender, Sexuality* (New York: Oxford University Press, 1998).

56. Lewis Erenberg, *Steppin' Out: New York Nightlife and the Transformation of American Culture, 1890–1930* (Chicago: University of Chicago Press, 1981), 183.

57. Badger, *A Life in Ragtime,* 82.

58. *New York Times,* January 4, 1914. Cook, "Passionless Dancing and Passionate Reform," 143. Erenberg, *Steppin' Out,* 164–165.

59. Erenberg, *Steppin' Out,* 73, xiii, emphasis mine.

60. *New York Age,* January 15, 1914; Badger, *A Life in Ragtime,* 89, 121.

61. Badger, *A Life in Ragtime,* 101; *New York Age,* March 26, 1914, April 2, 1914, for previews; *New York Age,* April 16, 1914, and October 15, 1914, for reviews.

62. *New York Age,* October 29, 1914. For a discussion of dance as work, see Robin D. G. Kelley, *Race Rebels: Culture, Politics, and the Black Working Class* (New York: Free Press, 1994), 48–49.

63. *New York Age,* November 16, 1911 as cited in Badger, *A Life in Ragtime,* 62.

64. W. C. Handy, *Father of the Blues: An Autobiography* (1941; repr., New York: Da Capo Press, 1969), 226; Castle scrapbooks, BRTC; Badger, *A Life in Ragtime,* 116.

65. Susan Cook, "Passionless Dancing and Passionate Reform," 146.

66. *New York Tribune,* November 22, 1914, as quoted in Badger, *A Life in Ragtime,* 120; *Indianapolis Freeman,* March 6, 1915, as quoted in Badger, *A Life in Ragtime,* 116.

67. *New York Age,* February 20, 1913.

68. *Indianapolis Freeman,* February 14, 1914, as published in Athelia Knight, "In Retrospect: Sherman H. Dudley, He Paved the Way for the T.O.B.A.," *Black Perspective in Music* (Fall 1987): 175.

69. For the Winslow quotation, see *New York Age,* February 6, 1911; on Will Marion Cook being robbed, see Abbie Mitchell to Mercer Cook, and Will Marion Cook to Senator Robert R. Reynolds, August 4, 1941, Mercer Cook Papers, Moorland-Spingarn Research Center, Howard University.

70. *New York Age,* July 24, 1913.

71. *Indianapolis Freeman,* November 28, 1908, as published in Sampson, *Ghost Walks,* 444.

72. *New York Age,* November 11, 1915, June 5, 1913, October 16, 1913.

73. The Walton quotation is in ibid., December 2, 1915. For the nickelodeons, see Erenberg, *Steppin' Out,* 69–71; David Nasaw, *Going Out: The Rise and Fall of Public Amusements* (New York: Basic Books, 1993), 114–116, 171–172.

74. Robin D. G. Kelley, "Without a Song: New York Musicians Strike Out against Technology," in Kelley, Howard Zinn, and Dana Frank, *Three Strikes: Miners, Musicians, Salesgirls, and the Fighting Spirit of Labor's Last Century* (Boston: Beacon, 2001), 126–127.

75. *Indianapolis Freeman,* August 6, 1908.

76. Ibid., March 7, 1908.

77. *New York Age,* October 17, 1912, March 13, 1913; *Crisis* 6, no. 4 (August 1913): 166–167.

78. *New York Age,* August 27, 1914.

79. Ibid., October 28, 1915.

80. Ibid., November 11, 1915, where a review from *Variety* was reprinted.

81. W. C. Handy, *Father of the Blues,* 87; Colin Palmer, *Passageways: An Interpretive History of Black America, 1865–1965* (New York: Harcourt Brace, 1998), 61.

82. *New York Age,* October 28, 1915.

83. Ibid.

84. As quoted in ibid., December 2, 1915.

85. *Indianapolis Freeman,* October 23, 1915, as quoted by Carter, "The Life and Music of Will Marion Cook," 95.

86. Ibid., December 2, 1915.

87. Ibid., February 27, 1913.

88. Ibid., December 9, 1915.

89. Rose, *Eubie Blake,* 82.

90. Allen Woll, *Black Musical Theater from 'Coontown' to 'Dreamgirls'* (Baton Rouge: Louisiana State University Press, 1989), 72.

91. David Levering Lewis, *W. E. B. Du Bois: The Fight for Equality and the American Century, 1919–1963* (New York: Henry Holt, 2000), 172; Langston Hughes, *The Big Sea* (1940; repr., New York: Thunder's Mouth Press, 1986), 223-224.

92. Rose, *Eubie Blake,* 42.

Coda

1. Evelyn Brooks Higginbotham borrows the term "rhetoric of violence" from Teresa de Lauretis to refer to the proliferation of racist stereotype. See Higginbotham, *Righteous Discontent: The Women's Movement in the Black Baptist Church, 1880–1920* (Cambridge, Mass.: Harvard University Press, 1993), 189, 282, n. 13; De Lauretis, *Technologies of Gender: Essays on Theory, Film, and Fiction* (Bloomington: Indiana University Press, 1987), 31-48.

2. The Alberta Roberts quotation is from John Langston Gwaltney, *Drylongso: A Self-Portrait of Black America* (New York: New Press, 1993) 105; Roberts is quoted in Robin D. G. Kelly, *Yo' Mama's Disfunktional! Fighting the Culture Wars in Urban America* (Boston: Beacon Press, 1997), 15; also see Robin D. G. Kelley, *Race Rebels: Culture, Politics, and the Black Working Class* (Boston: Free Press, 1993), 35. The lyrics are quoted in Lawrence Levine, *Black Culture and Black Consciousness: Afro-American Thought from Slavery to Freedom* (New York: Oxford University Press, 1977), xiii.

3. Nathan Irvin Huggins, *Harlem Renaissance* (New York: Oxford University Press, 1971), 88-89, 118, 241.

4. W. T. Lhamon, *Raising Cain: Blackface Performance from Jim Crow to Hip Hop* (Cambridge, Mass.: Harvard University Press, 1998), 180-195; W. T. Lhamon, *Jump Jim Crow: Lost Plays, Lyrics, and Street Prose of the First Atlantic Popular Culture* (Cambridge, Mass.: Harvard University Press, 2003); Eric Lott, *Love and Theft: Blackface Minstrelsy and the American Working Class* (New York: Oxford University Press, 1993), 8-9, 15-18.

5. Langston Hughes, "The Negro Artist and the Racial Mountain," 1926, published in 1925 in the *Nation* and reprinted in Addison Gayle Jr., ed., *The Black Aesthetic* (New York: Doubleday, 1971), 175–181; also see Philip Brian Harper, "Nationalism and Social Division in Black Arts Poetry of the 1960s," in Eddie Glaude Jr., ed., *Is It Nation Time? Contemporary Essays on Black Power and Black Nationalism* (Chicago: University of Chicago Press, 2002), 165–188. The black arts quotation is from Addison Gayle Jr.'s introduction to his *Black Aesthetic,* xxi–xxiii; see also Larry Neal, "The Black Arts Movement," in Gayle, *Black Aesthetic,* 272–277.

6. Tricia Rose, *Black Noise: Rap Music and Black Culture in Contemporary America* (Hanover, N.H.: Wesleyan University Press, 1994), 1–20; Kelley, *Race Rebels,* 183–227; Kelley, *Yo' Mama's Disfunktional!* 15–78; S. Craig Watkins, "'Black Is Back and It's Bound to Sell!' Nationalist Desire and the Production of Black Popular Culture," in Glande, *Is It Nation Time?* 189–214.

Index

Note: Page references to illustrations are in italic.